JONATHAN WALKER
the MAN with the
BRANDED HAND

An Historical Biography
by ALVIN F. OICKLE

LSP

First Edition

International Standard Book Number 0-9664556-0-6
Library of Congress Catalog Card Number 98-90402

Printed and bound in the United States of America
by BookCrafters, Post Office Box 370, Chelsea, Michigan 48118-7337

Cover Design by Jack Viall, West Harwich, MA 02671

Quantity discounts are available on bulk purchases of this book for educational purposes or for fund raising. An order form is printed in the back of this volume. For information, please contact:

Lorelli Slater Publisher, Post Office Box 69, Everett, MA 02149-0001
Telephone (617) 389-2532.   FAX (617) 389-1697.
E-MAIL: LSPub@juno.com

LSP

TABLE OF CONTENTS

PREFACE

Perhaps more than most writing projects, a work of history, especially that called biography, owes much to an ad hoc kind of team that develops among those who help the author.

Most important to me was the assistance of my wife, Lois A. Oickle. She has become my full partner, not only because of the major contributions she has made to this project but also because her support never wavered. She never stopped believing that the story of Jonathan Walker – my story – would be published.

My efforts in stringing together the many scattered and often unconnected pieces that make up this record of the lives of Jonathan Walker and his family were at times frustrating, yet seldom fruitless. Overall, a lasting reward has come from Walker family members and others who gladly shared documents collected over the generations, some more than a century old.

I tend to think of my sources in a geographical way. On Cape Cod, the most helpful contributions came from my son M. Scott Oickle, whose field work turned up several significant sources, and from Louise H. Kelley, whose genealogical resources provided background not otherwise available. Historical and genealogical information also was provided by Richard J. Besiak, Edward L. Etsten, Muriel Ellis Girard, Phyllis Horton, Dick Johnson, and Paul R. Mangelinkx.

In the Midwest, Elmer Koppelmann and Raymond Van Handel, Jr., provided information and sources that helped round out the Walkers' Wisconsin years. Elmer Koppelmann's book, *Branded Hand: The Struggles of an*

Preface

Abolitionist, was a principal historical source, and his willingness to share research material went beyond simple kindness. Similarly, Ray Van Handel made several excursions around the farmland where the Walkers worked and lived, and proudly provided maps and details of his beloved Wisconsin that were available nowhere else.

Tressa LaFayette brought the same generosity to assisting me in gathering information about the Walkers' years in Michigan. She scoured the files of the Muskegon *Chronicle* and made my searches her searches.

Family historians and genealogists in the Midwest who provided material included Gail Allred, Lois Wightman and her daughter, Bonnie Inskeep, Barbara Martin of the Muskegon County Museum, and Barbara Rams of the Muskegon County office of records.

Some of the Florida background was provided through three sources. Most notable was the work of Joe M. Richardson, of Florida State University. He created a valuable introduction to Jonathan Walker's account of his 1844-45 experiences for a 1974 reproduction published by the University Press of Florida. The National Archives' voluminous records included 1844-45 newspaper files and letters to federal officials, all of which helped provide a special glimpse of the determination of the pro-slavery citizens to recover what they considered stolen property. The third major source was Jean Ducey, a Michigan writer who had collected a trunkful of history from the Pensacola area for her children's book account of Captain Walker. Of the material she loaned me, the work of Leora Sutton, a Pensacola historian, was outstanding.

I am indebted also to Susan Johnson, curator of the Pensacola Historical Society Museum, and to Herb O'Neal, who volunteered to provide current maps and photocopies for me.

Helen E. Ellis and Virginia Doane deserve special recognition for their early reading and editing suggestions, and for their encouragement. Dick Risk, of Amrob Publishing, offered virtually unlimited assistance in bringing this book to publication. To Jack Viall, who designed the cover, goes a special salute for the painstaking care he took to assure accuracy and artistry.

Finally, it is important that readers recognize that the conclusions and conjectures that I express in the manuscript should not lead readers to conclude that I disagree with any source, material, or contributor. My interpretations of how Jonathan and Jane Walker may have made decisions are based on my having a great variety of information on which to develop these opinions. Others with access to the same background may have different conclusions.

In truth, none of us with access to the historical and family material available to us today can be certain of why stalwarts such as Jonathan Walker, and his loyal wife Jane Gage Walker, carried on as they did. We can, however, be grateful that they chose to act as they did.

INTRODUCTION

There must be dozens, or hundreds, or even thousands of men and women who never have been properly recognized for their contributions to the ripening but unfulfilled American quest for a society in which everyone has free and equal opportunity. They are history's forgotten people. This is the story of one of them.

Jonathan Walker was among the small army of white people who fought to abolish slavery throughout much of the 19th Century. Jailed in Pensacola, Florida, for a year because he was caught trying to help seven black men escape from slaveholders, he became "The Man with the Branded Hand." Proudly, he carried the mark – SS for slave stealer – the remaining thirty-three years of his life.

The story of this native of Massachusetts' Cape Cod may be as remarkable for its lack of widespread historical recognition as it is for its human adventure on behalf of equality. Walker's place in history would be understated if he had been, as one historical researcher claimed, "an obscure man who returned to obscurity" after his branding and a seven-year tour on the abolitionist lecture circuit. Similarly, his role would be overstated if he were presented as a

Introduction

major hero. Some writers, perhaps thinking to honor him, have linked him with those generally considered the prime movers in the anti-slavery action – Frederick Douglass and John Brown, Harriet Beecher Stowe and Harriet Tubman – and the many others, black and white, men and women, Southerner and Northerner. Walker was among a large group, and his contribution was more dramatic than most. Acknowledging his role only for the unique severity of his punishment, however, is a shallow recognition.

Like the land in which he was born at the end of the 18th Century, Jonathan Walker was to lead a tumultuous life well into his middle years. And then, his struggle on behalf of equality for all people was to continue less dramatically and openly, but with equal determination and involvement, into his senior years.

The new United States of America was fending off enemy attacks, exploring its own geographical and moral bounds, and growing ever larger during the years that the young man born on Massachusetts' Cape Cod was surviving disaster and disease in strange places around the world, helping to raise a family of nine children, and becoming a national figure – a white man prominent in the fight to abolish slavery and to establish equal rights for black people.

Jonathan Walker's role in helping bring an end to slavery in the United States was perhaps best summarized in 1878 by the noted African-American abolitionist, Frederick Douglass, who worked with Walker "for a time." He wrote, upon Walker's death: "I well remember the sensation produced by the exhibition of the branded hand. It was one of the few atrocities of slavery that aroused the justice and humanity of the North to a death struggle with slavery." J. C. Furnas, in *Goodbye to Uncle Tom*, termed Walker's branding "a medieval touch that made him a platform attraction as Exhibit A for Abolition."

Walker was more than simply a victim of an atrocity, or a public exhibit, although he willingly accepted recognition as something of a freak. He displayed his branded hand in order to arouse anti-slavery sentiment and to speed efforts to abolish slavery. But his role was even greater, perhaps because he was not an heroic figure with the stature of a Douglass or a Lincoln. He was, as Florida historian Joe M. Richardson concluded, an ordinary man. Clearly, however, this ordinary man devoted most of his adult life to an extraordinary effort. He had little to bring to his crusade except his valor and his dedication. He was not an inspiring figure; indeed, his long nose, receding chin, and rounded shoulders as pictured in old photographs may leave the impression of a man with a lack of will, even withdrawal. He was only a passable public speaker, and could not begin to stir a crowd the way New Hampshire's Stephen S. Foster did. Nor did he have the political genius of Abraham Lincoln and William H. Seward, or of Henry Clay and John C. Calhoun.

A few months after he died at age 79 in Muskegon County, Michigan, on April 30, 1878, six thousand people attended the unveiling of a monument in memory of Jonathan Walker's iconic, unflagging leadership in the long, difficult

Introduction

effort to outlaw slavery. Paid for by an American patriot adopted from his native Greece, the granite tower rises ten feet above Jonathan Walker's grave in an honored location just inside the main entrance gate of Evergreen Cemetery in the city of Muskegon. The obelisk and his casket were relocated in 1921, nearly a half-century after his death, from a donated plot in a more obscure site within the cemetery. The monument is marked on its sides: with his birth and death dates, with a quotation from a poem that John Greenleaf Whittier wrote about Walker's martyred moment in history, and with a replica of his right hand bearing the branded mark "SS" – burned there by order of an American jury and judge in Florida in 1844.

Some sources say his was the only branding ever ordered in a court under federal jurisdiction. The National Archives has no record to prove, or disprove, the claim. But it *was* a United States marshal who placed the hot iron on Walker's right hand in a courtroom serving the Territory of Florida. Nor does there seem to be a record of anyone else's having undergone such punishment. Walker himself alluded to the branding as the responsibility of the federal government. In a rare display of wit, Walker occasionally referred to the scars as "the seal, the coat of arms, of the United States."

He was a man whose career unfolded with the lurch and stagger of America's protracted founding. Massachusetts Historian Paul Gagnon explained the flaw in the national flowering: "The Union had to be made, but circumstances – the real balances of power in the society – determined that it would not be made without the fateful compromise on slavery... Many of [the Framers] hoped, of course, that the new government would manage to reduce, and ultimately to abolish, slavery. Their hopes were in vain. The tragedy wrapped inside the triumph would be played out for generations to come." Some went beyond hoping. In 1775, Benjamin Franklin and Benjamin Rush organized the first American society to abolish slavery.

By the standards of today, Walker – who would know both triumph and tragedy – would be considered a "free spirit," something like a "hippie." Eccentric would be a fair term. Wisconsin and Michigan neighbors seemed to hold him in the kind of uneasy respect – and wonderment – earned by his contemporary, Henry David Thoreau.

Writing in the South Bend (Indiana) *Tribune*, John D. Furbush claimed that Walker, during the more than fifteen years that he lived near Michigan's ocean-like lake shores, "took a daily plunge... even if he had to break ice to do so. Each day, except in winter months, he ferried his cattle to a small island because the grass was more lush." Walker in his final year wrote of himself in the third person, "He has used no intoxicating drinks or tobacco for the last forty years, and for more than thirty years has been a vegetarian, and now lives principally on the productions of his little fruit farm, with no lock on his cabin door to keep out a hungry stranger or other object of need." He had unsuccessfully attempted in the 1850s to establish a farming commune in Wisconsin, promising equality for all settlers.

Introduction

Walker was not a weakling. He was a six-footer, taller than most men of his generation were, and during his middle years and later, he displayed unusual physical strength. Beyond the homeliness of his facial features one saw piercing eyes that reflected intelligence and self-confidence.

Walker was a lonely figure in a melancholy campaign. *The Negro History Library* might have been writing about Walker in Volume 1: "During most of the period [of protest against slavery], the Negro had no allies, except an occasional white liberal who dared to face social disapproval, and frequently faced legal sanctions as well. The wonder is, against such odds and the certainty of swift and terrible reprisal, that protest occurred at all."

Jonathan Walker thought of himself not as a liberal but as a progressive "for human welfare." Not because he was that "occasional white liberal," or "progressive," but because he was just "ordinary" – and perhaps "braver five minutes longer," in Emerson's words – Jonathan Walker deserves greater recognition as an American hero than he has been given, and certainly more than he ever thought he deserved.

He was a patriot in the way Frances Wright suggested in her essay, "The Meaning of Patriotism in America." A 19th Century writer and social reformer, she came to the United States from Scotland in 1824. Through her essay, she encouraged the use of "patriot" and "patriotism" in a larger sense: "To express a love of the public good...to signify a lover of human liberty and human improvement, rather than a mere lover of the country in which he belongs." The patriot, she continued, "is capable of establishing fundamental principles and of merging his own interests, those of his associates, and those of his nation in the interests of the human race."

Walker often invoked Christianity during his early and mid-life years, but he came to regard Jesus not as God but as the world's greatest reformer. The contemporary reformer he followed directly was William Lloyd Garrison, the editor and owner of *The Liberator*, an abolitionist newspaper published in Boston. Walker considered himself a "Garrisonian." The editor's unshakable, religious-like zeal for equality attracted hundreds of faithful followers. And all of them were far outnumbered by thousands of the disdainful and disinterested. Some abolitionists were, in fact, carrying on a public ministry. A Unitarian clergyman who was at Walker's deathbed eulogized him as unchurched but the best Christian he had ever known.

Lesser men and women may have been attracted by the excitement at the vortex of organized abolitionist activity, perhaps by the controversy it created. Their admiration and appreciation of comrades in the cause would have been sufficient fuel to propel these agents in the noble swirl. They performed for the applause of what often was a small audience, sometimes only their colleagues.

Jonathan Walker was another kind of abolitionist. He asked no reward. For weary weeks fading into torturous months, he accepted indignities inflicted

Introduction

on few white men in antebellum America. For months compounding into years, he blazed an abolitionist trail, his family destitute, his spirits rich.

Walker's story, which inspired such famed abolitionists as Frederick Douglass and John Brown, is now barely a whisper in the shout of history that was culminated with the American Civil War. In his final resting place in Michigan, Jonathan Walker has been modestly celebrated for more than a century. Each year, he is remembered with respect and honor by the African American community in Muskegon, where he lived his final sixteen years. Beyond Muskegon, and Pensacola, where his flight with the seven black men was begun and ended, he has been remembered by few. And in his native Massachusetts, Jonathan Walker has been virtually overlooked. He is known now only by a few scholars, historians, and people who stumble upon references to him in old history books.

There is, of course, no need to rate Jonathan Walker on a scale with others. Did he accomplish more, or less, than Frederick Douglass, or Parker Pillsbury, or Abby Kelley? We do not need to make such measurements. It should be enough to be aware of his deep dedication to the promises for human equality that were made by a new nation's Founders.

It is not the aim of this account to glorify Jonathan Walker. His story needs no exaggeration to earn credence. The goal of this biography is to trace Walker's journey along the abolitionist trail, through the lonely and discouraging experiences as well as with the satisfaction and pleasure he found among those brave citizens who dared challenge the slavocracy of a steadily growing, often groping, young nation.

If there is inspiration for the reader to discover, it may come from understanding that one humble, determined human being did not flinch when, acting on simple faith in his need to challenge an insincere, precarious pledge on behalf of fairness, he was met with punishment and pain.

Jonathan Walker's story is one of the more remarkable in the human race's frustrating experience – and, ultimately, the never-ended poison – of racial discrimination in a nation founded on and dedicated to the belief that "all men are created equal." When that credo is truly accepted, Jonathan Walker of Harwich, Massachusetts, should be remembered as one of those who helped achieve that unreached noble goal.

> A hero is no braver than an ordinary man,
> but he is braver five minutes longer.
>
> **Ralph Waldo Emerson**

CHAPTER 1   Ordinary Man, Extraordinary Hero

Some of the men who were in the courtroom in Florida that dark morning in November 1844 later claimed they heard the white skin on Jonathan Walker's right hand sizzle when the United States marshal pressed the branding iron against the fleshy palm beneath the thumb. As the smoldering tool began burning, Walker held the hand steady.

One second, two, three, four...

There was no need to tie the hand, Walker had told Marshal Ebenezer Dorr as he prepared to administer this unusual punishment on a man he had known as a "close acquaintance" for nearly a decade. The marshal had gone silently about his job, securing the hand to a railing in the prisoner's box. Walker clenched his jaws. As he had promised, he did not flinch, nor did he cry out. He showed no pain, no resistance. But, Walker later recounted, the "pain was severe while the iron was on..."

Six, seven, eight...

The heated iron was searing, then penetrating the skin. Eben Dorr's assistant marshal, James Gonzalez, stood nearby, unneeded for this chore.

Ten seconds, eleven, twelve, thirteen...

One man in the small gathering standing around the courtroom leaned forward to get a better view. He was George Willis, one of three Pensacola white men who claimed to own seven black men who had sailed with Captain Walker for the Bahamas – and freedom.

Seventeen, eighteen seconds...

1

Jonathan Walker The Man with the Branded Hand

The heated iron, Walker was to write later, "made a spattering noise, like a handful of salt in the fire, as the skin seared and gave way to the hot iron."

Nineteen seconds, twenty...

The iron was lifted. The white skin was raw where the curving marks of the brand had left its mark – SS for slave stealer.

Walker already had been battered and vilified in the four months he had spent in the Florida jail. Now, he suffered this branding, which would make him a martyr in the cause of freeing America's slaves. Walker did not know that he was not yet halfway through the punishment the United States government and some of its citizens were to administer for his crime of stealing the human property that would not be declared "free and equal" for another twenty years. Not before hundreds of thousands of black slaves, and the white men who fought over the rights of these African Americans, had died on plantations and battlefields.

* * * *

Jonathan Walker traced his lineage to Pilgrim families that had come to this continent aboard the *Mayflower* in 1620 and the *Fortune* in 1621. He grew up in the region that has been called America's birthplace. His grandfather, briefly a soldier in the Revolution, was among the colonists who first read the words of the Declaration of Independence – "We hold these truths to be self-evident, that all Men are created equal, that they are endowed by their Creator with certain unalienable rights, that among these are Life, Liberty, and the Pursuit of Happiness..." Newspaper readers of 1776 would have seen this battle cry for freedom printed with advertising that mocked the philosophy and the language. The July 10 front page of the Pennsylvania *Gazette*, for example, printed the new document only two columns away from ads offering rewards for runaway slaves.

When Jonathan Walker was born in Harwich, Massachusetts, on March 22, 1799, George Washington was living in retirement at Mount Vernon with Martha and their slaves, as many as three hundred. John Adams was midway in his four-year term as the second president of the United States of America.

Walker's life was to span the administrations of nearly all the presidents elected during the first century of the joined colonies. Born nine months before Washington died, he lived during the White House terms of the next eighteen men who followed the first president. Through all of these historic years, Jonathan Walker was to fight against slavery and for equality.

The new nation's Constitution, adopted only eleven years before his birth, was a document providing a central theme of co-existence for thirteen independent nation-states. Before Walker was ten, the U.S. Supreme Court made clear, however, that the power of the federal government was to be greater than that of any individual state

The federal Bill of Rights had been added only eight years before Walker's birth. The nation's Congress, first located in New York City, had been moved temporarily to Pennsylvania, pending construction of a new capital city.

Ordinary Man, Extraordinary Hero

The village that was later named for "the father of his country" was still nearly wilderness in 1799. The ten-mile square site for "Federal City," its location chosen by Washington himself because it was hopefully midway among the uniting colonies, had been ceded by Maryland on December 23, 1788. Still, when Walker reached his first birthday more than a decade later, the forested area that was to become the District of Columbia had only dirt streets and a few buildings. They included "the President's House," the beginning of the complex that would later be called the White House.

Jonathan was not yet two years old on November 17, 1800, when Congress held its first session in the partially completed Capitol Building. George Washington had laid the cornerstone on September 18, 1793, using a silver trowel and marble-headed gavel. This was in accordance with a ritual of the Masonic organization. Like the Masons' membership then, only white males made such decisions throughout the land.

The bondage of black people was not an issue of consequence among Cape Cod's white population when Walker was born, although Massachusetts had long been involved with slavery. Historians often have cited Jamestown, Virginia, as the place and 1619 as the time when slavery was introduced, by a Dutch ship's crew, to the North American continent. But it was from Marblehead, a sailing community north of Boston, only eighteen years later, in 1637, that the first American-built slave ship, the *Desire*, set out for its human cargo from the west coast of Africa. It was not until 1783 that slavery was outlawed in Massachusetts. The state's Supreme Judicial Court ruled slavery illegal, citing the Massachusetts Bill of Rights: "All men are born free and equal." The kidnapping continued for nearly another century.

Jonathan Walker was a fifth generation native of Cape Cod. His family had pioneered living at the "elbow" of that muscled arm reaching out into the Atlantic Ocean. They and the nation struggled alike through these formative years. Jonathan believed in the concept behind this radical, experimental form of govern- ment, this democracy. His faith in it was to be strong, literal, and unyielding. For him, the Declaration of Independence and the Constitution of the United States meant exactly what they said: *all people* were born free and equal -- men and women, whatever their skin color. He was, however, to lose faith in the people who ran the government.

Young Jonathan came into manhood as the new nation's frontiers, like an inflating balloon, were being pushed deep into the South and outward to the West. The maturing youth yearned to help pioneer the settlement of the American western frontier, but first he was to follow the routine of generations of Cape Cod's young men and make a career at sea.

      *   *   *   *

Jonathan did not come by the sea through family tradition. His grandfather, Jeremiah Walker, Jr., maintained an active life in Harwich as farmer, millwright, husband, and father to five sons. He had carpentry skills that his sons and his grandson Jonathan were to develop. He also had ambition, and

3

in 1780, when his youngest son Seth was only twelve years old, Jeremiah built a windmill in Harwich on the north side of Mill Pond, now known as Bucks Pond. What became the family home for three generations of Walkers – Jeremiah, Jr. , his son, Seth, and his grandson, Jonathan, and their families – was, however, in a third location, about two miles south of Mill Pond. The unmarked site is on a two-lane state highway running parallel with the Atlantic Ocean shoreline, about a half-mile west of the Harwich-Chatham town line. This section of South Harwich includes a pond named for an original Indian resident, John Skinniquit. Skinniquit Pond, only a few hundred feet south of the Walker home site, was to play a part in Jonathan Walker's boyhood.

Chatham recorded marriage intentions filed on May 30, 1789, by Seth Walker of Harwich and Mercy Bassett of Chatham. She was descended through her mother's family from Pilgrims William Bassett and Thomas Rogers. Mercy and Seth were married in Harwich on June 18, 1789, by Joseph Doane, a justice of the peace who solemnized scores of 18th Century unions.

The newlyweds were living in stormy times. Great Britain and France resumed open warfare in 1793 and the United States, trying to develop its Atlantic trade, was caught in the middle. During the first decade of their marriage, Seth and Mercy were to have four sons. Jonathan, who arrived March 22, 1799, was the youngest, and the tenth consecutive Walker male baby on a direct line to grandfather Jeremiah, Jr. His older brothers were David, only a half-year from his tenth birthday; John, who would soon be celebrating his seventh birthday, and Nathan, nearly three and a half and until now the baby. Perhaps the old adage is true: The mold was broken after Jonathan was born. In the decade following his arrival, three daughters were born to Seth and Mercy.

During Jonathan's childhood years, the United States was in undeclared wars with both Great Britain and France. Spain sold the vast continental sweep called Louisiana Territory to the United States in 1803, when Jonathan was only four years old. "The Floridas," which was to become the place of Walker's torment in his middle years, was ceded by Spain to the new nation in 1819, when Walker was a young sailor.

The Walker boys were close enough in age to enjoy each other's company. When Jonathan was nearing ten, for example, all of his older brothers were still in their teens: David was nineteen, John was nearly seventeen, and Nathan, thirteen. The two older boys were to leave soon: David in 1811, when he and Hulda Phillips married, and John in 1813 with his marriage to Ruth Rogers. Jonathan and Nathan were not to be married for nearly another decade.

It is not likely that any of the Walker children went to school for more than a few years. Jonathan Walker attended classes approximately in the years 1805 to 1811, at about the same time as Aruna Ellis, who was born the year before Jonathan. Ellis wrote about attending classes in several places in Harwich, including "Mr. James Cahoon's kitchen [with] Eben Eldridge as teacher." Young Walker doubtless had a similar educational experience in Harwich. That he paid attention, and learned, is evident in his writings.

Ordinary Man, Extraordinary Hero

Not all of Jonathan's education came from school and church classes. Later to be eulogized as a model Christian, although he was unchurched as an adult, he attended the West Harwich Baptist Church as a boy. Jonathan also learned from neighborhood youths. Sidney Brooks, who founded the Harwich academy that came to bear his name, recalled the family of Samuel Moody, which had moved to Harwich in 1820 from Gorham, Maine. Jonathan Walker was already a veteran of three years at sea, but the activities of the boys as described by Brooks would have been popular when the Walker boys were growing up a few years earlier.

Brooks wrote of the Moody boys: "They had seen rather more of the world than we... We compared dialects, and the sharp discussions that arose upon each other's provincialisms and pronunciation were the most substantial and best remembered grammar lessons I ever learned."

Among the sixteen Moody children were two – Lucy and Loring – who were to become important in the lives of Seth and Mercy Walker's children. Nathan Walker, Jonathan's next older brother, and Lucy Moody were married in Harwich by the Reverend Nathan Underwood on January 11, 1821. Loring Moody became not only Nathan Walker's brother-in-law but, a quarter-century later, one of the most important people in Jonathan Walker's life. During the years after his branding in 1844, while Walker toured the abolitionist lecture circuit, Loring became an occasional companion, and something like a campaign manager. Moody was to become the general agent of the Massachusetts Anti-Slavery Society.

Jonathan would have known the Moodys as neighbors. The newly arrived family lived north of the Walkers, on a large plot that came to be called Samuel Moody's hill. Below lay a beautiful pond in winter and a cranberry meadow in summer. The boys had sport skating, and coasting on sleds they made. Sometimes, like youngsters of all ages, the boys had a near calamity. At age fifteen, Jonathan Walker was rescued from drowning in one of these Harwich ponds. In his 1845 autobiography, *Trial and Imprisonment*, Walker recounted his winter adventure. Since the Walkers lived only a few minutes' walk from Skinniquit Pond south of the farm, it seems likely that this was the scene of his chilling experience. As the boys were sliding over surface ice, Jonathan recalled, he broke through. He struggled to get out of the freezing water, and failed, until a companion was able to grasp him and pull him to safety. Walker credited the other boy, who was not named, with saving his life. Later, he called the incident the first of several escapes from death.

Cape Cod, although occupied by white people for more than 150 years, was still being settled as the young Walkers and Moodys and Brookses were growing up. Gone were the Old-comers, the name given early settlers – the Pilgrims and their offspring. But the Old-comers' great-grandchildren, and even some of the now elderly grandchildren, were there, passing along family stories about the early days of the new nation. Jonathan's parents had grown up during an economic era of trade by bartering.

5

Jonathan Walker The Man with the Branded Hand

As Jonathan and the Cape were developing, the United States was expanding. The total national land area when Walker was born was about 900,000 square miles. That is less than one fourth of the total in the late 20th Century. In 1803, when Jonathan was four years old, the vast continental acquisition called the Louisiana Purchase almost doubled the land area. Three weeks before his fourth birthday, the Union had admitted its seventeenth state, Ohio. Between 1788 and 1796, the original thirteen had been joined by Vermont, Kentucky, and Tennessee.

The new nation, despite having established governmental independence, was still in contention with Great Britain, Spain, and France for territorial control on the North American continent. White Americans in Georgia and Florida were fighting both Native Americans and the early arriving Spanish for the rights to claim Florida. Meantime, white settlers in the Northwest Territory believed that their difficulties with the Native Americans of the region were attributable to the British in Canada, who seemed to be supplying weapons and incentives for attacks on farms owned by white people.

Jonathan Walker was to settle in both Florida and the Old Northwest later in life, and to contribute to the early history of both regions. Labor and its management were as different in the North and South as were the harvesting of hay and cotton. Weather was a factor, but the main difference was the trend towards huge Southern plantations being developed literally on the backs of slaves. The U.S. census figures tell the story of slavery's growth: 757,208 in 1790, 893,602 in 1800, 1,191,362 in 1810, and in 1820.

Adopted in 1807, a federal law went into effect in 1808 banning the importation of slaves. Slave trading was not to end there, or elsewhere in the new nation. An estimated quarter- million blacks were illegally imported for indentured service over the next half-century, many of them through the Gulf of Mexico and Mobile Bay to the still undeveloped areas of Florida and Alabama. Hundreds of thousands of black children were born into American citizenship – and into slavery – after 1808. Despite the ban, kidnappings and smuggling continued, and the number of slaves counted in federal censuses increased from about 1.5 million in 1820 to two million in 1830, to nearly 2.5 million

In 1840, to 3.2 million in 1850, and in 1860, on the eve of the war that was to bring a halt to slavery, to nearly four million. Five million or more Africans were brought to the Americas as slaves, as many as a half-million to the South illegally before 1808, and thousands more illegally thereafter.

It is doubtful that the young Walker had opportunity to associate with many people of color. In the first national census in 1790, Harwich's population was 2,392. Listed under heads of households were a total of eleven "all other free people," a category for non-white. That was not unusual in New England. Three New England states – Massachusetts, Maine, and Vermont – had no slaves, and the entire state of Vermont had only sixteen "free colored" in 1790. The other three had nearly 4,000. New York had 21,324 slaves and New Jersey,

11,423, demonstrating that slavery was not confined to the South as the 19th Century neared.

The proportion of black slaves to free white people was remaining constant in the 16 to 20 percentile range. Jonathan Walker was growing up in a country where nearly one of every five residents was a black slave.

  *   *   *   *

Life in the new nation was, by any standards, difficult during the early years of Jonathan Walker's life. The men worked at the mill, on the farm, or at sea. The women cooked, cleaned, and took care of the children. On Cape Cod, sailing attracted the greatest number of young men, by far. One historian has estimated that as many as two thirds of the men were sailors. Indeed, the Walkers were unusual in not having had sailors for several generations. The Walker men had been surveyors, carpenters, farmers, and millers. Their home, and work, was on the land.

When Jonathan Walker was thirteen years old, the United States declared war on Great Britain. While probably not affected directly by the War of 1812, he was old enough by then to have been aware of what would have been the first major international activity to occupy his attention. Very likely he had completed his schooling and was working around the home farm. War news came ashore with the many Cape Cod sailors running the embargo. Harwich claimed two local men on board the *Constitution* in its famous duel with the *Guerriere*. That battle with the British frigate was fought east of Nova Scotia on August 19, 1812.

The older Walker boys did not participate in the War of 1812. They were either too busy working on the family farm or too young. In the winter of 1814, local excitement would have centered briefly around Jonathan's near drowning. While that event no doubt caused consternation in the Walker family, more generally exciting activity was being carried on around New England that year. The war was winding down, good news indeed for the Cape's many deep-water sailors. Disturbed by the British Navy's pesky patrols off shore, some action-prone New England citizens convened in Hartford, Connecticut. They hoped to rally support for their proposal to secede from the still shaky collection of colonies. They gave up the idea soon after. The end of the war, Cape Codders reasoned, would bring a welcome halt to British threats to bombard the shore communities if "tribute" were not paid. Such demands were not unprecedented. Great Britain and France, at war with each other, had found it cheaper to buy off Barbary States pirates than to fight them. And now, the British, began to seek this ransom from American communities that, like Cape Cod, had been left to fend for themselves by the time the War of 1812 was launched.

The British, under Admiral Lord Howe and Captain Richard Raggett, demanded "ransom" – protection money, really – to be given in exchange for the enemy navy's promise not to shell the towns, thus "to spare their ships and salt works." Eastham paid $1,200, and Brewster paid $4,000. In Barnstable, where "safety" would cost $6,000, Loring Crocker had four cannon brought from

7

Boston, and had them set up pointing into Cape Cod Bay. Barnstable was not troubled further.

In the final year of the War of 1812, the British marauders carried out their threats on two Cape Cod towns. Both Orleans and Falmouth had refused the extortion demands.

Falmouth was first. On January 28, 1814, a British cannonade damaged several buildings before the home militia drove off the invaders – and then went on the offensive. Thirty-one volunteers captured the British five-gun privateer, aptly named *Retaliation*, and sailed it to nearby Woods Hole.

The year-long siege of Cape Cod was concluded on December 19, 1814, at Orleans, where citizens had refused to pay a $2,000 tribute. Possibly annoyed because of their Falmouth defeat, and because only a few of their demands had been satisfied by the stubborn Cape Codders, the British decided to attack Orleans at Rock Harbor. They burned two Orleans sloops, *Washington* and *Nancy*, and captured the schooner *Betsy* and the sloop *Camel*.

Because of their unfamiliarity with the coastline, the British placed a Cape Codder who had been "impressed" into service in charge of the prized *Betsy* for the trip to Boston. This defiant Yankee ran the schooner aground in Yarmouth.

The *Betsy*'s British crew members were captured and sent to Salem for trial. The *Betsy*, meantime, was reclaimed by its American owner.

Such rebellion also was attributed to Eastham's Matthew "Hoppy" Mayo. Captured by the British and assigned to pilot a captured schooner, *Spencer*, commanded by Captain Raggett, Mayo ran the vessel ashore at First Encounter Beach, off his home shore in Eastham. Mayo escaped. Twenty-three British did not fare so well; they were taken prisoners.

War's end came with the Treaty of Ghent, signed only five days after Orleans' conflict.

The Battle of Rock Harbor was, without doubt, a major topic of conversation for Cape Codders that Christmastime of 1814. It is not unlikely that strong young men like Jonathan Walker and his brothers would have hiked the few miles from their Harwich home to Orleans to inspect the scene first-hand. Youngsters just as surely must have imagined themselves taking part in similar adventures.

    *   *   *   *

Danger came not from war alone. When Jonathan was sixteen years old, a hurricane swept off the sea and tore across Cape Cod, an event not unfamiliar then, or now, but always fearsome. "Unroofed" in what Harwich historian Josiah Paine called "the great gale of September 1815" was the windmill that Jonathan's grandfather had built thirty-five years earlier. on the thirty-acre Mill Pond in East Harwich. Grandfather Jeremiah Walker, Jr., had died in 1811, so the mill's operation probably had been taken over by Jonathan's father, Seth Walker, and Jonathan's brother, David, who at the time was twenty-five years old. Relocated a couple miles southward to the east of Salt Water

Pond, known now as Wychmere Harbor, the re-roofed wooden windmill stood another forty years, until 1855. The Walkers moved to a farmhouse on Chatham Road (Old County Road).

When Jonathan Walker was seventeen years old, he decided the time had come to begin a career. Like the generations of Walker men before him, his heart was in farming. But Jonathan was not to begin adulthood as a farmer. That career would be postponed. His life, for now, anyway, would be on the ocean. He had some of the spirit of his ancestors – the Stephen Hopkins family and William Walker, for example – who had left their native land two hundred years before and helped settle America.

The Walker family history is rife with the marbled streaks of impulsiveness and virtue associated with the Pilgrims: a zest for adventure, a spirit of compromise, a quest for equality, and a determination to pursue freedom. These are the qualities that Jonathan Walker was to demonstrate throughout his adult life. He followed in the pattern of his most famous ancestor, Stephen Hopkins. Margaret Hodges' biography, *Hopkins of the Mayflower*, was subtitled, *Portrait of a Dissenter*. The description also would fit Jonathan Walker.

Debating his choices for the future – on land or on sea – Jonathan Walker had major personal and practical considerations. Could he earn a living on the family farm, or in the mill? He was the youngest of four sons. Seth Walker probably was already sharing farm and mill duties, and the very modest rewards, with his three older sons. Was there enough for another, reducing each one's share from a fourth to a fifth? Had the youngest son asked, the family would have made room for him. They always had. But Jonathan also might have considered the possible resentment his older brothers would have endured, even if silently, for having to reduce their shared income. As well, Jonathan would expect more than a pittance; a full share for a full effort. He would want to begin saving money for his eventual marriage, and, in his youthful optimism, perhaps, even for the farm he was to long for throughout his early and middle years.

Facing the choice of a career, the young man was to decide not so much against farming as *for* sailing. Perhaps the most practical reason for Jonathan's postponing a farming venture was rooted in the sheer difficulty of the work on the sandy peninsula. Cape historian Paul Mangelinkx explained:

> Farming on Cape Cod had always been more of a struggle than anywhere else in New England. [The soil] was marginal, at best, especially on the south side [where the Walker family lived], due to its sandy nature... In addition, as the Western lands began to open and transportation improved, commercial farmers on Cape Cod faced increased competition from the Ohio River Valley or, in fact, were themselves lured to the frontier. Many farmers turned to the sea, to other trades, or to the "mainland," attracted by the economic opportunities offered during the early stages of the industrial revolution.

Jonathan Walker The Man with the Branded Hand

Running a mill did not interest young Jonathan, any more than farming did at that time in his life. This had nothing to do with money, although a hired hand could earn as much as sixty cents for a day of plowing, planting, or hoeing. What the seventeen-year-old Walker would have wanted was adventure. A boy living among sailors would know that adventure was at sea. Daniel Webster described the unobtrusive sophistication that sailors brought to 19th Century Cape Cod. He wrote a friend in Dennis:

> I was once engaged in the trial of a cause in your district, in which a question arose respecting the entrance into the harbor of Owhyee [Hawaii]... The counsel for the opposite party proposed to call witnesses to give information to the jury. I at once saw a gesture which I thought I understood, and suggested to the judge that very probably some of the jury had seen the entrance themselves. Upon which, seven of the twelve arose and said they were quite familiarly acquainted with it, having seen it often.

Deep-water sailing would take a young sailor to such faraway places in the Pacific Ocean. Old ports were being reopened. United States-China trade, begun from Boston only a quarter-century before, in 1790, had been halted during the war years while the British harassed American commercial vessels with sea blockades. But now, the ancient Asian nation wanted cotton from New England mills and other commodities. The intriguing experiences of Marco Polo, and Christopher Columbus, and countless other adventurers were likely being told again by Cape Cod's own legendary sailors. A young man would listen.

Perhaps the solution to this dilemma was not so complex after all. Perhaps Jonathan Walker simply wanted to be on the water. He was not uncommonly young to be leaving his parents' home. He probably had completed, four or five years earlier, the little education the town offered its children. Some of the boys he had attended classes with were probably on the water by now. In 19th Century Cape Cod, boys not even in their teen years regularly became sailors. Scores of cemetery stones throughout the region stand over barren plots, each with the stark line "Lost at Sea" carved beneath the name of a man-child. The youngest recruits usually began working in the ships' galleys, preparing food and carrying out other assignments not directly related to sailing. In 1842, eight-year-old Ambrose Snow, Jr., sailed with his father from Wellfleet for the Bay de Chaleur, Henry C. Kittredge wrote in *A History of Cape Cod*. In one of Cape Cod's most tragic storms, the October Gale of 1841, fifty-seven men and boys from Truro, a town east of Harwich, were lost in the wreckage of seven ships. Of the fifty-seven, fifteen were under the age of eighteen. Charles W. B. Nott was the youngest. He was eleven years old. Another town, Dennis to the west, counted twenty dead in that 1841 storm. Twelve of them were named Howes, according to Kittredge.

Ordinary Man, Extraordinary Hero

There were sometimes as many boys as there were men out on a whaling ship, hunting the ocean giants and returning with vital supplies of the lighting and heating fuel that the mammals' rich, heavy bodies supplied. Arthur Tarbell wrote in *Cape Cod Ahoy!*:

> There was a decade in the 1830s when the Cape, including her sister ports of New Bedford and Nantucket, boasted of having over 500 "blubber-boilers" in the Atlantic, Pacific, and Indian Oceans... Out of [these] harbors, whaler after whaler sailed, ugly in every line but stout and dependable in dirty weather, and built for capacity, not speed. It was a hard life that their crews had to face – cramped fo'castles, stale rations, bullying mates, frequent mutinies, rigors of Arctic icefields, cruises three and four years in length, and enormous physical hazards when at grips with their prey.

Not incidental to the career that young Jonathan Walker was to start soon, black men were among the crews on these whalers. Lorenzo Johnston Greene wrote in his study, *The Negro in Colonial New England*: Larger whaleships carried "twenty-one men, of whom nine are commonly blacks; the smaller, sixteen men, of whom seven are blacks." Quoting from the Massachusetts Historical Society Collections, he cited the whaler *Lion*, which had "three officers, eight white men, a boy, and nine Negroes."

Black men were getting little, if any, publicized credit in the early 19th Century. Yale's President Timoothy Dwight, after touring Massachusetts about 1815 during a summer vacation, wrote of Cape Cod's white sailors: "There are no more enterprising, active, skillful seamen perhaps in the world."

Farmers for generations, the Walkers nevertheless lived in the heart of a fishing community. In 1802, Harwich had between fifteen and twenty vessels in the range of forty tons each for shoal fishing and four one hundred-ton vessels that fished off the banks of Newfoundland and Belle Island. All together, they employed more than two hundred men and boys.

Surrounded by lakes and streams, and only a short walk from the Atlantic Ocean, the Walker family lived in a region that had turned out thousands of sailors in the two centuries between the arrival of Stephen Hopkins on the *Mayflower* and the adolescence of Jonathan Walker. But if any of those thousands of young men were Walkers, no record remains. Jonathan's grandfather, Jeremiah Walker, Jr., and his father, Seth Walker, were farmers and mill operators, and before them William, and Jabez, and the first Jeremiah Walker, also had provided for their families by farming.

Jonathan, in 1816 as he confronted his choices, could look to his family for land vocations, and almost anywhere else for maritime occupations. His family's traditional roots were in farming, just as many more families had the sailing tradition. Harwich had a notable example of the latter in the family of Job Chase, Jr. Six of his sons were lost at sea. Four of the six were masters of their own vessels.

Jonathan Walker The Man with the Branded Hand

Having no sailors in the contemporary family did not mean the Walkers lacked adventurers. Stephen Hopkins certainly qualified. Even William Walker, while not in the swashbuckling ilk of Hopkins, had the courage to leave his native England, and then the inland safety of Massachusetts Bay Colony, to help settle Cape Cod.

And, of course, Jonathan had come under the influence of the Cape's maritime culture. He wrote later, in *Trial and Imprisonment*, that Cape Cod had been

> ... the birthplace of many as bold, daring, and enterprising people as can be found in any part of the world. There is no navigable ocean, sea, lake, bay, or river anywhere on the globe that has not seen the Cape Cod man at the prow or at the helm. Though her sons are not exactly web-footed, yet, like ducks, they take early to the water for their support, and start out on ocean's wide domain in pursuit of the finny and feathered tribes. Nor do they turn back or fear to attack "Leviathan," though "he maketh the sea to boil like a pot." With all their exposure, poverty, poor soil, and other disadvantages, they have steadily made a due show of advancement with other parts of our common country, that have been favored with better natural and local surroundings.

Jonathan Walker left home when he was seventeen years old. He had grown to be a head higher than most of his contemporaries. The mature Walker was to be described as "a tall, large-framed man, curiously double-jointed, and exceedingly strong." Jonathan Walker, the last of a string of ten consecutive male Walkers, was to be the first in his branch of the Walker family on Cape Cod to become a sailor. Like the Chase brothers, but for a different reason, Walker was being drawn to the ocean.

Near the end of his life, Walker was to write of himself in 1816: "In early life, I, too, whirled about in the pursuit of knowledge, and, to gratify my love of adventures not found on Cape Cod, I scoured the [world's oceans]."

Long before poet Archibald MacLeish wrote his tribute to Gerald Murphy, called *American Letter*, Jonathan Walker's heart told him also that

> America is West and the wind blowing.
> America is a great word...
> A shining thing in the mind and the gulls' call.

Jonathan Walker had heard the gulls' call.

> To signify a lover of human liberty and human improvement
> rather than a mere lover of the country in which he belongs...
> [the patriot] is capable of establishing fundamental principles
> and of merging his own interests, those of his associates,
> and those of his nation in the interests of the human race.
> **Frances Wright, in an essay, "The Meaning of Patriotism in America"**

CHAPTER 2   The Making of a Patriot

About to become a sailor at the age of seventeen, Jonathan Walker was to develop the attitudes and moral strengths that would govern his life. As suggested by Frances Wright, a writer, lecturer, and social reformer who immigrated to the United States from Scotland in 1824, Walker was "establishing fundamental principles... in the interests of the human race."

In the process of becoming by Wright's standards a patriot, young Jonathan was going off to sea in 1816 at the same time as the sons of other Cape families. Adventure at sea came quickly, but where the six young sons of Job Chase, Jr., of West Harwich, were to die while sailing, Jonathan Walker was to encounter similarly extreme hazards and survive.

Another Cape Cod son, Edward Knight Collins of Truro, was to leave two years after Walker, when only fifteen years old. Collins was to become one of America's best known men of the sea during his lifetime. After leaving the Cape in 1818, Collins began work as a shipping clerk for his father, Captain Israel G. Collins, a Truro man who was founding his own firm as a shipping merchant in New York that year. When Israel Collins died in 1831, the twenty-eight-year-old Edward took over the business. Five years later, Collins had four passenger vessels built and began the Dramatic Line, naming the liners after eminent actors. In 1840, Edward Collins chose his uncle, John Collins, already captain of the firm's oldest vessel, the *Shakspeare* (as the name was spelled), as skipper for the *Roscius*, the largest American merchant ship afloat. John had shipped out from Truro, also at age fifteen, had been a British prisoner of war when captured as a blockage runner during the War of 1812, and had spent ten years in the Mexican trade. Edward Collins eventually took on the Cunard Line, abandoning sails for wooden side-wheeler steam packets carrying U.S. mail and passengers across the Atlantic. Collins was celebrated as America's most successful deep-water entrepreneur.

Like Collins, Jonathan Walker's career eventually would be generally land-based, but far more modest as he applied his carpentry skills as a shipwright. For the tall, restless Harwich lad, life for now was on the water. He had a choice: fishing, or merchant shipping. The whaling fleet had made the names of Nantucket, New Bedford, and Cape communities recognizable around the world and provided sailors a good income. But there was a catch: whaling voyages often ran into years – three to five were common. The rate of desertion was high. A whaling ship on a lengthy Pacific cruise frequently lost half the original crew. The men were expected to commit their labor to months away at sea and, worse, so far as Walker was concerned, to resign their spirits to continuous subordination.

No, that was not the kind of life, nor the kind of character, Jonathan Walker sought or possessed. Walker was like a Chatham young man named Samuel Atkins who, two generations earlier, "drew in his breath" and decided to "spend a portion of his youth at sea as a common laborer in the employ of merchant capital."

While Jonathan Walker was never to have the financial success of the Chases and the Collinses, he was to gain national recognition. Leaving Harwich to begin his career, however, he could not know that his success would come from a calamitous failure at sea.

*   *   *   *

Jonathan Walker was to continue maturing for a few years. At full growth, he stood six feet tall and was described as "stout" and "sturdy." From photographs taken at mid-life and into his seventies, it appears that he may have weighed between 180 and 200 pounds. That was large! Josiah Paine's *History of Harwich* included a 1780 roster of townsmen enlisting in the service. The tallest stood five feet ten inches; two were under five feet. The average height of fourteen enlistees was five feet four inches. If that was average for Jonathan Walker's time, he was at least a head taller, and probably forty to fifty pounds heavier, than the average young man.

His size was not to keep him from disease and disaster. In his first year on the ocean, soon after turning eighteen in 1817, he "lay dangerously ill with a raging fever for more than twenty days in an East Indian village," Walker reported in *Trial and Imprisonment*.

The Republic of India was called "East India" in the early American years to distinguish it from the Western Hemisphere's tropical islands called the "West Indies." It is fair to speculate that Walker's shipmates, unable to provide the care they thought a dying man should have, carried him ashore somewhere in the southern part of India. Joe M. Richardson, in his 1974 introduction to a

14

The Making of a Patriot

reprinting of Walker's book, suggested that this experience – a white man being attended by people of color while ill in a bamboo reed hut – may have helped develop Walker's respect for black people. Richardson wrote: "Probably he would later remember their kindness when he came in contact with American slaves."

It is possible he was cared for by natives of a subgroup of the Hindu race, the Dravidians of the South, described as dark-skinned, stocky, and having rather more Negroid features than other Indics.

Walker wrote in his autobiography, a quarter-century after the adventure:

> I was stretched upon a sick couch, in a thatched bamboo shantee [sic], suffering with, and but scarcely surviving, a violent and raging fever, more than 8,000 miles from home, kindred, and friends... Before I had so far recovered as to be able to prosecute any employment, my small purse was exhausted, and I was left... dependent upon the kindness of those whom I never saw before, and could neither speak their language nor they mine; but a kind Providence interposed, and I was soon again in comfortable circumstances.

      *   *   *   *

Over the next few years, Walker survived two major accidents at sea. The first was in March 1819, while the twenty-year-old Walker was aboard a ship riding out a storm in the English Channel. Walker wrote:

> A sea struck [the brig] midships with great violence, staving in much of the bulwarks and carrying with it all that was moveable, and me with the rest; and the next thing I knew, I was lying on the cabin floor, and was told that when the water had cleared from the decks, I was found crawling out between the lanyards of the lee main rigging, and would, if let alone, in a few seconds have been overboard, and clear of the vessel.

A year later, in 1820, Walker was, in fact, thrown clear of a brig returning to the United States from Europe. Walker's account continued:

> I was precipitated from the fore topsail yard-arm head-foremost overboard, in a dark night and gale of wind. The weather being cold, I had on at that time heavy boots and thick clothing, which greatly obstructed my exertions in the water; and the first thing I came in contact with was the bottom of the vessel, and after some struggling to gain the surface, and before I was sensible of reaching it, I caught a rope and seized it with my whole strength, and soon found myself raised partly out of water, and the next instant plunged under again and dragged forcibly through it, at a rapid rate. Thus, for three or four minutes, as near as I can judge, I remained in that situation, hallooing at the top of my voice whenever my head was above water, and was nearly losing my hold when I was seized by the captain, mate, and

another man, who, with some difficulty, succeeded in getting me on board. There were two men on the same yard, and a third coming up, when I fell off, and neither knew that I had fallen off until they had reefed the topsail and come down upon deck. Had I fallen on the vessel in my headlong position, it would have insured instant death. Had I fallen in any other position than I did in the water, the concussion would, in all probability, have rendered me incapable of immediate exertion. Had I gained the surface at any other place than I did, there would have been nothing to get hold of, and in less than one minute the vessel would have passed away from me altogether and forever; for there was no possibility of getting to me with vessel or boat at such a time as that, if such an attempt should have been thought of.

   *   *   *   *

Despite dangerous bouts at sea, and between long absences, Walker came home to New England often enough to meet and court the woman who was to be his faithful wife and supporter through the next half-century. Jane Gage was born June 28, 1803, in Harwich, the second daughter and the last of the six children of Mayo Gage and his wife, the former Zerviah Ellis, both of Harwich. Jane and Jonathan had in common strings of older brothers; she had four, he had three. The Gage family home, local historians seem to agree, was apparently in a Cape Cod section that was called Gageville for the obvious reason. When Jane's father, Mayo Gage, was born in 1769, Gageville was in the part of Yarmouth called East Parish, near the line dividing that town from Harwich. In 1793, when East Parish was incorporated as a new town called Dennis, Gageville went with it. The family enclave was so identified with all three places, in fact, that the history of the Thomas Gage descendants, compiled by Clyde VanTassel Gage, noted that Mayo Gage was born in "Yarmouth, Harwich, Dennis."

Jane and Jonathan filed their marriage intentions with both the Chatham and Harwich town clerks on September 21, 1822. The marriage of the twenty-three-year-old sailor and his twenty-year-old bride was, as the town clerk recorded it, "solemnized by the Reverend David Curtis" two weeks later, on October 8. The union was to last until Jane's death in 1871 in Michigan at the age of 68.

The year of his marriage was to be important for another reason for Jonathan Walker. He wrote: "From about the year 1822, I began to go amongst slavery, and from that time, on all occasions which presented, I tried to inform myself of its mode of operation, and have, in several of the slave states, scrutinized it in the parlor and in the kitchen, in the cottage and in the field, in the city and in the country..."

Newlyweds Jane and Jonathan left Harwich almost immediately and settled in New Bedford. It was Jane's first move away from her Cape Cod upbringing. The Cape was coming alive in this decade, but not with the kind of business that would interest a young farmer-turned-sailor. The residents began

The Making of a Patriot

to build factories; for example, the Chatham and Harwich Manufacturing Company, established in 1827 to make cotton and woolen cloth, and the Skinniquits Fishing Company, founded in 1828 at Harwich...

Jonathan Walker had other ideas about how to make a living, and he began to do so in New Bedford. This community, fifty miles southwest of rural Harwich, was one of America's major port cities early in the 19th Century. In his biography *Frederick Douglass*, historian William S. McFeely noted that

> From New Bedford harbor sailed a large fleet of whaling ships. ...the whaling industry had made New Bedford the richest city, per capita, in America... New Bedford, with its flourishing whaling industry, [was] particularly attractive to black families in the 1780s, when the abolition of slavery in Massachusetts made that state more hospitable than nearby Rhode Island... The black people of New Bedford [by 1838 had] achieved a measure of societal and psychological independence that made New Bedford the best city in America for an ambitious young black man.

Frederick Douglass, like other escaped Southern slaves and free blacks, was attracted there to work at his trade as a ship's caulker. Another man who relocated later to New Bedford, also to become well known, was Herman Melville. He was there in 1844, sailing on whalers and preparing to write *Typee*, his first book. Seven years later, his greatest novel, *Moby Dick*, was published. Melville did not ignore the heavy influence of slavery. Another of his books, *Benito Cereno*, concerns a slave revolt.

Here, in part, is how Melville described the Walkers' new hometown, New Bedford of the 1840s, in *Moby Dick*:

> The town itself is perhaps the dearest place to live in, in all New England. It is a land of [whale] oil, true enough; but not like Canaan; a land, also, of corn and wine... [N]owhere in all America will you find more patrician-like houses; parks and gardens more opulent, than in New Bedford... In summer time, the town is sweet to see; full of fine maples – long avenues of green and gold. And in August, high in air, the beautiful and bountiful horse-chestnuts, candelabra-wise, proffer the passerby their tapering upright cones of congregated blossoms.

In understanding Jonathan Walker, it is also helpful to know that New Bedford had been the home port of the sea captain and ship-owner, Paul Cuffe. Walker would have known about him. In *The Black Yankee*, George Arnold Salvador described Cuffe as "a half Indian, half Negro, Massachusetts Quaker... a free American Negro who dramatized the back-to-Africa movement in 1816, when he took thirty-eight American Negroes to Sierra Leone." Some historians have credited Cuffe with helping found Black Nationalism and another movement called "Colonization." While never as strong as the 1960s' and 1970s' "Black Pride" efforts, Black Nationalism was a revitalization movement among

Americans, emphasizing their African origins and identity, their pride in being black, and their desire to control their communities. Colonization was an effort to establish a black nation in Africa or some part of the United States. Cuffe was in his 50s, between 1811 and 1815, when he made the first attempts to establish a black American colony in Africa.

Such efforts, of course, did not always work in the best interests of African-Americans. The American Colonization Society's crusade, begun in 1817, led to the passage of laws in southern states prohibiting the education of Negroes, whether slave or free, under penalty of fine and imprisonment.

Cuffe, however, may have been one of a relatively few Americans, white or black, with a different reason for supporting the colonization movement. Salvador's study was devoted to the premise that the New Bedford captain was more practical than humanitarian. He concluded that Cuffe was interested in colonization for its income potential.

The idea of colonization did not fade quickly. Many supporters of the newly formed Republican Party in the 1860s thought that shipping all black people to Africa was the best solution to slavery. Among them was Benjamin Franklin Wade, elected to Congress from Ohio. Not without irony, Wade was considered, with Massachusetts' Charles Sumner, as among slavery's most outspoken opponents.

    *   *   *   *

Moving to New Bedford did not mean leaving Harwich for Jonathan and Jane Walker. Over the next thirty years, they and their growing family moved frequently between Harwich, New Bedford, and Plymouth along Massachusetts' southeastern coastline. Their "honeymoon" stay in New Bedford lasted only a few months. The birth of their first child was recorded on May 13, 1823, in Plymouth. Jonathan continued his sailing career and Jane tended their baby, who was named for John Bunyan (1628-1688), the author of *Pilgrim's Progress*. Bunyan wrote forty-three books and tracts, almost all while imprisoned for nonconformist beliefs. During his second jailing, when he was fifty years old, Bunyan published the religious allegory for which he was best known, and which attracted Jane and Jonathan Walker's admiration.

From 1816 to 1831, Jonathan was at sea regularly, "visiting all the Atlantic coasts and various Asiatic ports," the New Bedford *Republican Standard* wrote in 1877. When John Walker was a year old, and Jonathan himself only twenty-five, Jonathan met his fourth major calamity abroad. No doubt, people of color again came to his rescue. He was to recall the epidemic that struck mosquito-infested Cuba:

> I was at Havana in the sickly summer of 1824, when the yellow fever was multiplying its victims among foreigners at a fearful rate, and carrying them off with the black vomit, while death hoisted his desolating ensign over the fleet of shipping that was then in port, and sending its cart-loads daily of European and American citizens and seamen out of the city, and from on shipboard, to their last earthly

18

abode, no more to return to the social circle and their active vocations, in which they had acted their part; but leaving gloom and despair in the countenances of many a gallant crew. In some cases, there were not men enough left to pass their sleeping shipmates over the vessel's side into the waterman's boat, to be transferred to the dead-cart.

Walker described his own "unique" escape from death – he knew of no other who did not die, he said – in similarly florid language:

I too was singled out, and prostrated by that scourge of humanity, but after five days of severe conflict, the pale horse and his rider passed by, and permitted mercy to attend, and nature to revive again, contrary to human expectation; for I knew not the second one that could say that he was rescued from the clutches of the fell destroyer.

At home, the Walker family continued growing. John was three years old when the second Walker, Altamera, arrived – back in New Bedford. Less than a year later, Nancy Child Walker was born there, and two years after her, Sophia. In all, eight children were to follow John. Each year, it seems, there was a new, greater need to earn money for this family's survival. Jonathan did his best, while continuing his adventurous life with the support and encouragement of his understanding wife.

From 1831 to 1835, the Walkers lived in New Bedford and nearby Fairhaven. This was one of the few periods in his early life in which Jonathan spent most of his income-producing time on shore as a shipwright. As a result, during much of the early '30s, the growing family could settle into the routine of life with father. Reversing his earlier pattern, Jonathan was home now for longer stays, and then off on brief voyages.

    *   *   *   *

When he was in his twenties and thirties, Walker's concern for the plight of American slaves was deepening. As a sailor, he would meet and know black men. He wrote later that he had ...long since made up my mind that [slavery] ranked with the highest wrongs and crimes that ever were invented by the enemy of man, and ingeniously contrived to destroy the social and kind feelings existing between man and man, and the virtue and morals of both the master and the slave; subjecting one to the deepest degradation and misery, and the other to dissipation, and contempt of the laws and government of God. It is a family, community, political, and national poison; obstructing the circulation of friendly and Christian sympathy, and giving vent to the worst passions and most debasing and corroding feelings that human nature can experience.

Like the first crack of sunlight bringing promise of darkness' lifting, minor signs of slavery's end were appearing. On March 4, 1829, when Americans inaugurated the first president born in a log cabin, Andrew Jackson's calamitous White House reception led guest James Hamilton, Jr., to recall the people's wild party: "The mob broke in, in thousands. Spirits black, yellow, and gray poured in in one uninterrupted stream of mud and filth, among the throngs many subjects for the penitentiary..." Citing the spirit of the British Parliament's leading abolitionist, Hamilton added: "It would have done Mr. Wilberforce's heart good to have seen a stout black wench eating in this free country a jelly with a gold spoon at the President's House." Now, however, nearly forty years before the new Union was to settle the crisis of division, the stage was still being set.

Journalism was bringing forth a new single-issue press. As a traveler, Walker may have seen copies of the first newspaper edited for and by African Americans, *Freedom's Journal*, published in New York. In 1830, Daniel Webster provided the foundation for the dark decision he was to make years later in the United States Senate. Speaking on the threat of secession, the great orator declared: "Liberty and Union, now and forever, one and inseparable."

Jonathan Walker was not a man to sit aloof as such intense political and social strife rocked the changing nation. He never explained how he was attracted to the anti-slavery movement, although he claimed later in life that he had become an abolitionist in 1831. That would make Jonathan Walker a charter abolitionist, as it were. Historians generally consider that year as the beginning of the organized, and relentless, anti-slavery actions that led to the Emancipation Proclamation. Among the important events in the history of slavery that were recorded in 1831 were two would have influenced Walker:

- William Lloyd Garrison in January began publishing his immediately influential abolitionist newspaper, *The Liberator*, in Boston. Over the next thirty-five years, Walker was a faithful correspondent, providing scores of reports for publication.
- And Nat Turner, a black preacher in Southampton County, Virginia, led a local slave rebellion that August of 1831. Fifty-seven white people were killed before the federal government's troops suppressed the uprising and captured Turner. He was tried and hanged, becoming one of the abolitionist movement's earliest martyred heroes.

For years, such a revolt had been considered possible by Southern slaveholders, especially in areas where the black population outnumbered the whites. The Nat Turner rebellion, though quickly put down, spawned fears that another, greater insurrection, would explode. In 1831, a young entrepreneur named John Brown was raising a family in the Pennsylvania wilderness. Brown is said to have first seen *The Liberator* in 1833 or 1834. Insurrection at Harpers Ferry, Virginia, was not yet a dream.

The man whose destiny was to proclaim emancipation also was becoming more acquainted with slavery about this time. In 1831, Abraham Lincoln worked on a flatboat taking goods to New Orleans. It was there that Lincoln saw slaves in chains, being whipped, and on the auction block for sale.

Over the next few years, Jonathan Walker's interest would have been spurred by the developing abolitionist movement. The New England Anti-

The Making of a Patriot

Slavery Society was founded in 1832. The American Anti-Slavery Society, convening in Philadelphia on December 4, 1833, adopted a "declaration of sentiments" prepared by Garrison. The preamble reflected the reliance and dedication to religious roots, and the determination to overcome political and other more practical aspects of slavery, that abolitionists like Garrison and Walker brought to their efforts.

In 1834, Jonathan Walker was to recall later, abolitionist Samuel J. May "was the first man I ever heard lecture on the subject of slavery." The Reverend Mr. May was a Unitarian pastor in Syracuse, New York. His son, the Reverend Samuel May, Jr., became a Unitarian pastor in Leicester, Massachusetts.

Some parts of New England were welcoming abolition activists. While Boston was the major hub in this experience, as it has always been for the region, smaller communities, like Leicester, were also represented. For example, in Concord, New Hampshire, the state Anti-Slavery Society was putting out the weekly *Herald of Freedom*. Its editor was a former attorney from Plymouth, Massachusetts, Nathaniel Peabody Rogers. He was complimented by Henry David Thoreau, among others, for serving with "wit and fancy."

Editors were not always so honored. As Garrison's reputation for insisting on a complete end to slavery grew, so did public opposition to his virtually uncompromising demands on the clergy and government. The editor was threatened by a mob in 1835 and escaped only when authorities took him into Boston City Hall for protection. The mayor addressed the angry crowd while Garrison slipped out a side door.

*   *   *   *

During these years, Jonathan was still away most of the time. While Jane was often the only parent at home with the growing gang of youngsters. Jonathan was making his livelihood as a sailor and shipwright. In 1835, their eldest son, John, not unlike hundreds of Cape Cod's twelve-year-old boys in the 19th Century, left home to join his father at sea. Young John became a participant in what may have been Jonathan's most miraculous escape from death in a foreign land. This episode found the sea captain, nearly thirty-seven years old, chasing another dream to help settle a new frontier. Before father and son were able to return to Massachusetts, they were stranded in Mexico, attacked by bandits, escaped despite Jonathan's being wounded twice, and then walked, naked, forty miles before finding – again, for Jonathan – help in a small alien village.

The Mexican adventure was another product of Walker's lifelong desire to live in a pioneer community. In early 1835, he was still two decades from fulfilling that dream in the Old Northwest, but his desire and determination were strengthened when "I had some correspondence" with Benjamin Lundy, a Philadelphia philanthropist who had obtained a grant to establish a new colony in the northern Mexican province of Tamaulipas. The neighboring Spanish province, Texas, would break away from Mexico the following year and be an independent republic until becoming a United States territory in 1845. The very uncertainty of this frontier may have been another contribution to exciting the pioneer spirit of Jonathan Walker. "I had a mind to favor the scheme to the best of my ability," Walker wrote nearly ten years after, in a letter to a New Hampshire friend, "and began to look that way for my earthly home; but thought it best to *see* the promised land before adopting it as my local resting-place with my family."

There was an even stronger reason for an adventurous abolitionist. Walker described Lundy's idea as a proposal "to establish a refuge for blacks who wished to escape slavery and prejudice." The "refuge" was to be on 138,000 acres that Lundy had acquired in Mexico. That was equivalent to an area ten miles wide and twenty-one miles long, more than five times larger than Manhattan.

The man to whom Jonathan Walker had decided to trust his future was quite unlike himself. Benjamin Lundy, handicapped by deafness, was a wealthy Quaker who never married. He was like Walker, however, in being a man of action. The United States had 140 abolition societies in 1828, and many of them were credited to the efforts of Lundy.

Jonathan Walker had no reason to believe that such a man would not achieve his goal in Mexico. He set off with his twelve- year-old son, John, and a young friend, Richard Marvel, of Fairhaven, the Massachusetts community near New Bedford where the Walkers had been living. Walker identified this young man as a "mechanic" and misspelled his name as "R. Marble." Walker and the two young men sailed in November, 1835, from New Bedford, headed south along the Atlantic coast, rounded the Florida peninsula, and went into the Gulf of Mexico. They traveled, Walker wrote, "in a vessel of twelve tons, if so small a craft may be called a vessel." This was the first of at least two boats that Walker was to build – and to lose during adventures far from home. Walker built this boat in Fairhaven, probably with the help of John and young Marvel. He identified it as "a small sloop called the *Supply of New Bedford*."

"We had a long and rough passage, and encountered five gales before we reached Mexico," Walker wrote. Their arrival was just as stormy. They had left Massachusetts at the historical time (November 2-4) that Texans had proclaimed their right to secede from Mexico. An eagerly receptive United States placed in charge of the Texas army that November a man who had been elected to Congress from Tennessee when he was only thirty years old. Sam Houston, destined to be Texas' most glorified war hero, led the revolutionary forces in fierce battles during the winter of 1835-36 and throughout the territory.

And into this storm came a white Yankee idealist! Jonathan Walker sailed into the northeast corner of Mexico, landing only a few miles west of the community today known as Brownsville, Texas.

The Walker group put ashore that winter at Matamoros, which a decade later was to be the scene of major action in the U.S.- Mexican war. The conflict had already begun. About the time of the Walkers' landing came the famous

The Making of a Patriot

battle of the Alamo, February 23-March 6, 1836. The entire Texas garrison at San Antonio was killed. This battle seemed only to stiffen the determination of the breakaway Texans. They declared their independence from Mexico on March 2, during the Alamo fight, and, although they were badly beaten in that battle, General Houston and his Texas army did "remember the Alamo." On April 21, 1836, Texans seceded from the Mexican coalition and established their independence with a major victory at the battle of San Jacinto. The battle took place 375 miles northwest of Walker's position in Matamoros, but with the Mexicans' withdrawal to the land south of the Rio Grande River, Lundy's grant was now in Texas. Eventually, the international boundary was defined by treaty as the deepest channel of that long, coursing river called by the Mexicans, who were now to its south, *Rio Bravo del Norte*, Brave River of the North. Merton L. Dillon pointed out in his Lundy biography that Lundy abandoned his dream, "aware that Texans were unsympathetic to his abolitionist scheme." In fact, Texas' pro-slavery citizens' wrath exploded when Houston became the only Southern Democrat to oppose the Kansas-Nebraska Bill. This Congressional act had the effect of permitting new states, upon joining the Union, to decide for themselves if they wished to legalize slavery.

Walker, in his typically formal and understated way, wrote of his arrival in the thick of this war: "I found the country in a very unsettled state, and strong and growing prejudices were arrayed against citizens of the United States, on account of the war that was then raging between Mexico and her rebellious Texas, carried on mainly by assistance from the United States."

The Walkers and Marvel waited in vain for the Lundy colonists to join them. The charitable Jonathan concluded: "They were prevented doubtless by the war."

Ever the entrepreneur, never idle, Walker arranged that spring to operate courier charters from "mercantile houses in Matamoros," mainly carrying mail to New Orleans businesses. Now he was sailing the same Gulf of Mexico waters that Abraham Lincoln had worked five years earlier. Perhaps he tied up near one of Edward K. Collins' New Orleans Line ships captained by Nathaniel Brown Palmer. Palmer, who was about the same age as Cape Cod natives Collins and Walker, was a native of Stonington, Connecticut, another community known for producing sailors. Hired in 1833 by Collins, Palmer was to become commodore of Collins' Dramatic Line and sail the *Roscius*, at a thousand tons and with the greatest expanse of sail of any ship afloat, a giant compared to Walker's small craft.

*   *   *   *

On June 6, 1836, as best as Walker could later fix the date, the three Massachusetts adventurers were leaving their craft at the end of a run from New Orleans to Matamoros when they were attacked "by a gang of robbers." Walker described the scene this way:

> My young friend, R. Marble [sic], attempted to escape by flight, but was pursued by two of the armed assassins, and I saw him no more. My

son plunged into the surf and swam to sea. They fired at me, and I received two of their musket balls, and made supplication for mercy, but they soon convinced me, by attempting to use a pistol and their knives upon me, that if I looked to them for quarter, I looked in vain. My only chance to escape immediate death was to follow, if possible, the example of my son, and while they were making the attempt to dispatch me, I succeeded in gaining the surf, and joined my son in the offing. We found it necessary to divest ourselves of what clothing we had on, to enable us to exercise ourselves with more activity and ease.

As he attempted to stay afloat, Captain Walker may have recalled the story of Captain Freeman Mayo of Brewster, a Cape Cod town bordering on Walker's hometown of Harwich. Mayo was very likely a distant relative of Jane Walker. Pirates in 1822 had overtaken Captain Mayo's brig, *Iris*, off Cuba. Finding no money on the brig, the pirates allowed the captain to go to Matanzas to solicit funds while they held the crew hostage. When Mayo returned with $3,000, he found the *Iris* abandoned and the two pirate vessels gone. Returning to Matanzas, he was amazed to see his wounded crew. Led by Sylvanus Crosby, also of Brewster, they had overthrown the pirates and escaped as the United States schooner *Alligator* found the pirates' cove and took the pirates into custody.

Walker – swimming naked and bleeding, concerned for the welfare of his twelve-year-old-son – certainly would not have devoted much time, if any, to Captain Mayo. A good storyteller, he continued his account as a kind of afterthought in the appendix to his book, *Trial and Imprisonment*:

And now, let the reader imagine our situation. On one side was the shore, guarded by the robbers ready to butcher us if we landed, and on the other side was the whole bay of Mexico; and myself deprived of the use of one hand by a bullet, being shot through the wrist joint. The blood oozing freely from that and another bullet wound in the abdomen was well-suited to invite a greedy shark to finish the work of his two-legged brothers on shore.

Walker attributed their escape from sharks and robbers to "divine assistance." The father and son

treaded water until the darkness of night afforded us an opportunity to elude their vigilance, and land at some distance from the place where we first swam. We carefully surveyed the shore, before landing, to see that we were not observed by any of the *banditti*, and took the direction of the shore toward the nearest inhabited place I knew of, in search of aid and protection. It was nearly sundown when we were attacked, and I think we were in the water something over one hour. After travelling that night and the greater part of the next day, suffering severely from pain, raging thirst, weakness by loss of blood and the heat of a burning sun acting upon our naked bodies... we presented [on June 7, 1836] our miserable and almost exhausted persons at a rancho (small village) at the mouth of the Rio del Norte...

The wound in the wrist continued to bleed upwards of fifteen hours, and could only be stanched by keeping the wound higher than the shoulder, and in order to do that I was obliged to hold it up with the other hand. [Before reaching safety,] I was reeling and staggering like a drunken person, and could with difficulty make any progress.

The wound probably was in the left wrist. While that limb was permanently impaired, he continued writing with his right hand another thirty years. He estimated his loss of blood as "but very little, if any, short of four quarts..."

At the Mexican village,

... we found aid and hospitable treatment from its poor inhabitants, for which we were very grateful... Thus we were thrown upon the charity of strangers more than 2,000 miles from home, entirely naked, and penniless, myself severely wounded and in a very delicate state of health. The distance we had traveled was estimated by the inhabitants at forty miles, and we were unable to procure any fresh water during the whole distance.

Richardson, and other historians, have given special weight to Walker's words because the sea captain wrote with clear thoughts, moral opinions, and, it sometimes seems, an unfailing memory for facts. Richardson also praised Walker's account of his 1844-45 Florida imprisonment for its charitable regard for some of his tormentors. Walker was not always so considerate. Unexplainably, his journal dismissed Richard Marvel, the Fairhaven mechanic, with a single sentence: He was never seen again. Walker detailed his own difficulties while making his wounded way to the Mexican village, but referred to his son only inferentially. As bad as the trip was for Jonathan Walker, it must have been a terrifying experience for the two younger men. Marvel was given up for dead. Jonathan, who thought deeply about parents' roles in helping their children into adulthood, surely would have considered the impact on his twelve-year-old son of a young companion's disappearance, his father's wounding, and their escape by swimming in the Gulf of Mexico.

If Jonathan took any blame for the boys' experience, he did not mention it directly in his writings. Nearly a decade later, however, in his narrative, *Trial and Imprisonment*, the father seemed to be faulting his own judgment in permitting his son to accompany him in 1836 to Mexico:

When parents and guardians so far neglect their duty to their children and minors as to induce them to embark on the dangerous experiment, by their neglecting to aid them in some other pursuit or employment, or drive them away by improper treatment, they have no right to complain if they have to partake of the bitter cup of sorrow and remorse themselves, as the natural fruits of their unnatural conduct towards those for whom they are, by the laws of nature and of God, held accountable. I do not intend to charge the fact upon all the parents that have children who follow the seas; neither do I contend that there is anything dishonorable or improper necessarily connected with that vocation. But I do unhesitatingly, and without the fear of contradiction, say that no way of life in the United States places a young man in so critical a situation as is common to a seafaring life; or one in which he is so likely to make shipwreck of his soul, unless guarded by the strongest moral feelings, or mercifully dealt with by a kind and overruling Providence.

*   *   *   *

On top of all this, Walker claimed to have lost what would have been a small fortune in Mexico, not during the attack by bandits but from Mexican authorities. He told this story in 1849 in a letter to Horace Mann, then a member of Congress from Massachusetts:

[W]e succeeded in reaching the mouth of the Rio del Norte late the next day nearly exhausted. I then prevailed on five men (among whom were two custom house officials,) to accompany my son down the coast to my vessel. My son succeeded in getting one thousand forty-five dollars from the wreck, which the robbers had not discovered and taken away. But before he reached me with it, the custom house officers got possession of it, and lodged it in the custom house at Matamoros, and not a farthing of it was I able to get again, though it was often promised me.

One thousand dollars was a great deal of money in the middle years of the nineteenth century. Walker's fine and a year's jail costs in Pensacola eight years after the Mexican affair never reached that sum. To have hidden that much cash aboard *Supply of New Britain*, Captain Walker obviously had been working hard, and earning good fees, hauling mail and supplies between New Orleans and Matamoros during the preceding few months.

What followed Jonathan and John Walker's Mexican affair? Jonathan's journals do not mention what he did. Richardson summarized the next year's efforts: "After his wounds healed sufficiently... he built another boat and returned to the United States. In order to earn desperately needed money, Walker determined to engage in the Alabama-Florida coastal trade, rather than proceeding immediately to Massachusetts. While involved in this venture, he reputedly assisted several slaves who chanced to come aboard in obtaining their freedom."

It is not recorded that Walker did, as Richardson speculated, construct a boat before leaving the South. Walker would have left Mexico as soon as he was well enough to travel, his reason for being there shattered. In the letter to Horace

The Making of a Patriot

Mann, Walker said he stayed in Mexico "about three months in ill health and suspense, living on charity..." The suspense, no doubt, came from waiting for the return of his money, not from hoping to see Benjamin Lundy's first refugees from slavery.

Walker would have overcome quickly the problems of having no money. An old hand as resourceful as he was would have had no difficulty signing on for work aboard a vessel headed eastward in the Gulf of Mexico. Obtaining a trip to Florida's panhandle area would have been easy, and Walker would doubtless stop at a place that he was familiar with. More conscious now of young John's safety, he would have looked for a settled port, perhaps a place where, over the years of sailing, he had developed acquaintances. For these reasons, it is likely that Jonathan Walker, with his son at his side, chose to land in Pensacola and to build a boat. Whether he did, in fact, earn money sailing in coastal trade, or whether he smuggled any slaves to freedom, is not documented, although various accounts over the years have suggested the possibilities.

We can guess that Jonathan returned with young John to Harwich in the late fall of 1836, or even the early winter of 1837, having devoted perhaps six months to recovering his health, constructing a new boat, earning money in odd jobs, and sailing around the deep Florida peninsula and northward in the Atlantic Ocean.

He now had survived at least five life-threatening adventures while on the ocean. This Mexican affair had left him with a weak arm, a handicap that may have confined his future sailing to the boats he built himself. He had seldom sailed recently on a deep-water vessel, so this new injury would not have caused any change in his plans. More important to his immediate future, however, was the likelihood that he had already found a place where he wanted to move his family. He had sailed to Mexico to scout that country as a place to settle. Whatever he had lost by the adventure, it did not include his desire to live in the South. Now, it seems, Mexico had been replaced in his fancy by Florida.

Photo by M.E. Haskell; courtesy Massachusetts Historical Society

The Walker Family home on Cape Cod, like Jonathan himself, moved about. This photograph was made about 1991, probably less than a year before the building was razed. While living here about 1814, the teen-age Jonathan was rescued when he fell through thin ice at nearby Skinniquit Pond. Located in its last years in South Chatham, the farmhouse was originally a half-mile or so west near Route 28 in South Harwich. The photographer said she had often heard the Walker legend. Driving by one day, she decided to make this image.

> He preached to the Negroes and exhorted them
> with great brotherly affection,
> telling them that they were just as good as he was,
> and that the difference of color was a mere shadow, etc.
> **Pensacola** *Gazette*

CHAPTER 3   Settling Down in Florida

Wherever it was that Walker spent the late months of 1836, it is probable that when he did return to Massachusetts he and Jane would have reviewed their situation. We can imagine Jane, without withdrawing any of her support for her restless but industrious husband, stoutly pressing Jonathan to take stock of his life.

Their first consideration would have been their family. In 1837, Jonathan was thirty-eight years old and Jane was thirty-four. They had been married fifteen years and had five children, ranging in age from John, who had turned thirteen during his first long trip away from home, to four-year-old Mary Gage Walker. Born April 8, 1832, Mary was named for Jane's grandmother, the mother of her father, Mayo Gage.

The Walkers' second major consideration would be income. At this point in his life, Jonathan had developed two maritime careers. He had been a sailor and captain of his own vessels more than twenty years. During this time, he also had become an expert boat builder. He frequently hired on as a boatwright in seaport towns. When he was thus committed, working for others, he had a reliable income and was with Jane and the children every day. On the negative side, he apparently hired on for specific jobs – building a large boat, or even a ship, for example – and when each project ended, he would be looking for a new source of income. Work was not always available at the site of his last job, so he would search out other boatyards. Consequently, the family had lived up and down the Massachusetts coast, relocating to wherever Jonathan found work.

Had the time come to think about another type of work, a kind that would lead to his settling down permanently? Sailing, as Walker had noted in his journal, was a tough occupation. Death was a common hazard not unknown to the Walkers.

Jane's forty-two-year-old brother, Edward Gage, "was lost returning home from the Banks in 1837," according to Louise H. Kelley's notation in the Harwich Vital Records. The Grand Banks lay off Newfoundland's coast, a trip of a thousand miles each way and of many months for Cape fishermen. It's more likely that Edward Gage was returning from what Kittredge described as the "dangerous tide rips that criss-cross each other on the Georges Banks, only a little more than a day's sail from home [for Cape Codders]... These waters had always been held in an almost superstitious terror. Strange things happened on them."

When Jane's brother died, his wife became one of about a thousand widows counted on Cape Cod by the New England *Gazetteer*. Such matters would give Jane Walker renewed cause for worry, and could have led to persuasive discussion with Jonathan about the family's future.

As Walker had written in reflecting on the rugged life of the sailor "Jack," shipboard discipline was intimidating for men of gentle spirit. Without attribution, historian Kittredge quoted this verse about the crew of a whaling ship:

> She'd a crew of blacks from the Cape Verde Isles
> > That spoke in Portagee,
> With men from Norway, Finland, too,
> > And the shores of the Irish Sea.
> She'd whites from the rocky Yankee farms,
> > Mixed up with Sandwich brown,
> With a skipper who hailed from New Bedford
> > And a mate from Westport Town.

Captain Nathaniel Burgess, of Bourne, who once sailed with a crew representing nine nationalities, said discipline was a whaling captain's most serious problem.

In *The American Whaleman*, E. P. Hohman had nothing good to say about such sailors. Whaleships, he wrote, attracted only "immoral and unprincipled wretches... confirmed drunkards, vagrant ne'er-do-wells, unapprehended criminals, escaped convicts, and dissipated and diseased human derelicts of every description."

Compared to making a living on the ocean, working on shore seemed safe and pleasant.

"By this time – the 1830s and 1840s," Kittredge wrote, "halcyon days on the Cape had begun. Business of all sorts was booming; bridges and breakwaters were being built; banks and insurance companies were being incorporated; fisheries were in full swing; the caulker's mallet made music in a dozen small shipyards."

There was plenty of work in Harwich, and elsewhere on the Cape, for a man with Jonathan Walker's skills.

Another reminder that Jane's family was rooted on the Cape, while she was forever being transplanted, came in May of 1837. Jane's thirty-eight-year-old brother, Hiram Gage, was married to Remember Bowen. They were both Harwich natives, they were married in Harwich, and they intended to live in Harwich.

Perhaps Jane Walker suggested that Jonathan might wish to consider finding a permanent job in his native town of Harwich.

If Jonathan gave up sailing, he would be able to work full- time as a boatwright. But then, would the family want to be committed to residing briefly in a port community before moving on to the next job site?

While the need to feed his family required a decision and action, Jonathan Walker still harbored a dream: to help in settling the western frontier. He would have been enchanted by the idea of loading his family onto a "prairie schooner," the Conestoga wagons being made by Keith & Sons in Sagamore, Massachusetts, just twenty miles west of Harwich. But, as he revealed later, he had "begun to go among slavery." No, the time had not come to pursue this dream of pioneering the territories opening in the West.

Walker did not act immediately. While home in Harwich, he contacted Cape Cod's representative in Congress, John Reed of Yarmouth, and asked his help in recovering the money taken from him in Mexico. He later wrote Horace Mann:

> After my return home, by the advice of friends, I consulted John Read (sic) in relation to the subject and was advised by him and others to petition Congress to aid in recovering at least this part of my losses in the case. I accordingly had a petition drawn up, giving a full account of the circumstances, to which was affixed the affidavits of a number of merchants of New Bedford (where I then resided) and a protest duly acknowledged by a notary of public, which was delivered by myself to Mr. Read, who promised faithfully to attend to the case at Washington the earliest practicable opportunity.

So, what was this family of seven to do? Perhaps the Walkers reached a compromise: He would yield to Jane's wish, give up life on the ocean and find work on land – if he could choose the site. Thus, Jane would have her husband every night, home with her and the children regularly for family activities. But would they continue to live in Massachusetts? Jonathan had long fancied life in the South. If he were to make such a compromise, he would likely choose a place he was familiar with, perhaps a warm place.

Jonathan Walker The Man with the Branded Hand

Jonathan and Jane packed up the five youngsters and moved to Florida. Pensacola in 1837 was already one of the South's major ports on the Gulf of Mexico. Walker had been sailing in and around the region for years; probably he and son John had lived there the previous fall. Moving the family there would meet Jane's end of the bargain. His settling down would carry out his promise.

The Walkers sailed to Florida early in 1837, probably in the small sloop he had constructed in late 1836. The enterprising Jonathan brought a heavy load of goods as well as his family. The weekly newspaper, the Pensacola *Gazette*, was to report that Walker "first came to this city from down east in a little sloop with a cargo of about 4,000 bricks and a few potatoes, beets, and other 'notions.' He rented a small house in the suburbs and opened his cargo for retail."

That was not going to provide money for long. As part of being an accomplished boatwright, he was a skilled carpenter. He could make virtually any part of a boat out of wood. That skill, and his shipboard experiences as manager of men, was soon to be employed in helping Florida develop a railroad.

Charles H. Hildreth wrote for the *Florida Historical Quarterly*:

The opening of the three-mile Quincy (Massachusetts) railroad in 1827 marked a general change in emphasis in transportation in the United States. Visionaries suffering from "canal fever" discovered [that] "railroad fever"... allowed the mind to envision schemes not limited by the natural waterways of the nation. Florida, a [territory in] the Union for slightly more than a decade, became the setting in 1833 for one of the most ambitious of these early plans. The acquisition of Florida placed in the hands of the United States government one of the best natural harbors on the Gulf coast... Isolated from the rich cotton lands of southern Alabama and Georgia, the leading businessmen of the city felt that Pensacola could achieve its destiny only by linking the hinterland with its fine harbor. This was to be accomplished through the development of railroad communication.

With the introduction of the steam locomotive in 1830 and the flanged rail in 1831, Florida was among the earliest regions to consider building a railroad. Construction of an eight-mile line was opened by the Lake Wimico & St. Joseph Canal and Railroad Company, using mules, on April 14, 1836, about the time that Jonathan Walker had sailed hopefully into Matamoros, Mexico. That September, before Walker had returned to Massachusetts, Florida's first steam locomotive "drew a train of twelve cars and 300 passengers, hooting the distance in twenty-five minutes, and with a confident engineer believing he could cut the time to eight minutes." Similarly, the Tallahassee-St. Marks line, twenty-three-mile long and also opened in 1836, was for the next seventeen years to use mules driven by black slaves.

These were boom times for Florida's westernmost city. In that confident year of 1836, Pensacola erected "a good and substantial jail on the site of the old Spanish Calaboza. The jail is two stories high with piazza in the front and rear," historical researcher Leora M. Sutton wrote for Ernie Lee Magaha, clerk of Pensacola's circuit and county courts.

Jonathan Walker's role in helping Pensacola develop a railroad center was small. And, as it happened, his part was played only briefly. Florida had chartered the Florida, Alabama, & Georgia Railroad on February 14, 1834. Immediately, Mobile business leaders pressured Alabama's legislature to block the operation, and when finally, late in 1834, the new railroad company met Alabama's standards, the name had been changed to give that state top billing. Now it was "the Alabama, Florida, & Georgia Railroad Company," the AF&G. It would be forty years before Florida had carried out its work to build a cross-state line. Long after Walker had left Florida, two others from Massachusetts remained prominent in railroading. They were William H. Chase, a Massachusetts-born captain in the United States Army Corps of Engineers, who was elected president in 1834 when the renamed AF&G was organized, and Walter Gregory, a former Bostonian who was elected the first president of the new Bank of Pensacola at its organizing meeting in June 1833 and who was a charter member of the AF&G's Board of Directors. Among their colleagues on the railroad board was a local attorney, Thomas M. Blount, who a decade later was to have an important role in Jonathan Walker's life in jail.

Indeed, long before the term "interlocking boards" pointed to the power the action derives, Pensacola's leaders met each other regularly in the board rooms. Serving as stockholders of the Bank of Pensacola with Walter Gregory, for example, were George Chase, Hanson Kelly, Dr. John Parker, and Walker Anderson, a lawyer. Anderson was to have a part in the murder investigation of Dr. Parker and a major role in Jonathan Walker's "trial and imprisonment." And yet, while all of these business people were to be prominent in Pensacola's railroad and banking history, and while Walker's part in community growth was minuscule, none of them was to perform nearly so catalytic a role as Walker in the young city's social identification.

Before the Walkers' arrival in 1837, an AF&G crew had begun clearing land from Pensacola northward to the Alabama state line. Most of the work was done by black slaves.

It is possible that Jonathan Walker, when the time came to decide where to relocate with his family, knew of this effort, and so in 1837 he chose the West Florida port city for his family's next home. He could make the same argument for regional prosperity that Jane may have suggested as a reason to settle on Cape Cod. The advent of the railroad in Florida promised years of income for an ambitious, steady worker.

As so often happened, life's realities fell short of Walker's hopes. The Walkers had barely settled in when disaster smashed the nation's economic hopes. Called the Panic of 1837, the depression sent workers' pay to fifty cents a day. Bankruptcy was everywhere. The depression wrecked the Bank of Pensacola. On December 23, 1837, the Alabama Legislature reversed its earlier agreement to permit AF&G rails to run to Montgomery. The Walkers had arrived just in time to see the boom, like a pricked balloon, instantly lose its robust grandeur and fall helplessly flat.

*   *   *   *

Meantime, East and West Florida were bickering over the issues of slavery. In *Florida: The Long Frontier*, Marjory Stoneman Douglas reported:

...the cotton planters of middle Florida began to argue that Florida should be admitted into the Union as a slave state, to balance the admission of other territories as free, under a growing sentiment for abolition. Frontiersmen, however...on the east coast objected to statehood because they said it would raise taxes. They had been ruined in the freeze of 1835 in East Florida, the bank failures, and depression of 1837. Few new men were coming into their listless and stagnant villages...

For the first time, then, West and East Florida lined up to oppose rich middle Florida in its clamor for statehood. Some even agreed that West Florida could be a state if East Florida could be left a territory. The Legislative Assembly in 1837 passed an act providing for a census and a referendum on statehood. There were three negative votes. The census showed 48,223 people in the territory, of whom 21,132 were slaves and 958, free blacks.

"Rail-fever," as Bowden called it, was again to hit Pensacola with prosperity's return in the 1840s, after the Walker family had returned to Massachusetts to live. In the years between "fevers," construction slowed, then stopped. Walker survived as a caretaker. He was remembered by the *Gazette* as having been "employed after the bursting of the railroad and New Town bubble to live at the depot and take care of the railroad property." And, especially, he was remembered as the white man who hired black workers. These workers, it appears, were slaves, their services rented out by the white men who kept all or most of the pay that the black men earned. This was a common custom.

Sutton wrote in a paper, "Blacks and Slaves in Pensacola 1780-1880," prepared for the Pensacola Historical Society:

Walker lived... [with] his wife and three children. There was a time, during the five years he lived in Pensacola, that he had found it necessary to hire slaves to help him with some work for the railroad. The family broke with strong traditions of the South by having the slaves eat at the family table while the wife and daughters waited on the men. White neighbors strongly objected to this "social equality.

Jane Walker, who genealogist Louise H. Kelley believes "lost a male infant" during this period, was Jonathan's partner in efforts to recognize the abilities of African Americans and to treat them as equals. It was he, however, who was credited, or blamed, for fraternizing.

Henrietta Buckmaster wrote in her history of the underground railroad, *Let My People Go*: "[Walker] treated his black workers in the manner of a

Christian, allowing them to eat with him and pray with him...he won their friendship."

The Walkers were not alone in their dedication to equality. Marjory Stoneman Douglas in *The Long Frontier* wrote: "There were even men here and there, Scotch Presbyterians, Northern men, Quakers, men down the Keys from the Bahamas where the slaves had been free since early in the century, who did not believe in slavery."

The Pensacola *Gazette* later wrote of Walker:

He seemed a very devout Christian, and by his apparent uprightness and integrity had gained a confidence of many highly respectable members of our community. Whilst he lived at the depot, however, he had frequent occasions to have Negroes to work for him, and he associated with them on terms of equality and intimacy, seating them with him at his table while his daughters (half-grown girls) waited on the table. He preached to the Negroes and exhorted them with great brotherly affection, telling them that they were just as good as he was, and that the difference of color was a mere shadow, etc.

Walker characterized the newspaper's report of June 29, 1844, as "an attempt... to tell how and when I came there, and my business and course of conduct while there, etc.; but in that description they only succeeded in getting at now and then a truth." Walker did, however, cite the paragraph quoted above as containing "most of the truth in the statement..."

The *Gazette* reported that a slave named Charles Johnson "was employed by [Walker] at the depot, and was a ranting, shouting member of the church with him..." Charles Johnson was one of four brothers who were to attempt the flight to freedom with Walker in 1844.

In his book, *Trial and Imprisonment*, Walker wrote:

Twice, while living there, I was called upon by different persons – the chief executive officers or mayors for the time being – in consequence of the reports in circulation that I was on good terms with the colored people; and it was intimated that there was danger in regard to my peace and safety, for should the people be excited in any consequence of my discountenance of some of their rules and customs respecting the association of white with colored men, it would be out of their power to shield me from *violence*.

Walker was accused of far more than associating with people of color. In the "most of the truth" paragraph, the *Gazette* also wrote: "He was suspected of tampering with the Negroes and of being accessory to the concealment on board of a vessel and the escape of two slaves about three or four years ago." By so clearly pointing out this as among the few "truths" in the account, was Walker verifying the accusation or the act of helping escapees? None of Walker's papers has suggested he ever attempted to assist slaves to run away around 1840 or

1841, when the Walker family was living in Pensacola. As adventurous as he was, Jonathan would have placed the safety of Jane and the children first when they were together. As he was later to experience, to have been caught in such an illegal activity would have put his own freedom in jeopardy and stranded his wife and youngsters far from their New England home.

To help a later generation understand how intimidating pro-slavery people could be in that place at that time, historian Mark Der explained in his book, *Some Kind of Paradise*:

> The central fact of Florida society in the years 1821 to 1865 was human bondage. To the planters, slaves represented not just labor but the *sine qua non* of an aristocratic way of life. Slaves tended the fields [and] provided the skilled artisans, and unskilled laborers produced the goods and services that turned the profits and kept the larders full. To work in the field, even if next to slaves, was to be a lesser man, and, throughout the Florida Territory, many young heirs of the new gentry would turn to professions like law if they owned fewer than thirty slaves, which was deemed the minimum number for operating a plantation in proper style. Those with insufficient wealth to partake fully of leisure often pursued it nonetheless and drove themselves into bankruptcy.... The privileged white men and women of Tallahassee traveled between plantations to party and dine, to hunt, and to discuss the pressing affairs of the day – the value of Christian virtue and civilization; life in their summer homes in the mountains of Georgia, Carolina, Tennessee; politics; the threat of slave insurrection; and the need to remove the Indians.

*   *   *   *

Jonathan Walker was concerned with some of the same practical matters, but his sense of virtue took a different turn than Tallahassee's privileged people. He took an infirmed slave, William Cook, into his home and treated him with botanical medicine, a skill for which he became known.

Cook, a black man from Virginia, went to Pensacola without papers certifying he had been freed. In 1840, Sheriff Peter Woodbine arrested Cook, placed him in jail, and advertised him as a possible runaway slave. After Walker talked with Cook, a lawyer was hired to prove Cook was free. Eventually, Woodbine moved Cook from the jail and chained him in the Woodbines' attic for almost a year while the Virginia papers were being obtained. When Cook's health suffered and dropsy set in, Walker received permission to move Cook to his home. He cared for Cook with cayenne, lobelia, and steam treatments. When Cook had regained his health, he left Pensacola. And, foretelling the experience that Walker was to have with Pensacolans, Cook was again seized – this time for not paying the fees charged by the attorney who never obtained his free papers, by the jail physician who never cured his dropsy, by the Pensacola *Gazette* newspaper for running the ad identifying Cook as a possible fugitive, and by Sheriff Woodbine for performing his duties as jailer. Cook, of course, was unable to pay, so work was arranged at the U.S. Navy Yard. He would earn money to pay off his obligations.

The bills, exceeding $200, included $30 owed the newspaper and more than $100 owed the sheriff for food, charged at the rate of 37½ cents per day. This was a standard rate for feeding prisoners in Escambia County, Florida, during that decade.

Cook worked at the Pensacola docks for two years to pay his debts. Then, Sheriff Woodbine presented Cook another bill – for feeding and clothing the Virginia man while he was still working off his debt. Cook put in two more months and, aware that he would never earn enough to pay off the ongoing debts, ran away. Jonathan Walker must have applauded that bold decision.

Despite such egalitarian actions – or perhaps, for some Pensacolans, *because* of them – Jonathan Walker was generally well regarded in both the white and black communities. One reason was, no doubt, his quiet demeanor and gentle manner.

Walker was a living oxymoron: a former sea captain who did not swear, drink, or carouse, and he was shorebound in a frontier port community where men on shore-leave perfectly fitted the role of the legendary drunken sailors. Pensacola's U.S. Navy base, founded in 1826, regularly contributed furloughed sailors to the inmate rosters at the city jail. Civilians did the same, notably immigrants helping to build the railroad. Bowden reported: "Irishmen 'worked like beavers' but their usefulness was limited by fighting 'like devils'; and the Dutch gangs, imported from Europe as replacements, stopped work at 10 a.m. and 4 p.m. each day until every man's stein was filled with beer." Among such a force, the benign Jonathan Walker would have seemed acceptably strange to peaceful Pensacolans.

Walker maintained the spirit of the Quakers, who interpreted literally the words of Christ in Scripture, especially "Do not swear at all" and "Do not resist one who is evil." Walker did neither. His friendship was invested in a manner as egalitarian as his other attitudes towards fellow humans. As a result, his friends and acquaintances came from a great cross-section of any community in which he lived. In Pensacola, for example, he came to know the United States marshal, Ebenezer Dorr. Marshal Dorr was a native of Hallowell, Maine. He had married a woman named Walker and had a son given the name of Walker Dorr, perhaps providing Jonathan and Ebenezer a source for a running joke about being "cousins" of a sort.

Having a namesake also meant having heartache for Walker. In fact, Jonathan Walker was to lose three members of his family within eighteen months while living in Pensacola. They were a nephew named Jonathan Walker, a brother, and a niece. His brother Nathan, the closest to Jonathan as boys growing up on the farm, died on March 5, 1839, at the age of forty-three years. Nathan and his wife, the former Lucy Moody, had named their son, born only three months before, on November 19, 1838, Jonathan Walker, probably after the baby's world-travelling uncle. The sea captain was never to see his nephew.

Jonathan Walker The Man with the Branded Hand

The baby died on June 30, 1840, not yet two years old. Three months later, on September 26, 1840, death was to take Jonathan's niece, Betsy Moody Walker, the eighteen-year-old daughter of Nathan and Lucy.

*   *   *   *

While the Walker family was adjusting to life in the South, the Northern abolitionist movement continued through adolescent years. Pursuit of equality was, ironically, recognized as activity for men only in many organizations, including the British and Foreign Anti-Slavery Society. As host of the 1840 World Anti-Slavery Convention in London, the group ruled that women could not participate. Indignant, William Lloyd Garrison and another newspaper editor, Nathaniel P. Rogers of the *Herald of Freedom*, objected and sat in the gallery with women. In Rogers' absence, the New Hampshire-based newspaper was being edited by Parker Pillsbury, described by Sterling as "a youthful former minister who had come out of the church to preach freedom for the slave."

Pillsbury, who was to lecture on Cape Cod often, worked closely with Stephen Symonds Foster. Foster graduated from Dartmouth in 1838 and attended Union Theological Seminary in New York before returning to New Hampshire as an Anti-Slavery Society lecturing agent. During the Walkers' Florida years, Foster and Pillsbury were to become major figures in abolitionism. Ralph Waldo Emerson described Pillsbury as "a tough oak stick of a man"; Foster was jailed many times over the next decade for his actions in arousing Sunday worshippers against the clergy. He branded them "a brotherhood for thieves."

Another important figure was emerging during the five years the Walkers were in Pensacola. In August 1841, three years after his escape from slavery in Maryland, Frederick Douglass addressed an anti-slavery gathering on Nantucket island, beginning his long, unparalleled career as an abolitionist. A week after his appearance on the tiny island located near Cape Cod as a new lecturing agent, he "enthralled" the Massachusetts Anti-Slavery Society quarterly meeting in Millbury, Sterling wrote.

Meantime, many of the people of Cape Cod were attempting to sort out their attitudes about equality. In 1839, the Barnstable County Anti-Slavery Society came into being. By the time of its second annual meeting in Orleans, Massachusetts, on January 8 and 9, 1840, it had several major issues to decide. Prominent in the action were ordained clergymen, led by the Reverend James Barnaby of Harwich, the society's first president; the Reverend Joseph Mash of Sandwich; and a visitor from Providence, Rhode Island, the Reverend Charles T. Torrey. Before this new decade of the 1840s had ended, Mash and Torrey were to have roles affecting the way Jonathan Walker was regarded, both on Cape Cod and throughout the country.

For the Cape gathering of about a hundred, a major issue was the admission of women to the society. The convention was opened with a motion "that all gentlemen present... are hereby invited to... participate with us in the

38

proceedings of this meeting." A formal protest, because the vote had excluded women, was circulated and signed by eighteen. The petition cited arguments familiar to opponents of slavery: "...a deliberate and palpable violation of the constitutional rights... contrary to the lofty genius and spirit of the Anti-Slavery enterprise... sanctioning the sectarian principle that it is a sin and a shame for a woman to speak in a public meeting." The petition was dispatched by being "entered on the records."

Had he known about the meeting on Cape Cod, Jonathan Walker would have resented the exclusion of women, but would have understood why females were banned when informed that at least twenty ordained "gentlemen" had attended. He, like Foster, was not affectionate towards the "brotherhood."

*   *   *   *

Walker became a familiar figure in Pensacola during the years after the Panic of 1837, although he never referred to any of the white men he knew as friends. His friendship was extended, however, to black people, some of whom law-enforcement officials like Marshal Dorr rounded up in carrying out official duties. William Cook was one such example. Another was a slave identified only as Isaac. Sometime in late spring or early summer of 1841, Isaac was sentenced to death. Leora Sutton wrote:

> Walker also noted the flow of justice in the case of State vs. Isaac, a slave belonging to James Stokes of Milton... [Isaac] had been accused of the attempt to ravish and carnally know a white woman. Isaac endured three trials. The two first juries did not agree, but the third rendered a verdict of guilty. The death warrant was to be executed December 1, 1841, to be hung by [his] neck at the usual place of execution, but a petition signed by local citizens was sent to the governor asking for his pardon.

In *Trial and Imprisonment*, Walker picked up the story:
> The day before he was to be executed, I called to see him [in the Pensacola jail]. He had undergone three trials, charged with committing a rape upon a woman of doubtful character... He still persisted in his innocence, forgiving his accusers, and appeared much resigned to his expected fate. His mind appeared calm, and he manifested confidence in the mercy of God through his Son.

Walker arrived at the jail only hours before Isaac was to be hanged. It is possible that Walker, charged with getting laborers to construct some of the new railroad line, had hired Isaac among the black slaves who worked for him. He knew Isaac to be honest, and gentle, and never doubted his innocence. When Walker stepped into Pensacola's jail building, Isaac was being secured with chains around his ankles. Walker made special note of the heavy iron. His account continued:

39

Jonathan Walker The Man with the Branded Hand

I had conversed with the prisoner a few moments, and we had knelt together in supplication, in His name who is able to take away the sting of death and smooth its rough passage, by His own blood rendering it safe to all who truly and faithfully trust in Him for divine aid. We had scarcely risen when the marshal entered and read a letter from the governor containing the full pardon of the condemned man, and offered his irons to be taken off, and delivered him up to his master; and I saw him no more... But few, if any, believed Isaac to be guilty of the charge against him, but that the prosecution was raised, on pecuniary considerations, out of revenge towards his master.

Walker was suggesting, then, that vengeful acquaintances of the white man who held Isaac in bondage had made the accusation knowing it to be false, but knowing that white men's charges against black people were seldom questioned; and the reason the accusers blamed an assault on Isaac was not to harm the slave – they didn't care about him – but to hurt James Stokes, the slaveholder, who would be denied Isaac's services while he was in jail and if he were hanged. In other words, it did not matter if Isaac were falsely punished by death so long as the white master was to be "punished" by the loss of the slave's services and his monetary value as property.

Sutton concluded her account of this incident with an understatement: "The deep convictions of Jonathan Walker, a man from the North, lay in direct conflict with what the Southern gentlemen thought of slavery."

*   *   *   *

On July 19, 1841, in the Walkers' fourth year in Pensacola, Jane gave birth to twins. They were named for two of America's best-known abolitionists: Lloyd Garrison Walker, after the famed (in the North) and notorious (in the South), William Lloyd Garrison, editor of the anti-slavery weekly newspaper published in Boston, *The Liberator*; and Maria Child Walker, for Lydia Maria Child, a writer and editor whose books and magazines carried the abolitionist message throughout the land.

Now there were seven Walker children. Jonathan surely would have been earning money for his family's support by his carpentry skills. And he very likely was permitted to live without charge in the railroad depot building while serving as caretaker. But the railroad's work was at a halt. Although no one could have guessed it in 1842, the depot may be best known in Pensacola history for the Walkers' having lived there. When railroad construction was resumed in 1856, Hildreth reported in his Florida Historical Quarterly account, "the route of the railroad differed from that of its ill-fated predecessor," and with this new plan came another change. The old depot site was abandoned, and the new Union Depot was to be situated less than a mile from the beach.

The Walker family's adventure was ending. In 1842, the entire family sailed back to New England. Jonathan left no record of why they returned. Perhaps Jane or the children, or all of them, preferred New England's more moderate weather. Perhaps it was because Jane was pregnant – again – late that summer of 1842. She was now thirty-nine years old and the mother of seven, including twins barely a year old. She may have longed to be near her own family. Or, perhaps it was because Jonathan desired to return to the ocean. If he and Jane had struck a compromise in 1837 when they went to Florida, he had done his best to live up to the agreement. He apparently had stayed home, away from sailing, for five years. In such circumstances, perhaps Jane and Jonathan reached another compromise: He would help re-settle the family in Massachusetts, and then he would resume his life at sea. The patient Jane no doubt would have relented.

They returned to a Cape Cod still not completely free of slavery. The September 8, 1842, Yarmouth *Register* carried the following advertisement:

TWO CENTS REWARD

Run away from the subscriber, on the night of the 14th inst., Clarissa Harris, indented apprentice. Said girl is an Indian, about 16 years of age – has a scar on the left side of her neck. All persons are forbid harboring or trusting said girl on my account; and whoever will return her to the subscriber shall receive the above reward, but *no charges paid.*

JOSEPH B. HATCH
Falmouth, Aug. 15, 1842

*   *   *   *

On May 13, 1843, the eighth Walker child was born in Harwich. He was named for the famed British abolitionist, William Wilberforce. And when baby William was six months old, Jonathan Walker once more left Cape Cod. He sailed to Mobile, Alabama, and went to work north of Pensacola on Mobile Bay. Some accounts of Walker's life claim that his eldest son, John Bunyan Walker, accompanied him on this trip, as he had nearly eight years earlier for the Mexican adventure. Captain Walker, however, did not mention John in his account of the 1843 trip. Considering what was to occur within a year, it seems certain that Jonathan Walker had not returned to New England to settle down with Jane and the children. He intended to return to his first love of sailing.

Sailing had just such a way of attracting devotion. Others who were to become better known for their writings than Jonathan Walker also were experiencing life on the ocean. In 1841, Herman Melville had begun a four-year stint aboard the *Acushnet*, sailing out of Fairhaven, Massachusetts. From this came the classic novel, *Moby Dick*. Walker, writing in 1845, was echoing a popular effort begun by Richard Henry Dana with the publication of his book, *Two Years Before the Mast*. This account of Dana's voyage from Boston to California via Cape Horn was credited with influencing legislation to improve the conditions of seamen. Dana followed up his biographical report in 1841 with a handbook, *The Seamen's Friend*.

Jonathan Walker The Man with the Branded Hand

Despite his frightening adventures, Jonathan Walker claimed that his life was not much different from other sailors' lives. In *Trial and Imprisonment,* Walker wrote: "... I do not suppose that I have experienced anything more or stranger than thousands of others, who, like myself, have passed upwards of ten years of their lives on the salt blue sea, and gone among as many different nations..."

In a sentence evocative and graceful, even with the weight of more than one hundred and fifty words, Walker continued by describing what surely were his own first-hand experiences:

...inhaling the atmosphere of each quarter of the globe; sometimes shivering with Russia's cold, piercing winds in her ice-bound seas, and anon wilting under a burning vertical sun; whilst gliding through the torrid zone, gently moved along by the refreshing breeze that always blows one way; and at other times scarcely able to turn the weather-beaten face to the furious howling blasts, while my habitation majestically mounted the lofty wave which it had hove up, the next instant rushing down its declivity with the rapidity of thought, as if bound in haste to the nether regions, almost engulfed between two water hills; tumbling, careening, and again, rearing the summit, like a thing of life.

Later in this same tribute to all deep-water sailors, Walker had a passage that would have served as a forewarning to himself, could he have read it before sailing in 1843 for Mobile and Pensacola, and toward the branding that was to make him a national figure in the anti-slavery campaign. He was writing about sailors' ignorance of maritime laws and ships' regulations; but, unintentionally, he was describing the way his Pensacola experience was to come about:

Many serious occurrences and difficulties have passed under my own observation, both at sea and in port, in consequence of [sailors'] ignorance of the purport of the articles of agreement, and the law by which they are bound and by which they are to be governed; and this, consequently, is the means of constantly furnishing jails and prisons with inmates, and courts with employment; which attempted remedy often proves worse than the disease.

He could not have known it in November 1843, when he left New England for Alabama, but Jonathan Walker's "remedy" for seven freedom-seeking slaves in Florida was, cruelly for him, to seem for many months at least as bad as "the disease."

> Under a government which imprisons any unjustly,
> the true place for a just man is also a prison
> ...the only house in a slave state
> in which a free man can abide with honor.
> **Henry David Thoreau, in an essay, "The Duty of Civil Disobedience"**

CHAPTER 4   The Unforgivable Crime

"Late in the fall of 1843, I left my home in Harwich, Massachusetts, and took passage on board of a vessel bound for Mobile, where I spent the winter and spring – mostly in working at the shipwright business, which is my trade."

So Jonathan Walker began his report on the adventure that was to make him briefly famous. In a single sentence, he covered the seven or eight months between Harwich and Pensacola and the fall, winter, and spring of 1843-1844. He tended in his autobiographical accounts to skip over long periods of time, and large amounts of work.

His next sentence reported: "I left Mobile on the 2nd of June, 1844, for Pensacola, in a boat belonging to myself; chiefly for the purpose of raising a part of the wreck of a vessel sunk near the latter place, for the sake of getting the copper that was attached to it."

Walker needed only two sentences to cover the half-year he stayed in Alabama as well as the important acquisition of a boat. He never explained how that came about. Perhaps he bought this boat, using money or by the exchange of his labor. More likely, he built the boat. He had noted matter of factly in his account that "the shipwright business... is my trade." For him, building a boat was not worth explaining; it was, after all, "my trade." That's what shipwrights did; they built boats.

Also unexplained was how he knew about the sunken boat, although this information most likely was gained during his five years' residency in Florida. It was part of his squirrelly characteristic to maintain in memory a list

43

of potential sources of income. When he judged the time had come to leave the city on Mobile Bay, he would naturally turn towards a place with potential for income. He worried about his family and their survival.

*   *   *   *

One of Jonathan Walker's lifelong concerns was finding the money to meet his family's needs for shelter, food, and clothing. He was, nevertheless, almost careless, it seems, about the handling of money. As desperate as Jane and the children always seemed for the bare essentials of survival, Jonathan somehow managed during his year away from Florida to find a rather large amount of money to loan his brother, David. The Barnstable County Registry of Deeds on Cape Cod contains a "mortgage deed" dated originally on December 29, 1842, which was not long after Jonathan and Jane returned with their children from Pensacola. The document was witnessed by Obed Brooks, justice of the peace, and Obed, Jr., on February 13, 1843, but not filed at the Registry until January 18, 1844. By then, Jonathan was in Mobile.

The deed from David Walker acknowledged the loan of $164 from Jonathan and his friend, Nathan Underwood. The hand-written deed granted them "a certain piece of cleared land, young woodland, and swamp, situated in Harwich," the transfer of ownership to be made final only if David failed to repay the loan within two years, or by January 18, 1846.

Jonathan Walker had loaned his brother $117.59; Underwood made up the balance of $46.41. The shares work out to an odd percentage, which suggests Jonathan put up what he could afford to lend David, right down to the fifty-nine cents beyond $117, and relied on Underwood to provide the balance.

This is the only Cape Cod record of Jonathan Walker's having title to property. The Barnstable County Registry has several dozen deeds recording land transactions by members of Jonathan's family, beginning in 1790. David had acquired land in 1825 from Seth Walker, his and Jonathan's father, and had taken title in four deeds from others between 1829 and 1844. Seth was a frequent trader between 1797, before Jonathan's birth, and 1825. Seth's father and grandfather, both named Jeremiah Walker, also were frequent buyers and sellers. But the only deed involving Jonathan was this paper called a "mortgage deed." It was, in reality, an I.O.U. in which David put up one of his properties as security.

Walker's journals never mentioned the transaction, which would not have been a noteworthy event for Jonathan, especially during his quest for income in Florida that winter of 1843-1844.

Walker spent a half-year at the northernmost point of Mobile Bay, forty miles from the barrier beaches that stretch like fingertips to nearly touch the tip of Perdido Bay's slender island protecting Pensacola to the west. Sailing the bay was a trip that Walker had made often in the past and, although he didn't know it in early June when he headed southward, he was to return within the month on a mysterious mission that apparently was planned to disguise his real intent. But now, Walker was to leave Mobile to answer a call from Pensacola, a call like others familiar only to him.

He wrote about his Pensacola trip with equal brevity:

I arrived on the 4th [of June 1844], made some examination and some inquiry about the wreck, and was informed that it was claimed by a citizen of the place. Although it had been sunk there more than thirty years, no effort had been made to raise it. I called on the person who claimed it, but we could not agree on terms.

In his book, *Trial and Imprisonment*, Walker used words carefully chosen to describe how, about a week after arriving in Pensacola, he came to be involved with seven runaway slaves. As was his custom in writing, he seemed almost nonchalant about the matter that was, literally, to brand him for life.

"Soon after [returning from visiting friends 'up the bay']," his account began, "I had an interview with three or four persons that were disposed to leave the place. I gave them to understand that if they chose to go to the Bahama Islands in my boat, I would share the risk with them."

Walker used similarly neutral language in telling his wife about this episode in his life. He did not identify the "persons," nor did he suggest who had approached whom for the "interview." Writing from his jail cell in Pensacola on July 29, 1844, to "Dear Wife and Children," he reported: "About... the 18th of June, I had made some arrangements to take some passengers to Nassau, New Providence, a little to the eastward of Cape Florida." Walker's words – purposely chosen, probably – do not incriminate him; he did not report who initiated the idea of going to the Bahamas. He mentioned only "passengers," nothing about slaves preparing to run away, or former slaves who were then fugitives. They were, simply, "persons that were disposed to leave the place."

Aside from his own inclination to paucity of detail, Walker had another, important reason to write carefully about this meeting. The account for Jane and the children was written in jail, and he knew that his mail was being read by Jailmaster Francis Torward. Torward would have passed along to U.S. Marshal Ebenezer Dorr, or even to the district attorney, any information he acquired that would help convict Walker.

It isn't likely that Walker would have sought out his Pensacola friends to suggest that they attempt an escape. During his long residence in Florida he would have had many opportunities for such activity. That he did not attempt to escort runaway slaves to freedom – there surely would be some record, had he done so – suggests that he may not have thought of initiating such an adventure, or, if he did, had rejected the idea because his family needed his presence and his income.

Walker, however, would find it hard to turn down his friends if they had come to him for help. Historian Der gave that view: "During his stop in Pensacola, his former workers pleaded with him to take them to freedom and he agreed to sail them to the Bahamas."

Jonathan Walker The Man with the Branded Hand

Harriet Buckmaster argued in her book: "Wasn't it natural – the story passing from ear to ear – for those black men to come to him when they wanted to leave the prison house of Florida? And wasn't it natural that such a man as Captain Walker would agree to help them?"

Joe M. Richardson, citing as sources several contemporary newspaper accounts, said the slaves "asked his assistance in going North. Walker was fearful of detection on a long coastal trip to the North in his small boat and declined, but he offered to share the risk of a trip to Nassau, from which the men could go in any direction they pleased."

That version assigns to Walker some of the blame, or credit, for the destination – the Bahamas, where freedom awaited.

Walker's being asked to take the men North would also help explain some of the confusion that developed during the hours immediately after the trip was suddenly halted near Biscayne Bay.

Walker knew that a trip in any direction with runaways was unlawful. He explained in the first letter to his wife that he "would share the risk with them." Walker's risk lay in a white man's being seen on a boat with seven African-Americans, almost a certain tip-off to an attempted escape. Risk for him lay also in being caught and charged with violating the federal law against assisting in an escape. He decided to take that chance.

For the slaves, the risk of recapture must also have seemed worth taking. If they didn't run away, they would never know freedom. If they were caught, they would be punished and then be no worse off by resuming their miserable working and living conditions.

It is not likely that Walker considered as a dangerous sailing challenge the planned coastal route around the peninsula, and then a half-day's dash "a little to the eastward of Cape Florida." Danger, Walker knew, lay in getting caught. He would favor the safest route, and he decided that was to follow the coastline. Whichever way he chose, he had already passed his own test of courage. He would challenge the laws.

"The [slave] codes were quite unmerciful towards whites who interfered with slave disciplines..." Kenneth Stampp reported in *The Peculiar Institution.* "Aiding or encouraging a bondsman to rebel was the most heinous crime of all."

Alabama's code read: "If a free person advise or conspire with a slave to... make... insurrection... he shall be punished with death, whether such rebellion or insurrection be made or not."

Under Florida's law, assisting a runaway was "stealing," and the punishment was not death but imprisonment and a fine, and, although never given out, standing in a pillory and being branded.

Marjory Stoneman Douglas, in her book, *Florida: The Long Frontier,* wrote: "The Criminal Code was constantly violated without punishment, even for murder, and never for murder of a Negro by a white man. White men were never imprisoned. Jails were reserved for rebellious runaway or murderous Negroes. The unforgivable crime was slave stealing."

*   *   *   *

Jonathan Walker was about to commit the unforgivable crime. However it was arranged, the bargain had been struck. Captain Walker went to work preparing for the voyage. The trip could be expected to take two weeks and cover a thousand miles, possibly more. Florida's coastline totals 1,350 miles, second only to Alaska's as the longest in the United States; and of that, 770 miles border the Gulf of Mexico. Jonathan Walker proposed to sail and row along almost all of the Gulf Coast, and then continue another couple hundred miles beneath the peninsula, northward towards the point that is now Miami, and then eastward to the Bahamas.

Joseph Quigles, who was hired to help recover the fugitives by two of the slaveholders, R. C. Caldwell and George Willis, wrote about Walker in a public notice posted three days after the escape:

> He came to this city about three weeks since from sea in a whale boat, he said from Mobile. He seems to have had no reasonable or proper business here. His boat is about twenty-five or thirty feet long, with plenty of beam, clinker built, and very light. When she came here, she had three oars and was schooner rigged, with fore and main sprit-sails, hull and spars painted green, the inside of the boat lead color. He hired board and lodging of a colored woman, whose lot runs to the beach, and hauled up his boat to be worked upon under the shade of trees in the lot.

"And," the *Gazette* added to the listings of suspicious behavior, "Walker was seen frequently during his recent sojourn here in close conversation with Negro men. He took lodgings with a quatroon woman and had no white associates during his stay."

That Walker stayed in a black woman's home is not surprising. Nor would it be unusual for black friends to visit Jonathan's hostess, whether or not she had a guest -- white or black. In fact, the Pensacola *Gazette* reported later that Walker's slave friend, Charles Johnson, was a visitor there: "[T]his boy was with Walker, lying under the trees in the lot where he was working on his boat, nearly all of the day on Sunday, the 16th inst."

The seven fugitives included Charles Johnson and three of his brothers, two Scott brothers, and Anthony Catlett. Charles, Phillip, and Leonard Johnson were claimed by George Willis; Moses Johnson, along with the Scotts – Harry, sometimes called Henry, and Silas – were claimed by Navy Lieutenant Commander and Mrs. Caldwell. Anthony Catlett was a slave of Byrd C. Willis.

It wouldn't bother Walker that his association with black people offended many of Pensacola's white citizens. Walker had long since decided how he stood on the subject of slavery. He wrote later that on this journey, as he had "on other occasions, came to the conclusion that slavery was evil, and only evil, and that continually; and that any mode or process of emancipation, short of bloodshed or the sacrifice of principle, would not be in violation of right or duty..."

Quigles' public notice continued:
For several days, he employed himself in making an additional sail for his boat, which was either a very large jib or square sail, two additional oars, and two paddles; lockers or water-tight boxes to fit in the bow and stern, and under thwarts. He laid in on Wednesday last [June 19, 1844] nearly two barrels of breads, about 120 pounds of pork and bacon, a keg of molasses, a cheese, and some other articles of mess stores, a compass, and a binnacle lantern, and a barrel and a demijohn of water.

The *Gazette* added: "He said he was making the locker to fit in his bows to hold some tools. He said he intended filling the empty barrel he bought with salt water for ballast, but was afterwards seen to go to the spring branch and fill it with fresh water and take it on board his boat."

Walker probably had no more than seventy gallons of drinking water – one barrel and the large glass jug that could be used to haul fresh supplies of water to the heavier barrel from ports along the way. Such stops would be necessary every few days. This "recruiting" of water, as he called it, contributed to both his illness and a general slowdown of the trip itself. In addition, the benefits to the men of being able to exercise their legs on land was offset for the runaways by the risk of being seen.

Quigles' account goes on to reflect the detective work involved in tracking down the runaways:
On Thursday [June 20, 1844], his boat being provisioned and equipped as above, he set sail, but instead of going to sea, stood up the bay. Before sunrise on Friday morning, he was seen close under the land inside of Santa Rosa Island, abreast of Town Point, by two fishermen from the Navy Yard, who asked him where he was going; he said to Mobile, but inquired where he could get water, and was told nearby on Santa Rosa by the sand hills. He immediately set sail and steered towards the place indicated; but soon altered his course to nearly the opposite direction, and when last seen by the fishermen, about an hour afterwards, was standing up the bay.

Santa Rosa is a long, thin barrier island running several miles from the east to westward and southward of both the secondary barrier island called Gulf Breeze as well as the United States Navy's station, which is on the mainland south of Pensacola city. Quigley used the phrases "up" and "down the bay" to mean north and south in Pensacola Bay.

Quigles continued:
On Saturday [June 22], he was seen beating down the bay, and that night the Negroes disappeared, and neither Walker, nor the boat, nor

48

the Negroes have been seen here since, excepting that Silas and Harry [Scott] were seen and recognized by some servants very late (say eleven o'clock) that night, passing down a street towards the [bay].

$1,700 Reward!

For the apprehension and delivery at Pensacola of SEVEN NEGRO SLAVES, who absconded on the night of Saturday the 22d inst. a reward of Seven Hundred Dollars will be paid by the subscribers, (or One Hundred Dollars for either of them) if taken beyond the limits of the Territory; and if taken within the Territory $50 each. Their names and description are as follows, viz:

MOSES JOHNSON is very black, with a full round face and pleasing expression—is stout built and about five feet four inches in height, talks rather rapidly and a little indistinctly—is fond of tobacco and occasionally drinks too much whiskey, is about 35 years of age, is a Blacksmith, basket maker and a great chopper. Belongs to Mr. R. C. Caldwell.

CHARLES, PHIL. and LEN. JOHNSON, are younger brothers of Moses, and the description of Moses answers for them, excepting that they are younger-looking and Philip not quite so stout in person, and Charles has several lumps or scrofulous risings on his breast; they are excellent labourers. Belong to Mr. Geo. Willis.

SILES SCOTT is about 5 feet 2 inches in height, very muscular and considerably bow-legged—is of brown complexion and has a small mark of a burn on his face of which the skin is not the same shade with the remainder of his face; the mark it is believed is on the right side of his nose—has a cut in the palm of his hand, done with a sickle about a week since and still sore and will probaly leave a scar—is somewhat hard of hearing, and has a slight hissing lisp with some words, and is about 25 years old, is a fisherman and a dining room servant. Belongs to Mr. R. C. Caldwell.

Jonathan Walker,

The notice "offered a reward of $1,700," Walker noted,

...for the apprehension and delivery at Pensacola of seven slaves, at one hundred dollars each, if taken out of the territory; and if within its limits, fifty dollars each... From these and other circumstances, the belief exists that said Jonathan Walker has carried these slaves off in his boat. And therefore, for his apprehension and conviction of said offense, the subscribers will pay a further reward of *one thousand dollars*. (The italics are Walker's.)

Captain Walker had prepared for a rendezvous with "three or four persons," but more showed up. He never offered comment, or explanation. Confirming Quigles' estimate of the rendezvous' timing, Walker wrote that "on the evening of the 22nd, seven men came on board the boat, and we left the place, went out of the harbor, and followed in the direction of the coast to the eastward." As Harriet Buckmaster suggested, word had apparently been spread "from ear to ear." Walker had rigged his boat, and brought on food and water, to accommodate only a few passengers. That number was doubled now, a change certain to cause the travelers difficulty. In addition, Walker was not feeling well. "I had for two days been somewhat unwell, having been much exposed to the violence of the sun, and had been what is called sun-struck, and was now exposed to the sudden changing elements night and day in an open boat," he wrote.

Despite "strong head winds, with frequent squalls and rain" over the first several days, the boat arrived in St. Andre's harbor on Wednesday, June 26, 1844. There, Walker wrote, "we stopped part of the day, dried our clothing, cooked some provisions, recruited the water-barrel, and I took an emetic."

Walker was regarded among some of his acquaintances, black and white, as an amateur physician, able to heal minor ailments and fend off internal distresses. In his own case, he prescribed an emetic such as salt or hot pepper, any agent that had the effect of irritating stomach nerves, inducing vomiting, and, he believed, thus purged him of his sickness.

The group filled the water barrel, stretched their legs, had a hot meal, and, that evening, left the coastal community that is today east of Panama City and called St. Andrews.

Captain Walker did not know it, but a false alarm had already been raised. While in fact Walker was one hundred miles east of Pensacola on Wednesday, the fourth day of the flight, news was being flashed about that his small vessel was spotted only a few miles away near Perdido Key, part of the barrier beach south and west of Pensacola.

This alarm led slaveholders Caldwell and George Willis to seek help from no less than the president of the United States. Through agent Quigles, they sent a letter on June 28 to James Tyler, a Tennessee slaveholder who had become the tenth United States president in 1841, and the first to advance from the vice-presidency. He succeeded William Henry Harrison, the first president to die in office. Tyler, having reluctantly decided to seek election in November 1844 and stay in office, had been nominated on May 27 by the Whig party. They had met in Baltimore the same day the Democrats nominated James K. Polk.

Now, his political plans temporarily settled, Tyler left Washington about the time that Walker left Pensacola. Tyler and Julia Gardiner, of the wealthy Long Island family, were married in New York City on June 26. Perhaps learning that Tyler was out of town, and unavailable to help them during his honeymoon, Quigles sent a similar letter on June 29 to the man Tyler had appointed only the previous April as his new secretary of state, John C. Calhoun. Quigles would have felt hopeful of action in writing Calhoun. The North Carolinian was considered slavocracy's leading intellectual.

In the correspondence, now preserved in the National Archives, Caldwell and George Willis apparently wanted the federal government to order one of its ships, the *Poinset,* to join the hunt for Walker and his passengers. On

The Unforgivable Crime

June 29, the Pensacola *Gazette*, probably informed by the publicity-conscious Quigles, reported

> a sloop... which put into our harbor on Wednesday evening [June 26] saw a boat about noon that day at sea, answering in every particular to the description of Walker's boat, with persons on board, beating to the eastward, but she was at such a distance that the number of persons on board or their color could not be seen. She was about ten miles to the southward of our bar, and on the sloop's nearing her she kept away to the south and west. As the weather was very heavy from the eastward since, it is thought that she cannot have made headway and must have made a harbor, the most eastwardly one that she could well have made is the mouth of Perdido.

Quigles, and the newspaper writer, obviously did not know of Captain Walker's sailing skills. That was to Walker's advantage. While the search was being focused for a few days near Perdido, he and his passengers were moving farther away to the east.

*   *   *   *

On Thursday, June 27, 1844, Walker's journal reported, they "run up St. Joseph's Bay, with the intention of taking the boat across into St. George's Sound, to avoid going around Cape St. Blass, but we found the distance too great, abandoned the idea, and passed out of the bay again and [on June 28-29] went around the cape." The places around St. Joseph's Bay that he mentioned are today known as Port St. Joe and Cape San Blas.

Several of the slaves later were to be quoted in the *Gazette* on a close brush with another boat there:

> They saw a small fishing boat in St. Joseph's Bay, where they stopped a day to bake some corn bread and boil some pork. When the boat began to come towards them, Walker ordered five of them to hide in the bushes and two of them to stand by him. The boat, however, changed her course and let go her anchor and went to fishing, not having discovered them.

It is possible that this incident led the slaves later to lend credence to the false alarm about their being near Perdido Key the previous Wednesday. They could have been confused, or they could have simply played along with the story, silently enjoying the consternation the mix-up had caused.

According to the slaves' story, the sight of other vessels did not always alert Walker to the threat of capture. At one point, perhaps when he was delirious, or when desperate for a new supply of water, he actually went after a sloop whose crew Walker's band outnumbered. "The next vessel they fell in with," the *Gazette* wrote, "was a sloop with apparently only two men on board. To this Walker gave chase – the Negroes did not know why – but the sloop outsailed them."

Jonathan Walker The Man with the Branded Hand

About thirty miles east of Port St. Joe, they landed at St. George Island, "stopping a few hours... to cook a little, and recruit our water."

The next day, Walker wrote, "We passed Apalacha Bay, following somewhat the direction of the coast..." The captain and his passengers had now traveled the entire distance from Pensacola along the southern shore of the Florida panhandle, had skirted Apalachicola Bay to the north, and were about to begin the long journey southward along the west coast.

In its edition of June 29, one week after Walker's boat had left Pensacola, the *Gazette* reported the news to those who had not already heard:

> The most daring and impudent outrage upon the peace and dignity of the Territory is thought to have been perpetrated by the abduction of seven negro slaves on the night of Saturday last. For the main particulars that have given rise to the suspicion that the slaves have been stolen, we refer our readers to the handbills of Messrs. Caldwell and Willis, which have been pretty generally distributed. As further matter for suspicion, besides what they there enumerate, we would state that the man (Walker)... is suspected...

The newspaper claimed, without giving further details, that Walker had been suspected earlier, about 1841 – but never formally accused – "of being accessory to the concealment on board of a vessel and the escape of two slaves..."

The *Gazette* scoffed at any suggestion that Walker was, as the newspaper claimed he had said, "only going to Mobile to sell his boat and proceed by steamboat to the western country." The paper wrote:

> *Quere?* – what could he have expected to want with five oars and two paddles with cross pieces for rowers to brace their feet against, and two boat hooks, with two harpoons for catching turtle, with two large sprit-sails and a large jib of square sail, with all the room in his boat saved by exchanging shingle ballast for iron, with making tight boxes to fit under the thwarts and in the bows and stern-sheets, with four months' bread and meat and a liberal supply of small stores, with a compass and binnacle lantern, with a gun and ammunition?

The newspaper continued in editorial style:

> Verily, we say, that if notwithstanding all the suspicious circumstances that seem to link themselves together to establish his guilt, he yet is innocent, he is the most unfortunate of men! But if he is guilty, is <u>he</u> alone to blame? Where is our police? Where is our patrol? How is it that numbers of Negroes can prowl unmolested the limits of the Corporation and from our very dwellings, while persons are in the pay of the Corporation to see that no Negro is at large after bell ring? We forbear further comment, from the conviction that this most daring outrage will induce the adoption of more vigorous measures on the part

The Unforgivable Crime

of the Mayor and Aldermen and stir up the watchmen to greater vigilance.

The *Gazette*'s editor was not alone in condemning Walker's "impudent outrage" on the peace of Pensacola. "By the 1830s," Stampp explained, "the fateful decision had been made. Slavery, now an integral part of the Southern way of life, was to be preserved, not as a transitory evil, an unfortunate legacy of the past, but as a permanent institution – a positive good. To think of abolition was an idle dream. Now even native Southerners criticized the peculiar institution at their peril."

Obviously alarmed at Walker's audacious action, the *Gazette* in its June 29 edition also went hunting for other suspects:

The abduction of the Negroes of Messrs. Willis and Caldwell has set an intelligent friend of ours to thinking of the probable connection between this event and the presence here, some time ago, of certain agents for Northern newspapers and periodicals. We mention this now for the double purpose of putting our own citizens on their guard, in reference to these itinerant gentry, and of cautioning *honest* publishers at the North to employ none but honest and right-feeling people in their business here.

*   *   *   *

By Monday, July 1, on their tenth day at sea, Jonathan Walker and the seven black men were in the vicinity of Cedar Key. Walker, aware that he was writing for a primarily Northern audience, explained in his account of the escape: "From the shore of the west and south part of the peninsula of Florida, shoal ground extends to a considerable distance, on which are numerous small islands denominated Keys, each having its own separate name."

Cedar Key lies along Florida's west coast, about parallel with today's city of Ocala. This north central community was to become a thriving port city after the completion in 1861 of the cross-state railroad carrying cotton, lumber, and turpentine to the Atlantic coast near the Georgia line. But in 1844, it was a dot on a map that Jonathan Walker was to remember primarily because he had become so ill there that he had to quit directing the escape flight. By spells, he wrote, "I was somewhat delirious. I remember looking at the red horizon in the West, soon after sundown, as I thought for the last time in this world, not expecting to behold that glorious luminary shedding its scorching rays on me more."

Walker was possessed with more than fever. "Among other things," he wrote, "my mind was occupied on [the subject of slavery] also, and I calmly and deliberately thought it over; and ... came to the conclusion that slavery was evil... and therefore calculated to secure the approbation of that great 'Judge of all the earth, who doeth right,' and before whose presence I soon expected to appear."

Jonathan Walker The Man with the Branded Hand

Once more, Walker was a survivor: "After passing this night, I scarcely know how, the next morning I found myself more comfortable, and felt some relief."

The passage had slowed. Walker's boat was only thirty miles south of the Cedar Keys around Thursday, July 4, 1844, the twelfth day out of Pensacola. Walker would have applauded the sixty-eighth anniversary observance of America's Declaration of Independence on Cape Cod by the Friends of Liberty. The Barnstable *Patriot*, the community's weekly newspaper, reported the group discussed "the all-important subject of American slavery." One of the twelve resolutions adopted by the group noted "...the people appear to be waking up to remove this curse from our land."

* * * *

That Fourth of July was not being celebrated by the Walker group in the Gulf of Mexico. The party landed on one of St. Martin's Keys in Homosassa Bay, about ten miles offshore from today's Citrus City, approximately fifty miles north of Clearwater. Supplies were now critically short. Walker had planned on accommodating no more than five people; instead, he had eight. They cooked a meal that Fourth of July at St. Martin's but found no fresh water.

The captain was having difficulty breathing, and his face "was nearly covered with sores," he wrote. The sores probably were from sunburn, and although the burn was to be relieved, Walker and the men had another painful distraction over the next eight days. "[After] leaving St. Martin's Keys," he wrote, "whenever we landed, we were harassed with swarms of mosquitoes, each anxious to have his bill entered without examination or delay."

Walker was still prescribing successfully for himself. "For several days," he wrote, "nature and my disease seemed to be about on a balance, and it was doubtful which would rule the day; I took another emetic, made free use of cayenne pepper and bitters, which appeared to have a good effect, and in a few days... my whole system, which had been so much oppressed that I could with difficulty respire, felt most relieved."

Such "medicaments" as pepper and bitters were common, especially for sailors. In *Pieces of Old Cape Cod*, Josephine Buck Ivanoff reported two remedies as advised in *The Improved Housewife* in 1843: For relieving delirium tremens, "drink plentifully of strong wormwood tea"; and for "weakness... a delicious brew of good port wine, cinnamon, and steel filings!"

Walker was to point out that the cure was almost as challenging as the illness: "But my strength and flesh were nearly gone, and the system so much reduced that it is a wonder to me how, after undergoing so much privation, exposure, and the treatment that followed, I was enabled to recover at all."

Despite Walker's recuperation, the party's luck was not improving, however. Their water supply was almost gone, and their efforts at continuing the journey without being detected were complicated by the need to put in at potential sites of potable water, knowing that such places were visited by sailors who regularly followed the coastal route. Driven to desperation, Walker's crew made several stops, more than they would have elected to make in safety, while continuing to sail and row south and then around Cape Sable. They tacked eastward through the Straits of Florida and the northern chain of tiny islands that drip off the southeast tip of Florida for a hundred miles to Key West. That first week in July of 1844 was, no doubt, typical of all Florida summers – scorching heat and little rainfall. Such weather doubled the pain of the dry ride: their bodies demanded fluids to offset the loss from perspiration, and the cloudless skies denied them even the opportunity to catch rain water in pails and makeshift containers. The recovering captain, still weak from his heat stroke, guided the open boat around the Mangrove Swamp, threading his way between Sandy and Clive Keys, and on beyond Eagle Key.

Passing out of the Gulf of Mexico, beneath the peninsula's southern tip, and into the Atlantic Ocean must have heartened Walker and his passengers. On Sunday, July 7, they had begun the fifteenth day of their flight to freedom. The captain reckoned that they had come about 700 miles. They were averaging nearly fifty miles a day.

As dawn awakened them on Monday, July 8, they were fifteen miles from the lightship on Carysfort Reef. This giant coral barrier lies in shoal water off the east coast of Key Largo, which is the largest and northernmost of the eastern keys. Carysfort had been named – and presumably better charted on maps – before the Revolution, after a British twenty-gun frigate had run "a-coral" nearly seven miles off shore.

Walker, who had rounded the peninsula many times, knew it was necessary to give the reef a wide berth. In so doing, he soon would be steering northeastward into Biscayne Bay. The bay had been known to sailors for more than three centuries. Ponce de Leon had named this area in 1513 on his first expedition to the land he called Florida. The Walker party were at most a day's sail from Cape Florida, at the southernmost point of Key Biscayne just south of today's Miami. A tall, brick lighthouse guarded Cape Florida, and Jonathan Walker very likely had been guided by the light since it had begun sending out its signal of safety in 1825.

Walker knew that Cape Florida had drinking water, so his spirits were bound to be improved. At last, journey's end was straight ahead, no more than two days' sailing, and their bad luck seemed to be behind them. From Key Biscayne they were only a half-day's journey to the Bahama Islands. These British possessions were the site of Christopher Columbus' first landfall in the Western Hemisphere. British subjects had settled there in 1647, and Parliament formally declared the islands a colony in 1783. Great Britain had outlawed slavery in the British West Indies in 1833, making the larger of the Bahamas' 700 islands an attractive goal for runaway slaves. Nassau, the capital city on the island of New Providence, represented the ultimate freedom for seven tired, thirsty slaves in an open boat from Pensacola.

The promise of the new sunrise on that Monday morning was soon blackened for Walker and his passengers. Jonathan Walker recalled it this way:

Jonathan Walker The Man with the Branded Hand

"Fortunately, or unfortunately, which I cannot tell, at daybreak on the morning of July the 8th, we saw two sloops within a short distance, standing towards us."

Some of the slaves were later to remember this differently. The *Gazette*, using the Southern euphemism "boys" for the grown men, reported:

> At daylight, one of the boys on the look-out espied "a sail." Walker looked at her and said she was nothing but a small thing, she wouldn't interfere with them. All he was afraid of was a Revenue Cutter or a Man-of-War. The sloop, however, made for them, and on coming near hailed the boat three times before Walker answered, "From St. Joseph bound to Cape Florida," and said he was out of provisions and water and wished to be supplied, while he had a large supply of both.

Walker's version of the capture was more detailed and slightly different:

> In a few moments they came within hail, and inquired, "Where are you from, and where are you bound?" I answered, "From St. Joseph's, bound to Cape Florida." The captain of one of the sloops said, "I am going that way, and will give you a tow;" at the same time, he ran alongside of the boat and made a rope fast to it, and invited us on board the sloop.

This captain was Richard Roberts, employed by Tift & Geiger, the owner of the *Eliza Catherine* and the *Reform*.

Walker seemed to know immediately that he was in trouble. Even if the captains of the sloops were not aware that a reward had been posted for the capture of the white captain and his seven black passengers, they would have had reason to suspect them as runaways. Walker's vessel clearly had only one cargo. Moreover, the small boat that Walker had sailed out of Mobile only five weeks earlier was greatly outclassed by the sloops. He described them as "wrecking vessels of eighty or ninety tons, manned with fifteen or twenty men each, and sailed very fast. They are employed for the sake of saving or getting what they can from vessels wrecked on the coast. They hailed from Key West."

Now, here was Roberts having Walker's boat tied to the larger sloop. Surely Walker knew immediately that his trip was ending. "The men were going on board [the *Eliza Catherine*]," he wrote of his passengers,

> when I advised them to stay in the boat. Four of them had stepped on board, but one immediately returned. The others were not allowed to [return]. The sloop directly reversed her course and run back where she had come from, and anchored. I requested the captain to allow the men to return in the boat; he made no reply, but took his boat and went on board of the other sloop, which had followed him back to the anchorage. Soon after he returned and requested me to come on board the vessel. I, being then exposed to the violent heat of the sun, thought it prudent to comply, confident that we should be detained at all events.

The Unforgivable Crime

Walker's "confidence" was well placed. It would be nearly a full year before his detainment was to end. His first few hours, at least, were to be spent in relative comfort. "While on board [the *Eliza Catherine*]," Walker wrote, "I was treated with civility, and permitted to pass the time in the cabin or on deck, as I chose for my convenience or comfort.

Walker could be expected to reflect on what was happening. Noting that Captain Roberts had consulted the captain of the second vessel, *Reform*, he could surmise they concurred that they had come upon the freedom flight from Pensacola, and knew a reward in excess of a thousand dollars had been posted.

The sun that had sent Captain Walker its beacon rays over the eastern horizon only a few hours before now beat down on him the heat of disappointment and failure. "We were then forty or fifty miles from Cape Florida," he wrote, "and if we had not been detained, would have got there before night, and been ready to cross the gulf the next morning. But our voyage was up, and we had other prospects now before us."

He concluded with a checklist of nautical benefits and hindrances. Delivered with an accountant's dispassionate rundown of a column of figures, this was his litany:

> We had now been fourteen days on our passage, and had sailed and rowed more than seven hundred miles; but for the last eight or ten days the weather had proved more uniform and mild, and the winds favorable but light. Had I been well, it is probable we should not have been more than ten or twelve days to this place, and saved much distance by running more direct courses. If we had been one hour sooner or later in passing this place, we should not have come in contact with those vessels.

*   *   *   *

The Pensacola *Gazette* reported the news on July 20, 1844:

> The man Jonathan Walker who recently abducted the seven Negro slaves belonging to Messrs. Willis and Caldwell was captured with the Negroes in his whale boat about fifteen miles from the lightboat at Caryfort's Reef on the 8th inst. by the wrecking sloop *Eliza Catherine* and brought to Key West on the 9th. The Negroes are on board the sloop *Reform* and are expected every hour.

The *Light of the Reef*, the newspaper published in Key West, apparently had Captain Roberts as the primary source of its information. It reported:

> On the 8th inst., Richard Roberts... discovered a boat having aboard suspicious appearance with seven Negroes on board... Whereupon the mate of the sloop was directed to jump into the boat and make her fast, suspecting them to be runaway slaves. The white man who had charge of the boat and Negroes was induced to come on board of the sloop under a promise of being taken to Cape Florida; and on being inter-

57

rogated gave his name as Jonathan Walker, and was employed by two men, the owners of the Negroes, to convey them to Cape Florida for the purpose of selecting land for their owners.

Walker had, apparently, come up with an explanation that he could have used anywhere along the trip's route. He was simply transporting the men for their masters, he said. But the slaves, also seeking an acceptable explanation, told Captain Roberts something else. *Light of the Reef* wrote:

> Upon questioning the Negroes, they said the man in the boat was their owner. Their statement not agreeing with that of the white man, Captain Roberts was induced to detain them on board for the purpose of bringing them to Key West for examination; well knowing that a few hours liberty would have placed them beyond the reach of such examination, for in a passage of twelve hours they could have reached Nassau, New Providence.

The *Gazette* quoted the slaves on another version of what they claimed Walker told Captain Richards, a version that, if true, revealed Walker's getting into trouble with the slaves whom he was attempting to help. The newspaper wrote:

> He said he was employed by two men, the owners of the Negroes, to carry their servants round while they themselves went directly by land; that he was going to select lands for them on the Miami River and open a plantation. This made a portion of the Negroes who heard it tremble, for they thought at once that the story about their going upon a plantation on the Miami was no fiction. They believed he was going to sell them, and were glad to reveal their true character and get back home...

Roberts was using a technique familiar to modern detectives: question the involved participants separately, compare their stories, and exploit discrepancies. Jonathan Walker, generally honest and upright, even in committing an unlawful act, was equal to the battle of wits. The Key West newspaper reported: "Captain Roberts having made known his determination to bring them to this place, Jonathan Walker, the white man, confessed himself an abolitionist from Massachusetts; and that he had induced the Negroes to run away from Pensacola."

From Walker's viewpoint, it made no difference whether he had in fact induced the slaves to leave their owners or whether he had yielded to their pleading, as some contemporary accounts had it. What would have been important to Walker would be to find a way to ameliorate the punishment awaiting the runaway slaves. By "confessing," as Roberts apparently told the Key West paper, Walker was taking full blame. The slaves were in trouble simply for leaving. They represented cash value to R. C. Caldwell, George

The Unforgivable Crime

Willis, and Byrd C. Willis, and their fleeing put that investment in jeopardy. Moreover, each day off the plantation represented further loss, the money that their services could earn. If the men admitted to running away, the three white Pensacolans probably would feel obliged to uphold one of slavery's codes and punish them more harshly than if the white Walker took the blame for inducing them to escape.

Later, some of the slaves told stories that supported Walker's claim to enticement. The Pensacola *Gazette* reported, "We take [their] story with some degree of allowance, but with far less than we should otherwise do in consequence of the several stories of the Negroes, separately given, coinciding with such precision as to force us to the belief of them."

Here is the story as logged by the newspaper:

They say that Walker commenced his negotiations with one, by whom he sent for another and by him for another and so on until he had seen them all. He told them that he had provided the means by which they could obtain their freedom, and he wanted eight stout and likely men, of good character, who did not get drunk, etc., that he would take them to Nassau and thence to Massachusetts. After they had gotten outside, he began asking them what they could do, whether they were mechanics or laborers, or what had always been their occupation, whether they knew anything about planting and a great many other questions, where were all answered agreeably to the facts. After they had been one or two days out, he began to be very fretful and crabbed, telling them that they were not what he expected to find them; they were not so prompt and active as he had looked for, etc. They coasted it all the way around, running day and night, closing in and running by the land at nightfall, and standing out further during the day. Walker lost their confidence, it seems, by telling them, for instance, in the evening it was so many miles to such a place, then in the morning, after running all night with a fair wind, he would give the distance often twice as great as it was the evening before. This made the shrewder of them begin to think that he was not to be trusted, and in proportion as this conviction grew upon them they began to give themselves up as lost and wish themselves home again.

The *Gazette* seemed to accept the possibility that Walker would actually have entrapped the slaves, in effect stealing them so that he could sell them. The newspaper scoffed:

It is a little singular that Walker's philanthropy should not lead him to free the weak as well as the strong, but not so: he selected his gang, strong, hearty, good- looking fellows, sober and industrious, just such as would bring the best price in the market. He could afford to sell them cheap on the Miami [River], then run across to the Bahamas, and take passage for his own beloved Massachusetts.

How much slaveholders reckoned the worth of any black man was dependent upon the very qualities the newspaper cited. White people controlled black slaves not only for labor but also for the breeding of more slaves. Nate Shaw, the son of two slaves who grew up in Alabama during Reconstruction years, described this process in his oral autobiography, *All God's Dangers,* compiled by Theodore Rosengarten, Shaw was quoted:

[I]f that marster had a nice-lookin, healthy colored man, I'd give him a pile of money for that big Negro, carry him home and put him with my crowd, and produce a mess of young-uns like hisself. They [slaveholders] didn't like so much the little scrawny colored people, weren't able to work much. If the marster caught a little, bitty, scrawny nigger foolin round amongst his women, there'd be no holdin up on the whippin he'd get. They wanted these big healthy fellows, big healthy women; they wanted to create a race of people to suit em... They told me that good able-bodied Negroes, and Negroes with good health, sold for a pretty penny. I might be a carpenter, I might be a blacksmith, or I might just work in the field. You'd sell me accordin to what I was worth to you... It run that way for years, they tell me, it run that way for years. A time of brutish acts, brutish acts.

Walker was also accused of dissembling in answering Captain Roberts' question about their port of origin and destination. Walker rationalized in his account of the trip: "The reader has seen that St. Joseph's was the last port we left, and we intended to call at Cape Florida. This has been used to make it appear that I resorted to falsehood, because we had started from Pensacola and were bound, ultimately, to Nassau, New Providence."

*   *   *   *

In his usual to-the-point reportage, Jonathan Walker completed the story of his capture this way: "The sloop lay at anchor until night, then got under way and run for Key West, with the boat in tow, where she arrived the next day afternoon."

Walker was never again to captain "the boat," nor even to ride in it. The courtesies given him over the first forty-eight hours after his capture were to end in Key West.

The indignation felt by this community
on the subject of this outrage is very great.
Pensacola *Gazette*, **July 22, 1844**

CHAPTER 5   **The Pensacola Calaboza**

Jonathan Walker was lying in the United States marshal's cart, being pushed on Intedencia Street towards Calaboza Square. Looking up, at the corner of Alcaniz Street, he saw the plain, brick building that had been serving the West Florida community of Pensacola as a jail for more than six years.

Even before entering a primitive cell on the other side of jail's front double doors, he had several major worries. The most immediate and personal were for shedding his own "unwellness," which had lingered now nearly a month, and for informing his family. The Cape Codders had not yet learned of his adventure fifteen hundred miles from home. Less pressing on this hot nineteenth day of July in 1844 was his hope for an early release from jail.

It is not likely that Walker was much concerned about his appearance. When healthy, he was clean shaven. His hair was dark, thinning on top but worn thick and to the top of his collar in the back. He had high cheekbones, and the prominent wear lines around his mouth gave him the appearance of perpetual patience. Arriving in Pensacola, he must have looked unkempt. His illness while sailing along the Gulf Coast for nearly a month would have left him with a beard covering his lower face. The hollows of his cheeks would have reflected his weight loss. His eyes would not have seemed so intently peering, as they usually were.

He knew that he could do little about his appearance until he had regained his strength.

Jonathan Walker The Man with the Branded Hand

Walker had additional problems, all legal, although he would not have known that while United States Marshal Ebenezer Dorr and City Constable-Jailer Francis Torward wheeled him in the cart in front of the jail over a sidewalk that had been constructed of "the best heart pine" seven years before. So weak that he needed help in walking from the Navy Yard docks to the court building, and now, being wheeled from the courthouse to the jail, Jonathan Walker did not seem much of a threat to harm anyone, let alone attempting escape. How severe his crime was regarded was to be made ever clearer to the prisoner when the cart was halted and he was helped to his feet.

"I was," he wrote, "placed in a room by myself, and secured to a ring-bolt by a large size log-chain, and a shackle of round iron, weighing about five pounds, 'round the ankle... The floor was my bed, seat, and table..."

Jonathan Walker was not being treated as a common criminal; worse, he was a stealer of slaves, unfaithful to the traditions and laws of the South. He could expect no more special treatment now than he had received on the painful trips from the place of his capture to Key West, and then from Key West to Pensacola.

Unable to administer his own medication, Walker had lost strength again in the sweltering July heat of Florida's keys. He had put up a good show of being a captain in charge when Richard Roberts took his boat in tow, although he knew he was too ill to resist. He never admitted that, but his account of the trip suggests it in several places. For example, he introduced his report of the capture by noting "fortunately, or unfortunately, I cannot tell which," his captors came in view. He offered no explanation for the remark. Yet, how could being found out be considered "fortunate"? One explanation would be that Walker's valiant efforts were no match for his serious illness.

A direct reference to his physical condition was in his report of arriving at Key West on Tuesday, July 9, 1844: "I was now taken before a magistrate, borne by two men, not being able to walk alone."

The newspaper, *Light of the Reef*, reported on July 13: "Upon arriving at Key West, on the 9th inst., he was given up to the civil authorities and committed to prison to await his trial at the next term of the Superior Court for Monroe [County]. The Negroes are to be sent today [by the sloop *Reform*, Captain Noyes, to Pensacola." This was the same boat on which they had been taken after capture to Key West.

The purpose of the Key West court appearance, the first of several in Florida for Walker, was changed from awaiting trial in the islands to simply setting the amount of bail so he could be held for trial and punishment in Pensacola. Bail was one thousand dollars, "but being unable to do so, I was committed to jail..."

Light of the Reef explained the change in court procedure: "The magistrate, with the advice of the district attorney, has concluded to send the prisoner, Walker, to Pensacola..." Walker recalled:

The Pensacola Calaboza

Esquire Balany (I think that was the name of the magistrate to whom my case was submitted) manifested no unkind feelings towards me, and allowed me as much indulgence as circumstances would admit of. But the district attorney, whom I saw on two occasions, appeared to have 'taken pepper in his nose,' and soon gave me to understand that I had no favors to expect from that quarter. I also received kind treatment from the jailer at that place – but did not stay long enough at the soldiers' barracks to form any acquaintance there.

Walker was "jailed" in the house in which the constable lived:
I was placed in a small room on the second floor, with three other prisoners, but slept in the room with the constable and family; the prisoners eat at the same table the family did, after they had eaten. I was handcuffed one night, but was permitted to use my hands the rest of the time while there, in fighting mosquitoes, which were very annoying at all times... Most of my things which I had in the boat were brought from the vessel by the sheriff and placed in charge of the constable, with the exception of a trunk and bundle of clothing which I was allowed to retain for my own use. I begged to be allowed to retain a small trunk of botanic medicine which I had, but was refused.

Walker still had, nominally at least, the boat he had acquired in Mobile.
On July 13, Walker reported, "[T]he seven men were put on board of another sloop (named the *Reform*) and sent to Pensacola previous to my leaving Key West." He departed later on that Saturday, leaving behind the last civility he was to enjoy for some time.
Walker described his first experience at real penal hardship – nearly a year of it lay before him – in this way: "I was placed down the hold of the steamboat, on the ceiling, where it was very filthy, and put in double irons (both hands and feet), where I was kept for six days, with the exception of being permitted to come on deck a few hours in a day, and sit or lie upon the hatches. The food given me was salt beef, pork, and navy-bread, with a slight exception."
In his account of this episode in his life, Walker claimed he made great effort to avoid exaggeration. He did allow himself some wry humor, however. About his trip from Key West he wrote:
As to Commander Ferrand, of the steamboat *General Taylor*, on board of which I was shipped to Pensacola, he did not make any great display of good feeling in my behalf, although he indulged me in a steam bath a considerable part of the passage, by having me placed in the hold of the boat, where the engine and fire were, to my no small discomfort. Also good care was taken that I should neither dance nor play on the fiddle, by closely confining both hands and feet in irons. The lieutenant was a South Carolina chicken, well stuffed with McDuffie-ism, from whom no answer to any question could be obtained, or any reply directly to

me. His name, I think, was Anderson. He had got his lesson from the nullification roost, and was prepared to look daggers at everything in the shape of abolition.

The trip up Florida's west coast was interrupted at Tampa Bay, where the steamer took on a load of wood. Five days after departing Key West, the *General Taylor* anchored at the Pensacola Navy Yard on Thursday evening, July 18, 1844.

*   *   *   *

During this long trip in a "steam bath," Jonathan Walker had much uninterrupted time to consider what was happening to him. How had a man who had grown up in the place of the Pilgrims come to be in chains for helping a small group of men seek freedom? Was there anything in the background of a white man from Cape Cod that could have foretold his interest in helping black people?

When Jonathan went through his adolescence, there were few people of color in Barnstable County, Massachusetts. In a 1764 count, Cape Cod towns had recorded twice as many Indians, five hundred sixteen, as black people, two hundred thirty-one. In 1801, when Walker was two years old, only five surviving members of the Potonumecot tribe lived in Harwich. By 1820, the town authorized a committee of three – Jonathan's uncle, the second Jeremiah Walker, Jr., was one of them – to sell land claimed by the Potonumecots in Brewster, Harwich, and Orleans. Divided into lots, the land brought three hundred dollars, which was "to be paid to the [town] treasurers toward the support of the Indians."

The growing Jonathan may have had chance encounters with these few people of color in his hometown, the people of Native American descent and former slaves, freed after 1783 by law, or released earlier by slaveholders, as well as offspring of former slaves.

One reason so few African-Americans were living on Cape Cod may be that Massachusetts had effectively outlawed slavery in 1783, when Jonathan's father was a teen-age boy. Earlier, however, in most Cape Cod communities, "all the inhabitants of means kept slaves," Annie C. Keene reported in *Early Days of Manomet*.

Some runaway slaves came to Cape Cod on their way to freedom. For example, shipmasters in the employ of George Lovell reportedly brought former slaves to the Cape. The fugitives were taken by the Underground Railroad to Barnstable village. Among the "conductors" on the railroad, Mr. and Mrs. Alvin Howes and Mr. and Mrs. Ezekiel Thatcher were said to avoid church services because preachers never condemned slavery.

That there were Harwich participants in the Underground Railroad is difficult to prove from written records. The very nature of the effort – helping escaped slaves make their way to freedom in the northern states and Canada – required secrecy for success, especially during the years when Jonathan Walker

The Pensacola Calaboza

was going out to sea. Perhaps the best known Harwich "stop" on the Underground Railroad is still in use as a family home at 254 Bank Street. Beneath a second-floor bathroom is a small "room" that, according to a legend passed on by a former occupant, was used to hide fugitive slaves. The area measures thirty-four inches wide, ten feet long, and forty-two inches high -- large enough to hide several people in a cramped but out-of-sight space. The room is reached through a trap-door in the bathroom floor. When the house was built, about 1840, the architectural design provided for two first-floor closets beneath the hidden space. These closets are noticeably shorter than the first floor hallway and a room on which the closets front.

As he considered his plight, lying in chains on the trip through the Gulf of Mexico, Walker may have taken solace in the knowledge that none of his ancestors had kept slaves. Stephen Hopkins' servants were white men who, in the English tradition, hired out their services in exchange for room, board, and, in the cases of Edward Leister and Edward Doty, the freedom they sought in New England.

*   *   *   *

Arriving in Pensacola that hot 18th of July in 1844, Jonathan Walker was kept aboard ship for the night. He wrote: "The next day I was conducted to Pensacola by the deputy marshal [James Gonzalez] in a small boat, and in a rain storm (distance eight miles). On landing at the wharf, there was a large collection of people, who appeared to be very talkative, and some were noisy; but no violence was attempted."

This account was amplified by several others, including the Pensacola *Gazette*'s report. Writing later about the newspaper and editor John McKinlay, Walker excoriated him for almost everything except one paragraph:

> Although he had no control over me, yet as he had control over the only paper published in Pensacola, it was in his power to give an unfair statement of the circumstances, which he did not fail to do. But feeling perfectly willing to credit him with truth when he utters it, I here annex a paragraph in the *Gazette* of July 22d – only remarking that the last word is incorrect. But unfortunately, in the next number (July 27th) he crowded into a part of a column of that small paper twenty odd *lies* at my expense. Whether that libelous statement was voluntary on the part of its crouching editor, or whether he was dictated to, I know not. But to the [July 22] paragraph...

Here is how McKinlay's paper reported Walker's return to Pensacola:

> The indignation felt by this community on the subject of this outrage is very great. When the prisoner landed on the wharf, the crowd was immense, and as he was escorted to the courthouse by the deputy marshal the crowd thronged the streets and sidewalks, and the courtroom was filled to overflowing with a highly excited mass of people. Great as the excitement was, however, and aggravated as its

65

cause, to the credit of our good citizens, be it said, not the least attempt was made to commit violence upon the person of the offender; on the contrary, while a few could not refrain from openly expressing their feelings of resentment, the great body seemed to look upon the prisoner as a miserable object of pity. How far he is truly to be pitied, however, we are not prepared to say, for the *General Taylor* brings rumor from Key West that Walker said his conduct was rash, but that he had done nothing wrong, and that he would do the same again if he had opportunity.

Walker continued his own account of his return to Pensacola: "By summoning all the strength I could muster, I succeeded in walking to the courthouse."

The trip from the wharf was the equivalent of several blocks, a considerable distance for a man in Walker's weakened condition. "The court was already convened," Walker said, "whether solely on my account or not, I do not know. My trunk and bundle were searched, but nothing taken therefrom."

The arraignment was carried out swiftly. "I was required to give bail in the sum of $10,000, or be committed to prison to await my trial whenever it should take place: with me there was no alternative but to comply with the latter," Walker wrote.

The Pensacola *Gazette* explained, in its July 27 edition, why the hearing against Walker was being put off. "As the sloop *Reform* has brought no witnesses from Key West against Walker, there will be no special term of the Superior Court for his trial."

The sloop did, of course, carry the seven slaves back to Pensacola, arriving "three or four days after I had arrived in Pensacola," Walker wrote. But, as the *Gazette* had noted without explanation, the sloop carried "no witnesses." The newspaper editor didn't bother to state what his readers would have known. African-Americans, as everyone knew, were not permitted to testify against white people, even if a white man had committed "the unforgivable crime."

The bail of $10,000 suggests how serious the crime charged to Walker was regarded. He had been ordered held in $1,000 bail in Key West. Either sum might as well have been a million dollars for all the hope Walker had of posting it and being freed. Certain of that, the July 27 *Gazette* reported, "He will remain in prison to take his trial at the next regular term commencing on the first Monday in November next."

Now, having "succeeded in walking to the courthouse," Walker was unable to go farther. "I attempted to walk to the jail in company with the marshal and constable, but gave out by the way, and was carried there in a cart..."

The Escambia County courthouse was a Main Street building about four blocks east of the railroad depot where the Walker family had once lived. Now Jonathan was headed north some five blocks to the city jail.

The Pensacola Calaboza

As the makeshift ambulance was halted on Intedencia Street, at the corner of Alcaniz Street, Jonathan Walker looked up at a two-story brick building. This was the Pensacola jail, the place where Walker would wait more than three months for a jury to hear testimony against him, the place where he would make his home for more than 300 days, the place where he would accrue the blame and the glory that would yield him a modest place in the history of American slavery.

Walker's new home was not unknown to him. He had visited at least one of his black friends there during the five years he had lived in Pensacola with Jane and the children. In fact, Jane Walker also had seen the building, she later told one of her husband's Cape Cod supporters.

Walker shared the jail that first night with one other man, a slave who had been placed in the second room, away from Walker. Upstairs were nine people: City Marshal and Mrs. Francis Torward and their five children; "the mulatto slave cook," whom Sutton identified as "Joaquina," and her screaming infant, then about six months old.

The Calaboza Square neighborhood had long been home to both Torward and his wife, Maria. Both had grown up on the east side of Alcaniz Street, within sight of the jail. He was born Francisco Touard, Jr., the son of a native of France. He had inherited his father's property when a young man, in 1825, and married Maria Quina, whose family lived next door. Maria, born about 1814, was also known as Mary. Her father, Desiderio Quina, had been born in Genoa, Italy, in 1775, and came to America as a Spanish soldier. Settling in Florida, Desiderio married Margarita Bobe and became an apothecary. When the elder Touard died, Quina had served as executor of the estate and as guardian of the young Touard brothers, Francisco, Jr., and Louis. One of the executor's first decisions after the death of Touard, Sr., was to sell the family slave, Patty, a forty-one-year-old woman "guaranteed to be free from disease and infirmity," according to Pensacola historian Leora M. Sutton.

Maria Quina Torward was identified by Walker in his journal only as "L.T." Perhaps he did not wish to cause her embarrassment by naming her, although Pensacolans of that time would have identified the wife of the man who was now known as Francis Torward. In his own wry way, Walker might have used the initials to represent "Lady Torward."

Walker wrote, "with some reluctance," about Torward, who was called

...the jailer, or constable, but more commonly designated by the title of city marshal. The jail is the property of the city, and the jailer (city marshal) is chosen yearly by a vote of the city, and is paid a salary per month. His duty is to look after the peace and quiet of the city; to commit and release all prisoners; to ring the city bell on all proper occasions, especially at the hours of 8 p.m. in winter and 9 p.m. in summer; and to take up all slaves found in the streets without a pass after the bell has been rung, etc. He provides the prisoners with their food and drink, for which he is allowed 37 1/2 cents each, per day. He also inflicts punishment upon slaves sent there by their masters or mistresses to be punished.

During Walker's stay in Torward's jail, more than one hundred other prisoners came and went from the second cell. Most of them were slaves. An occasional sailor was held for a day or two after a shore-leave celebration. At various times, two or three prisoners, and occasionally more, were locked in that room. On October 3, while Walker was still alone in his jail room, the population reached a high: "The whole number now confined in the adjoining room is seven," he wrote.

Walker's jailing was not, strictly speaking, in solitary confinement. He had an occasional cell mate, and he was able to communicate with the prisoners in the other ground-floor room. He wrote, for example, that a Navy boatswain, upon being released, after five days in jail, "made me a present of a pair of blankets."

All of these people lived in Pensacola's "new" jail, which had been constructed in 1837 to replace the old Spanish calaboza. The new building's ground dimensions were about the size of a two-stall garage. Walker put the measurements at approximately

...eighteen feet by thirty-six feet, having upon each floor two rooms, the lower part for the occupation of the prisoners, and the upper part for the jailer's family. The rooms for the prisoners are fifteen to sixteen feet square, with double doors, and two small grated windows from six to eight feet from the lower floor. Overhead is a single board floor, which but little obstructs the noise of the upper part from being distinctly heard below, and vice versa.

About twenty feet from the jail, and fronting the windows, was a wooden building denominated the kitchen. Its door having previously taken refuge in the fire, and the wooden windows shutting only as the wind blew them to, I had a pretty fair view of what was transacted there from the only window which I could look out of, and from which I was often compelled to turn away, for the scene was too disgusting to look upon. There was scolding and cow-hiding dealt out without measure, and the filthiness far exceeded anything I ever saw before connected with cooking. The place was a common resort for all the lank and starving domestics about the premises, seeking to pacify their hungry rage where the cook performed; and one might truly say that

"The cook and the hens for the kitchen went snacks,

"With two horses, three dogs, and five cats;"

for there the cook, the poultry, and the horse might be seen helping themselves from the same meal barrel, and the dogs cleaning the cooking utensils, and sometimes taking a favorite bit from the market-basket, before its contents had been otherwise disposed of. The board on which the food was prepared for cooking was common to the tread of the cats and the poultry.

The cook was a slave woman, and had a small, straight- haired child whose lungs were the strongest of any human being I ever saw of its size, and it made the freest use of them. For hours and hours of each day, for months, my ears rang with its tormenting screams, for it could not be called crying. And to make the matter still worse, there were three more small children of the family, all, alas! having the same habits; and no reasonable means or effort appeared to be put forth to reduce their noise. The young band were allowed to continue or to cease their music at their pleasure.

For many years I have been in the habit of being much among children, and am passionately fond of them, and delight to mingle in their company and sports; and I well know that children will cry, and to stop them entirely could only be done by stopping their breath. But there is a vast difference between crying naturally and occasionally, and screaming at the top of one's voice with rage and passion, trying at each breath to exceed the previous note, for hours together. I do not wish to exaggerate, but to speak within bounds, I honestly think that for the first three months I was there crying would occupy six hours per day; and frequently two or three would be under way at a time.

Walker wrote of Joaquina, the cook: "Of course, the work about the yard and kitchen devolved on the slave woman, who, by the bye, was not without her faults. She had been brought up in the family under the lash as the only stimulant, which, as a natural consequence, had instilled the most bitter hatred and carelessness, with other kindred qualifications."

The cook may have been the eldest of four young people brought up in servitude by "an extraordinary woman of color" about whom Pensacola historian Leora Sutton wrote a short biography. Euphrasine Hinnard "could have been born to free mulatto parents living in New Orleans," Sutton said. She noted that Louisiana in 1776, when Hinnard was born, was a French province that granted legal rights to all subjects, white and black. By 1812, Hinnard was living in Pensacola, "free and independent," and making a living buying and selling real estate. In 1828, Sutton said,

Euphrasine changed her investment procedure. Buying slaves was far more profitable ... [They] would receive board and shelter where they worked, and she would receive at least fifty cents a day for [males'] labor, the regular fee. She also had another motive for her purchases... [T]he slaves would mortgage themselves to her for ten to twenty years of service. At the completion of this tenure, she considered their debt paid" and would free them.

Jonathan Walker The Man with the Branded Hand

If the Joaquina listed in the 1820 federal census as a fifteen-year-old living with Euphrasine Hinnard was the same person as the Torwards' slave cook, she would have been almost forty years old in 1844.

Sick and weak in his cell during these early weeks in the jail, Jonathan Walker had little capacity for compassion. His first and immediate need was to doctor his illness: "Although the rage of my disease had much abated, I was still kept low, and suffered from alternate chills and fever, attended with much pain in the head and distress at the stomach..."

Years later, Walker described his plight for a granddaughter: "[S]evere treatment in jail reduced me very near to a skeleton. Many a time have I grasped around my leg above the knee joint, over my pants, with one hand so as to meet thumb and finger."

On July 29, ten days after being committed, he wrote in his journal: "My health a little improved; could sit up half the day." Later, he wrote, "I gradually gained strength, and by eating a large quantity of red peppers got rid of the chills, and in about three months was nearly restored to health again."

He continued: "[I]t was nearly a month before I could procure anything to lie upon, other than a few clothes which I had with me. But I finally succeeded in getting a chair, small table, and some straw, of which I made a pallet on the floor, and it served for my bed during my imprisonment."

With the little money that came his way, Walker was able to buy his botanical medicine and, later, food more to his taste than the jail fare. The day he was committed, he wrote, "The marshal searched my person, found on me about fifteen dollars in money, which he took but afterwards gave me again." Once word of his capture and jailing was reported, Walker was helped by friends. For example, he wrote in his journal for September 3, 1844: "Received twenty-five dollars cash, from an old shipmate, by remittance from New York." Later, "Received a visit and some money from a Naval officer who had witnessed the acts of attempted degradation which I had undergone and expressed his sympathy in my behalf."

Walker apparently called on his long acquaintanceship with Pensacolans to help provide food he considered more suitable than the jail diet. He wrote:

One of my first objects after I was incarcerated was to procure such nourishment as would not quarrel with nature, and this I found rather difficult at first; a part of the jail feed I could not relish, and if I attempted to eat it, it would sicken and distress me. The bread, a dish of soup once a day, and sometimes a little fish, was all that I could eat of my rations, and it was difficult to get anyone to bring me anything for two or three weeks. But I finally succeeded in getting a Dane, who kept a grocery, to let his boy bring me such things as I needed, and by this means I obtained much relief and accommodation throughout my confinement; and both the father and his little son, who was very attentive to my wants, are entitled to my grateful and warmest thanks.

The Pensacola Calaboza

Among Pensacolans with whom Walker was acquainted were two men prominent in his jailing, District Attorney Walker Anderson and U.S. Marshal Ebenezer Dorr. A friendly visit from Anderson was not unusual. "For a considerable part of my confinement," Walker explained, "he furnished me with reading matter and the news of the day; and in his absence, his kind and amiable wife would supply me with literary food." The two men had met during Walker's earlier years in Pensacola, and possibly the Yankee captain enjoyed joking with the Florida attorney about their sharing the name Walker, as he might have done with Ebenezer Dorr and his son. Walker Dorr had been only fourteen years old when the Jonathan Walker family had arrived in Pensacola in 1837.

Marshal Dorr appeared to have some sympathy for Jonathan Walker, although he was not so solicitous for Walker's comfort as was Anderson. Dorr was quoted in the Boston *Emancipator and Weekly Chronicle* as writing in September: "I am extremely sorry, as well as almost every other person in this community, that a man so much respected as Captain Walker was in this city should have placed himself in so terrible a situation."

Nevertheless, Anderson, Dorr, and Deputy Marshal James Gonzalez had sworn to uphold the laws, and it was their duty to bring to justice a man accused of stealing valuable property, as slaves were regarded. Both Anderson and Gonzalez had for years been involved in Pensacola police and court cases. Both had had roles in the investigation of the murder of Dr. John Parker in 1837, when the Walker family were newly settled in the community. Court records show that James Gonzalez "must have moved Dr. Parker's body from where he was murdered," Leora Sutton wrote in *Blacks and Slavery in Pensacola, 1780-1880*. "He used his own horse, and a wagon with two horses, used a few Negro men, purchased tobacco for them, and covered the wagon with lime for a trip out of town, then to the graveyard. His bill was eighty dollars."

Anderson, practicing law privately, had been commissioned to defend one of two slaves accused of Parker's murder. His client, identified only as "Lewis," allegedly confessed during the four months he was jailed before the trial. Sutton wrote:

> The usual sentence of the court was read by the judge: "You will be taken from the public prison, to which you are now remanded, to a suitable place, in this city or its vicinity, and there, by the proper officer, publicly hanged by the neck until you shall be dead." To a white person, he would add, "and may God have mercy on you!", but a Negro was without soul, and this would have been omitted. The executioner was paid the usual fee of a bit less than one hundred dollars. One dollar twenty-five cents was allowed for cartage to the graveyard. Anderson was paid fifty dollars for losing the case.

Now, in the matter of Jonathan Walker, Deputy Gonzalez was not hauling victims but a criminal, and Walker Anderson was not the defense counsel but the prosecutor.

*   *   *   *

About Wednesday, July 24, 1844, the *Reform* docked at Pensacola, bringing the seven men who had sailed with Jonathan Walker, as well as the boat that Walker had made or bought in Mobile, Alabama. The slaves were returned to the three white men who claimed ownership.

Joseph Quigles, the agent hired by Caldwell and George Willis to locate the runaway slaves, apparently interviewed the slaves and wrote another letter on the white men's behalf to United States Secretary of State Calhoun: "We feel it is our duty to apprise you at this the earliest practicable date of the return of our Negroes... The man 'Walker' was captured in his whaleboat with the seven Negroes by a wrecker from Key West on the 8th inst. and is now secured in the jail of this county to await his trial. And the Negroes are again in our possession."

Quigles went on to complain politely about the government's failure to help hunt the runaways. He wrote:

We are induced to believe from what the Negroes tell us (of course from their memory) that the boat which the packet-sloop reported on the 27th ult. off Pensacola Bar was the boat of the said Jonathan Walker and if so that there is scarcely room for a doubt that the *Poinset* could have overhauled her in a few hours, and have saved us the delay, trouble, and expense to which we have been subjected by the application for the services of that vessel being refused. As our present misfortune is, however, an evil past being remedied we are chiefly solicitous for the action of the Government so that we may entertain the hope of succor in a similar emergency that may occur in future.

Joseph Quigles' follow-up letter demonstrated the thoroughness with which he carried out his task. Nevertheless, apparently he was unsuccessful. The National Archives has no record that Calhoun – or President Tyler – ever responded.

On the same day that the slaves were returned, July 24, Caldwell visited Walker in jail. "[He] appeared very friendly, saying that he did not intend to punish his servants for going away with me," Walker wrote.

Three of Navy Lieutenant and Mrs. Caldwell's "servants" – Harry and Silas Scott and Moses Johnson – had sailed with Walker. A safe and unpunished return for the seven slaves he had helped was of importance to Walker. Throughout his tribulation, he maintained concern for their welfare. Although he did not say so in his journal, it is likely that Walker would have considered their welfare when confronted next with Caldwell's offer to "help" him.

Walker wrote: "[Caldwell] intimated that the custom-house and the wreckers both had claims on the boat [that Walker owned], and it was very

The Pensacola Calaboza

doubtful whether I should be able to realize anything for her; and as he had lost a good deal by his servants' going away with me, if I would consent for him to have the boat, he would try to compromise with the claimants, and might get something for it."

What if he were to reject Caldwell's offer? Walker thought that "a refusal might excite a spirit of revenge, and that if disposed, he could make my situation more desperate than it was already, and being of the opinion that I should not be able to realize anything from it if I refused him..."

He decided then: "Placing some confidence in what he said... I consented for him to get what he could from it..."

By then, Walker had learned that his personal belongings had been sold in Key West. He reported, "I subsequently wrote twice to the sheriff [Page], but received no answer. They were of no great value, but to one in my circumstances, it was a good deal. I had an excellent spy-glass, for which I paid twenty dollars, and a chest of carpenter's tools, and several other articles, besides some things that the sheriff said he could not find on board of the sloop."

In an example of his habit of turning the other cheek, Walker wrote: "The treatment of Sheriff Page, at Key West, was kind and obliging, and of him I should have no occasion to complain if he had, as I requested, informed me what disposition was made of my effects which were in his charge."

Now, with the yielding of his boat to Caldwell, Walker wrote, he had "put an end to what I had there [Florida] in the shape of property. I should be no further harassed on that point."

Indeed, he was not "further harassed." He now had lost his boat, surely his most valuable possession, in effect offering it to offset the lost wages of Caldwell's three slaves. In addition, Walker had lost the carpenter's tools that he needed to earn a living as a boatswain. His only belongings now were what he wore and the clothing he had brought in a sack. Now he rolled up the sack for use as a pillow.

In Caldwell's behalf, it should be recorded that he kept his word and did not jail the three slaves he claimed – Moses Johnson and the Scott brothers. However, the four men claimed by George and Byrd Willis were taken to the jail on July 28, 1844, and kept in the second prisoners' room for nearly two weeks. On August 5, each was given fifty blows by paddle. They were released on August 8, Anthony Catlett to the custody of Byrd Willis, and Moses Johnson's brothers, Charles, Phillip, and Leonard, to George Willis. Walker's log described the departure of the four slaves: "Were taken out; with much difficulty could walk, being very sore."

*   *   *   *

Walker wrote to his family as soon as he was able. His letter, written the first time he could sit up for half a day, was dated July 29, 1844. The contents were reprinted in several New England newspapers, including the Boston *Morning Chronicle*, Garrison's *Liberator*, the *Emancipator and Weekly Chronicle*, the Yarmouth *Register*, and the Barnstable *Patriot*. The Reverend

Jonathan Walker The Man with the Branded Hand

Joseph Mash of Sandwich, one of Cape Cod's leading abolitionists, helped distribute copies.

Addressed to "Dear Wife and Children," the letter reported on Walker's departure from Pensacola five weeks earlier, on June 23, "with seven colored persons in my boat." He reported their July 8 capture off Key Largo and being taken "by force" to Key West. "In about one day more, if we had not fallen in with an enemy, we should have been out of their way altogether," he added.

Back in Pensacola, he wrote, he was secured to a chain that weighed twenty-two and a half pounds and a shackle that weighed about five pounds. Walker later explained how he determined weights: "By the use of a small stick and a little paper and twine, I made a balance, and for weights I used silver coin; and in this way I... weighed the chain attached to my leg, by weighing one link of medium size, and multiplying the others by that, which product was twenty-two and one-half pounds, beside the shackle which encircled my ankle."

His letter continued: "If I could walk the room, it would afford me great relief. I fast, but from the 25th of June until the 23rd of July, I was not able to sit up three hours in a day, and nearly all the time very much exposed [to the hot sun and rain]."

He added, "I cannot say when I shall have my trial, nor what the result will be." Then, somewhat hopefully: "The regular term of court does not come on until November, but the judge does not know but that he shall appoint a special term before that time."

And finally, in anguish:

Jane! what is to become of you and the children? I have lost nearly what little I had in the fracas, and I am confident that you are needy at this time. You had better send and get the proceeds of that iron and spars which I sent to Fall River [a maritime city in southeastern Massachusetts], and do as well as you can. Write me as soon as you get this, that I may know how it is. The Lord Jesus has been abundantly good to me through all my afflictions thus far, and I feel and trust that his Spirit will accompany me through, for I cannot let Him go. Should I be taken away today, I feel that all will be well beyond the grave. My confidence is strong in Him, for He has purchased redemption by His blood for such vile sinners as me.

Prisoner Walker later noted: "My correspondence had to pass under [Marshal Dorr's] inspection, and for one or two words in a private letter to my wife, respecting my situation, I received from him a severe reprimand."

Jonathan's parents, Seth and Mercy Walker, were then seventy-six years old and were to live more than a decade longer. A thoughtful son, Jonathan concluded his first letter home: "O! my dear parents, don't worry about me, for I am in good spirits, and shall weather the storm."

Once more, Jonathan Walker was on the threshold of a major change. He was about to become a national figure in the battle for equality.

...if ye suffer for righteousness' sake, happy
are ye: and be not afraid of their terror...

2 Peter 3:14

Chapter 6   National Recognition

W illiam Lloyd Garrison and *The Liberator* made a major issue of Walker's
jailing. Immediately, Walker's adventure captured the front pages of abolitionist
newspapers throughout the nation. Only a week after the end of his trip off
Carysfort Reef on July 8, the Boston *Emancipator and Weekly Chronicle* had a
brief note. *The Liberator* reported his capture on August 2. *The Liberator's*
August 9 edition noted that a resolution supporting Walker had been adopted at
the annual Emancipation Day program on August 1 in New Bedford. Early in
the day-long event, the gathering – held in honor of the end of slavery in the
British West Indies – had also expressed sympathy for the Reverend Charles T.
Torrey, the Congregational minister who had participated in Cape Cod
abolitionist gatherings a decade before. Torrey had left his pastorate in
Providence, Rhode Island, to take up abolition's cause, and now he was in a
Baltimore jail for assisting a slave woman and her two children to escape.

In speaking for the New Bedford resolutions supporting Torrey, *The
Liberator* reported, Garrison also alluded to the case of... Walker... concerning
whom the meeting passed a resolution as follows, drawn up by Mr. Garrison:

> Whereas this meeting has heard, since it has been convened, that
> another citizen of Massachusetts, Captain Jonathan Walker... has been
> arrested and thrown into jail in Pensacola, Florida, on a charge
> precisely identical with that which is brought against Mr. Torrey – and
> it is highly probable that he will not be able to escape from a terrible
> doom; therefore,

Resolved, That we feel an equal amount of sympathy for this worthy but unfortunate friend of the human race, and pledge ourselves to cooperate with our brethren elsewhere, as far as practicable, to secure for him the best aid and counsel, that he may happily obtain his deliverance.

While Walker began to displace Torrey as a prime subject in the abolitionist press, the weekly newspapers of Cape Cod were more restrained in their coverage. The Yarmouth *Register* finally took note of Walker's jailing in its edition of August 15, 1844. Besides the news report of his capture, the newspaper had an editorial: "However imprudently Mr. W. may have acted in thus risking himself, he certainly deserves our warmest sympathy; for if he has violated the despotic laws of the South, it does not follow that he has performed an unworthy deed."

The Register noted also that a meeting was being scheduled in Harwich's Congregational Meetinghouse to consider what local residents might do to help the Walker family.

Garrison wanted more action. He wrote in his August 9 newspaper: "Every town on Cape Cod ought to hold a public meeting and pass strong resolutions on the subject."

The Reverend Mr. Mash echoed the call in the cover letter that he sent with the Walker letter to *The Register* and *Patriot*:

Will the people of Cape Cod suffer one of their worthy fellow citizens to be in chains in a loathsome dungeon, in a strange land, among slaveholders and petty tyrants, without an effort to obtain his deliverance? Forbid it, Heaven! Let public meetings be called all over the Cape (it will be done elsewhere) to adopt such measures as shall appear feasible to accomplish the noble object, viz.: THE DELIVERANCE OF CAPT. JONA. WALKER FROM PRISON AND DEATH! Let the very best counsel be employed and, if need be, carry the case up to the Supreme Court of the United States. Let us see whether the law of Florida, under which Capt. Walker was arrested, is constitutional.

The edition of the Yarmouth newspaper with Mash's letter, dated September 5, 1844, also contained a letter from Ebenezer Hussey, a Quaker from Lynn, Massachusetts, whose "able and eloquent speech at the District convention" the previous March "was copied with approbation into many papers abroad." Hussey's letter revealed his belief that Congress and the people should "strike from the Constitution every blot which slavery has imprinted upon its fair fame." *The Register* suggested its stand against slavery with its introduction to the Hussey letter:

We commend his views to the consideration of those who think with him on the subject of Slavery, generally, but who are not willing to

National Recognition

reject a positive and practical good, and inflict a positive evil, in the vain attempt to grasp a mere abstraction – who are not willing to throw away the substance and pursue the shadow.

If Cape Cod readers had opinions on the subject, they were not represented in succeeding editions of that newspaper. Garrison's readers responded quickly. James Fuller of New York sent Walker twenty dollars. Samuel E. Sewall proclaimed, "Walker *must be* defended. He is a fellow soldier with us in the great moral warfare against slavery... Neither money nor labor must be spared to obtain his deliverance." Lewis Tappan, treasurer of the American and Foreign Antislavery Society, printed an appeal for money.

Thus began efforts on Walker's behalf. With them came the publicity that would make an obscure Cape Cod sailor a major figure in the abolitionist movement. Over the summer and autumn months, news of his escapade, his plight, and efforts to free him were to extend across the young country's states and territories and even to Europe. It would, nevertheless, be many more months before substantial support arrived.

Joseph Mash continued his efforts on Cape Cod. He wrote an evocative letter to Garrison on September 10, 1844. Published in *The Liberator* on September 27, the letter began:

I have this moment left the hearthstone of Captain Jonathan Walker... Sitting in the midst of his distressed family, my heart ached while I was inquiring into their circumstances, and the ages and names of his children. There are three names among the eight which are significant of the father's views and sympathy for the oppressed. William Wilberforce is playing with his toys; William Lloyd Garrison, a child at the breast, is calling for his father; and Lydia M. Child has gone to school, a privilege the poor colored child of the land of chains has never enjoyed.

Mash actually was identifying the famous egalitarians for whom the children were named. The children's names were William Wilberforce Walker, Lloyd Garrison Walker, and Maria Child Walker. The custom of naming children after well-known reformers was popular among abolitionists: Mr. and Mrs. Garrison named a son for abolitionist Wendell Phillips.

Mash continued:

...[T]his, and other disasters, have reduced [the Walker] family to poverty. They are needy. I shall do what I can for them on my tour down the Cape. Whatever help the benevolent wish to furnish may be forwarded to Joseph P. Nickerson, Esq., South Harwich, who will gladly place it in the possession of Mrs. Jane Walker... Any thing, such as clothing and other necessaries forwarded to me at Sandwich, will find its way to them. Yours for justice.

Jonathan Walker The Man with the Branded Hand

Dramatically, Mash had contrasted the "hearthstone" scene of children playing around their nursing mother and the "small, dark, dirty" jail in which this "good, honest, humane, upright man" was chained.

*　　　　*　　　　*　　　　*

One of the conditions that most distressed Jonathan Walker during his jail term was the routine, impersonal torture of slaves. For weeks, he recorded in a journal he kept each beating of the Torward family's cook-slave. He described in detail the kinds of weapons used for punishment. His book, *Trial and Imprisonment*, included a drawing of a prostrate slave, her buttocks bared, being paddled by a white man. Observing the punishment are two white men, wearing striped trousers and buttoned jackets.

Walker introduced the subject of whippings in his book with this report:

I had scarcely been secured in my cage like some rabid, dangerous animal, before I found I had to encounter a species of torment which I had not counted on, in the terrible amount of noise from the domestics about the premises...

The paddles which I have seen are about twenty inches in length, made of pitch-pine board, from an inch to an inch and a quarter thick, and seven or eight inches of one end is three and a half or four inches wide, having from ten to fifteen holes through it the size of a small nail gimlet, and the other part is made round for the handle. The unfortunate subjects who are to feel the effects of this inhuman drubbing are first tied, his or her wrists together, then made to sit down on the floor or ground, and put the knees through between the arms, then a stick or broom-handle is inserted through the angle of the legs, directly under the knees and over the arms, which confines them in a doubled and helpless condition. Previous to this arrange- ment, the victims are made naked from the waist down. The operator now takes hold with one hand of one end of the stick which has been inserted to confine the legs and arms together, and cants them on one side, and in the other holds the before-mentioned paddle, which he applies to the backside of his helpless fellow-creature; stopping at short intervals to allow the sufferer to answer questions as are asked, or make such promises as it is thought best to extort; and to give the numbness which has been excited by repeated blows time to subside, which renders the next blows more acute and painful. After a requisite number of blows with the paddle are given, which is generally from ten to fifty, as the master or mistress may dictate, the raw-hide switch is next applied to the bruised and blistered parts, with as many or more blows laid on; after which the sufferer is loosed and suffered to get over it the best way they can.

Common mode of whipping with the paddle.

Illustration from *Trial and Imprisonment of Jonathan Walker* (1845)

This drawing appeared in Jonathan Walker's own account of his observations while in jail awaiting court action in Florida. It depicts a woman being "whipped with the paddle." The white male brandishing the two-foot long paddle probably was drawn to represent City Marshal Francis Toward. Walker said slaveholders, like the two figures at right, paid Toward to punish the men and women they claimed to own as slaves.

Jonathan Walker The Man with the Branded Hand

Walker began his log on Monday, July 22, his third day in the jail, with a note that "L.T." – jailer Francis Torward's wife, Maria – "whipped the cook." He added: "Whenever the cook was whipped, it was done, with a few exceptions, with a raw-hide switch, about three feet in length, generally from twenty to fifty strokes at a time."

Walker's log was continued for sixteen weeks, through November 15. During that time, Joaquina was beaten thirty-three times, an average of twice weekly. On two occasions punishment was administered by Constable Torward himself, and once each by Maria Torward's mother and brother. All the other whippings – twenty-nine in sixteen weeks – were made by the arm of Maria Torward. Walker's log included additional information and comments; for example, after noting that the slave was beaten four times in one day, August 17, Walker added: "mistress dreadfully cross." Multiple beatings of Joaquina were not unusual. During this period, he logged two each on three different occasions. On October 25, he wrote: "Rather squally overhead and about the kitchen. L.T. whipped the cook twice, and another servant once; the children got some scolding, dealt out unsparingly."

Maria Torward's health during a pregnancy did not seem to reduce her strength or her determination to carry out punishment. After recording an August 30 beating of Joaquina, Walker noted: "L.T. confined; brought forth a fine boy." Now there were ten second-floor residents. The new baby was probably Stephen Torward, the sixth of the ten children Maria was to bear, and the fifth of her eight sons. Although Maria Torward apparently was not "confined" long, she did permit temporary assistants to beat the slave in the following weeks. Walker logged the cook's beating on September 13 "by L.T.'s brother at her request" and on October 15 by "L.T.'s mother." Walker recorded three beatings for the cook on November 26, once each by Mr. and Mrs. Torward and Maria's mother. Maria Torward eventually slowed down. Walker noted that the cook was punished less after that. He logged "only" six beatings, all by Maria Torward, in the succeeding three months until the family moved out of the jail building in February 1845.

Maria Torward occasionally had difficulty coping with her own unhappy existence. Walker wrote on November 3: "L.T. whipped the cook severely with a broomstick; scolds tremendously; gives unlimited scope to passion, and tapers off by crying herself."

Like the measured pace of a relentless whipping, Walker's impersonal itemizing of beatings took on a chilling rhythm – swish, snap, scream; swish, snap, scream. In its way, such a simple repetition of violence can be viewed as more evocative of pain than the melodrama imagined and described by abolitionist Abby Kelley, as reported in Dorothy Sterling's *Ahead of Her Time*:

> When I come to sit down in the cool of the day, alone with none but God to hold communion with, and in the exercise of love to him, become myself the slave – when at such a moment I feel the fetters wearing away the flesh and grating on my bare ankle bone, when I feel

the naked cords of my neck shrinking away from the rough edge of the iron collar, when my flesh quivers beneath the lash, too, in anguish, I feel portions of it cut from my back...

Sutton's *Blacks and Slavery in Pensacola, 1780-1880,* has the unemotional documentary tone of Walker's. In a section on punishment given slaves, Sutton wrote:

For the habitual runaway, it could mean back to the shackles and chains, or worse, the loss of a foot. The thief could lose a finger or hand. The amputations were expediently executed with the aid of a sharp meat cleaver or axe. There was a guillotine, French in origin, located in the basement of a prominent Pensacola physician's home that served a dual purpose: merciful and unmerciful, therapeutic or sadistic!

....The law was the law. For a simple pleasure, such as swimming in the bay, a slave could expect ten lashes across the back. If they were away from their master's compound without a pass, or unaccompanied, twenty lashes... It was their neck, stretched in a long, straight line from the end of a rope, for raping a white woman, though the same was not true if the circumstances were reversed by a white man. Then it was only a matter of "borrowing someone else's property."

*   *   *   *

Leave it to Garrison and his *Liberator* to find a way to agitate on Walker's behalf, even if it meant bringing a negative edge to an otherwise positive action. It was not enough for Garrison that the Glasgow Emancipation Society had denounced American laws that had resulted in the Baltimore jailing of the Reverend Charles T. Torrey, and the jailing in Missouri of three other American abolitionists. Writing in his newspaper on August 23, 1844, Garrison welcomed the news from Glasgow – "but," he persisted,

...as yet the still more afflicting and hopeless case of the unfortunate Walker... appears to attract very little attention. Something ought to be done in his behalf immediately... If in Scotland – in a foreign land – across the wide Atlantic – the public feeling has been promptly roused to an earnest expression in a case like this, shall there not be some stir at home – a meeting in THE OLD CRADLE OF LIBERTY?

The "cradle" nickname for Boston's Faneuil Hall originated from a patriotic address given there by Barnstable's James Otis.

The week after Garrison's nagging appeal, John Bailey of New Bedford wrote "friend Garrison" about

...calling a meeting, to be held in Faneuil Hall, to take into consideration the case of Jonathan Walker. We are anxious, here, to do something for him, if anything can be done. I have consulted some of the friends of liberty upon the subject, who think a public meeting ought to be called, to express our sympathy, at least, for a very worthy man (as some here know him to be) and one who is in imminent danger of suffering, if not martyrdom, imprisonment perhaps for life. But we wish our Boston friends to take the lead...

Noting that a meeting had been scheduled on Torrey's behalf at Faneuil Hall on September 6, Bailey assumed Walker's case also would be discussed. "But why is the meeting delayed to that time? The public expression of our sympathy, it appears to me, should go abroad immediately, that the whole country may be electrified before it is too late." Bailey signed his letter, "Thine, for suffering humanity."

Walker family friends in Harwich were acting as quickly as the communications of the times permitted. The first mail delivered to Walker came on his forty-fifth day in jail.

Walker received four letters on September 2. They came from his wife, parents, and children, and offers of help from J. P. Nickerson, Sidney Underwood, and Elkanah Nickerson, Jr., all of Harwich.

The letter from Elkanah Nickerson, dated August 17, offered news and inspiration. Addressing "my dear suffering friend Jonathan," Nickerson began with the news: "Thy family are all in health. Some days after the news of thy capture came, I went over to see thy wife and thy parents, and they expressed much concern about thee..."

Walker and many abolitionists, although not formally Quakers, nevertheless used the plain speech adopted by members of the Society of Friends. Quakers employed "thee" as opposed to the more formal "you" to represent the leveling of social classes and the spirit of fellowship.

The news from Nickerson continued: "At a meeting, on the first day of August, we made a small collection for thy family. We also chose a committee to see thy family. It was a consolation to many to have a letter from thee; many sympathize with thee."

The inspiration from Nickerson came from the Bible: "I mentioned to [your family] the well-known passage of Scripture: 'if ye suffer for righteousness, happy are ye'..."

More news of community action in Harwich came in an August 20 letter from Sidney Underwood and Elkanah Nickerson, Jr. They wrote:

> When your condition became known here, a good deal of interest was excited in your behalf. A meeting of the citizens was held at the Congregational Meetinghouse yesterday (19th), agreeably to previous notice, to take into consideration your case; and the undersigned were made a committee to ascertain through you, your friends, or the authorities of Pensacola, in what way, if at all, your condition may be ameliorated.

Underwood and Nickerson were prominent young men well into their careers as Harwich community leaders. Underwood, at age forty the elder of the two, was the fifth of the seven sons of Susanna Underwood and the Reverend Nathan Underwood. It was probably another son, also named Nathan, and not the minister, who had joined Jonathan Walker in lending money to David Walker.

Sidney Underwood, who was born on June 15, 1804, had grown up with Jonathan. At the time he was working on Walker's behalf, he and his wife, Lucy, had three children, ages one, four, and six. Sidney was apparently active in abolitionism only during Jonathan's imprisonment but, like his father, he never gave up his service to the Congregational parish. He was the first Sunday school superintendent and teacher of record, and perhaps the best remembered of the church's early deacons.

Elkanah Nickerson, Jr., was born November 13, 1806, the second of nine children of Elkanah and Elizabeth Nickerson. He had married the former Hannah Doane of Harwich in 1829 and their three children were fourteen, eleven, and five years old when Elkanah, Jr., reached out to help Jonathan Walker. His letter continued:

> We learn that you were committed to prison for want of bail; and we wish to know whether you would be now released from confinement if the necessary bail should be obtained? Do you wish for bail? or had you rather remain confined until your trial? Have you any counsel? And if not, do you wish for any? And if so, have you the means of employing counsel? Or does the government furnish counsel for you?... Will there be a special court for your trial, or shall you wait till the regular term in November? An early answer to the above inquiries, or so many of them as may be of importance to you, is desired...

Nickerson and Underwood obviously had sympathy for Walker and his family. Nevertheless, their letter went on to echo the somewhat stiff reserve sounded that same week by the Yarmouth *Register* editorial. Both the newspaper and the two-member Harwich citizens committee backed away from supporting Walker's illegal act in assisting slaves to run away. The Harwich letter stated:

> From our long acquaintance with you, we are assured that the act for which you have been arrested and are now suffering was done under a high sense of moral obligation. How far that sense has been mistaken is not for us to determine. We can only regret the occurrence; leaving the adjustment of its morality between you and your own conscience.

The *Register*, having recorded Walker's arrest in early August, 1844, did not mention him again until after his release nearly one year later. Some people, and some newspapers, were more direct in expressing their lack of sympathy. The *Christian Witness* of Boston commented that "if Walker did not appreciate Florida slave laws, he should never have gone there." Even in New Bedford, where the Walkers had lived, support for Jonathan was not unanimous;

the Reverend Henry Jackson said, "Walker had no more than his just deserts for breaking the laws of the government."

Walker's friends did not turn away. They continued to provide funds for Jane and the children, and that fall raised a large sum – seven hundred fifty dollars – for Jonathan's legal assistance.

*   *   *   *

Jonathan Walker, meantime, was immersed in the brutality of slavery. Not only was he living in chains, himself a slave to suspicion, but he was in a jail where slaves were brought almost daily for punishment for fee, or for violating laws and regulations made by white men to keep black people in line.

On September 1, one of the seven slaves who had attempted escape with Walker – the captain never identified this man in his writings – was "committed on suspicion of larceny." Like the trained dogs used in pursuit of runaway slaves, trouble had found it an easy task to track this miserable man. He must be guilty; he was black. No trial was necessary.

In his typically stark, dramatic way, Walker wrote in his journal of how the accumulation of grief affected his escape companion when jailed for theft on September 1, 1844: "[H]e committed suicide same day by cutting his throat and belly open, and lived but two or three hours after." Later, Walker recorded the haunting post-mortem discovery: the article that the slave was suspected of stealing had been found. It had simply been misplaced. Desperate enough earlier for freedom to attempt the flight with Walker, undoubtedly punished upon being returned to Pensacola, and then to be accused of a crime he did not commit, this man had made one of the few decisions that a slave could make without reprimand or contradiction. He had concluded that his life was not worth continuing.

Three days after this man's death, Walker was moved from the room in which he had been held for six weeks to the second cell. He wrote: "[H]ere were two objects which attracted my attention. On one side of the room, much of the floor was stained with the blood of [the] slave who had... committed suicide... The other object was the chain to which I was attached, it being the same which I had noticed fastened to the leg of Isaac, a slave man under sentence, nearly three years previous."

Walker recorded his experience of kneeling in prayer with Isaac in that cell in 1841, and then hearing that the governor had granted a pardon for Isaac.

"But while I am writing this," Walker's said in his 1844 journal, "I can see and feel the same chain attached to my leg."

Here, Walker yielded to a rare moment of self-righteousness:

And what is my crime? What have I done? I have attempted to assist a few of my fellow-beings to escape from bondage, to which they were subjected for no cause over which they or their ancestors had any control; but because they were of the weaker party, and had not the power to assert their rights among men.

National Recognition

Throughout Jonathan Walker's confinement, the jail was a busy place. In the few months' log items that he reprinted in his own book, he recorded the confinement of many people, white and black, male and female. The unenamored reportage captures the horror of being a black person accused of attempting to run away, stealing money, failing to work hard enough, or, saddest of all, of being old and failing to bring a satisfactory bid when put up for sale at auction. Here are some samples from the late summer of 1844:

> [August] 12. A fugitive slave man caught and committed....

> 22. The slave man committed on the 12th taken out and sent to Alabama.

> 28. ...Slave woman committed; had been brought from New Orleans by mistake on board steamboat....

> 31. The slave woman, put in the 28th, was taken out and sent back....

> [September] 11. A slave man brought to jail – whipped twenty blows with a paddle, and sent back.

This last entry was one of many in Walker's journal to refer to a legal disciplinary service provided for fee by Jailmaster Torward. His charge for one beating: seventy-five cents. Walker's log continued its grim picture of Pensacola life:

> [September] 25. A large fire in the city. A number of houses burnt. A white man committed on suspicion of setting the fire. He was examined and discharged.

> 26. A slave man committed, charged with attempting to steal fruit. He was whipped four blows with a paddle, and twenty-four with the cow-hide, and let out.

> 29. Slave man committed; did not stay at home enough on the Sabbath to do chores; next morning, let out.

> [October] 2. ...A slave man committed for debt...

> 4. The slave man, put in on the 29th, discharged....

> 9. A white man committed on suspicion of participating in murder....

> 11. The white man committed the 9th, on suspicion, discharged....

> 27. A white man committed for fighting.

> 28. Discharged. At night, the prisoner in the adjoining room broke out and went off....

> [November] 9. A slave man committed for leaving wood at the wrong place.

> 11. The slave man committed on the [9th] discharged, and a free colored woman put in for allowing the slave man to put wood in her yard...

12. The colored woman, committed yesterday, discharged, and another committed for attempting to defend herself when about to be flogged by a Naval officer, but discharged same day.

*   *   *   *

United States Navy personnel contributed to the heavy traffic in and out of the Pensacola Jail during Walker's confinement. Here are a few relevant entries from Walker's 1844 log:

[October] 3. Two sailors from brig *Wetomka* committed; they were intoxicated, and quarreled. Three sailors committed, who had taken French leave from U.S. steamer *Union*...

4. ...A sailor belonging to the U.S. vessel *Vandalia,* committed, and taken out the same day.

7. Three men, attached to the U.S. steamer *Union* [and committed October 3], taken out and sent on board....

9. ...Three seamen from the U.S. steamer *General Taylor,* committed for having some difficulty with the clerk on shore.

10. Two of them taken out and sent on board. The two seamen from brig *Wetomka*, committed on the 3d, were let out....

14. The other man, (the boatswain,) belonging to the U.S. steamer *General Taylor*, let out. He went on board, and made me a present of a pair of blankets. One white man in the adjoining room and myself are the only remaining prisoners....

17. A sailor, a deserter from the U.S. service, caught and committed....

20. The other prisoner discharged.

*   *   *   *

The Boston meeting that editor Garrison and letter writer Bailey had urged was held in Boston on September 21, not at the "Cradle of Liberty" but at Marlboro Chapel. This was one of Loring Moody's first public appearances on behalf of his brother-in-law Nathan Walker's brother, Jonathan. This was the Loring Moody who grew up in Harwich, the youngster who would rather read than rake hay threatened with a cloudburst. "Mr. Loring Moody, a delegate to the meeting from Harwich," *The Liberator* reported, "bore ample testimony to the character of Captain Walker, and read several very affecting letters from him to his family and friends." The Boston meeting unanimously adopted resolutions which, in summary, held that:

- Walker "had... been unlawfully seized... and there... with circumstances of the greatest cruelty, imprisoned for a pretended offense, for an act justified by the law of the land, and required by the law of God."
- "Congress has no authority to establish or permit slavery... that the Governor and Council of Florida... have no authority to establish slave laws therein, or to make it a crime to assist such *inhabitants* held in bondage under such laws to escape therefrom... and that all such acts of pretended

legislation are, and ought by Congress and the Supreme Judiciary of the United States to be, adjudged null and void."

- The "master and crew of the wrecking schooner *Eliza Catherine...* committed acts of piracy, justly subjecting them to penalties of the laws provided in such cases."

- "...Jonathan Walker as a citizen of Massachusetts... is entitled to the official interposition of the State to secure the rights that belong to him, and that the committee be directed to bring the matter before the governor and legislature."

- "...a committee of five persons be now appointed, to act for the friends of humanity in this case, in raising and disbursing funds, employing counsel, and other aid, providing for the personal relief of Mr. Walker and his suffering family."

A sixth resolution authorized "a subscription and collection," which amounted to $108 that evening. Copies of the resolutions, prepared by the Reverend Joshua Leavitt, were sent to Jonathan Walker in Pensacola and to Jane Walker in Harwich.

* * * *

In the October 11 *Liberator*, Henry Ingersoll Bowditch and Henry W. Williams, "for the Committee at Harwich," reported on a trip on Walker's behalf that Loring Moody was about to take, visiting thirteen Massachusetts towns in fifteen days. Between October 14 and October 28, he would speak in a new community each day, resting only on the two Sundays. Moody was referred to as "LORING MOODY, Esq., Chairman of the Committee of Citizens of Harwich." He was, Bowditch and Williams wrote, "to go, for the two or three following months, as agent through various Counties in our State." They asked that "funds without measure will be forthcoming from every man, woman, and child who have a farthing to spare to aid this righteous cause. Money will be needed for the assistance of Captain Walker... and for sustaining his numerous family, now deprived of their only means of support."

The committee also urged Plymouth County residents "to make arrangement whereby Mr. Moody may be amply accommodated... [and] conveyed from town to town, free of expense." Such an arrangement was common in the years long before telephones; newspapers listed dates and requested residents to rent a hall and provide bed and board for the traveling speaker in each community.

The notice also indicated that Walker's supporters had no hope that he would be acquitted of the charges against him in the Pensacola court. They wrote that funds were needed "to test the important questions which the case involves, by an appeal to the Supreme Court of the United States." It is possible, of course, that the Massachusetts supporters mistakenly believed that Florida, like some other states, imposed the death penalty for stealing slaves, and therefore were anxious to have the nation's highest court decide what they saw as a constitutional question.

This news coverage was taking place in mid-October. Walker already had been in jail three months. His first trial was a month away. And no one, especially the loyal friends preparing to take on the highest court in the young land, could have guessed that the final adjudication in Walker's lower court case would not be settled for another eight months.

*   *   *   *

Boston's five-member committee apparently acted quickly to obtain for citizen Walker "the official interposition of [Massachusetts] to secure the rights that belong to him." The petitioners asked Governor George N. Briggs to furnish counsel and "other means of relief."

Just how to execute "official interposition" on behalf of Jonathan Walker was not clear in 1844 on Boston's Beacon Hill. The citizens' petition went to the Governor's Council, an executive group headed by John Reed, the lieutenant governor. Reed had been elected with Governor Briggs and both had been sworn in on January 10, 1844. Supporting Reed, the Yarmouth *Register* called him "our nigh neighbor," and added, "We need not speak in his praise, since the citizens of this county have proved their confidence in him by electing him some dozen times to represent them in the Congress of the United States." This was the Yarmouth resident to whom Walker had appealed personally in 1837 for Congressional help in regaining the money that Walker claimed had been stolen from him and his son, John, during their Mexican adventure. Reed, who served as a representative from Massachusetts for eleven terms, had instead shipped Walker's case to the State Department.

If the new lieutenant governor felt any obligation to help his fellow Cape Codder, little was offered through the group over which he presided. The Governor's Council, on October 1, 1844, appointed a committee, headed by Reed, to act on "a petition of John Pierpont and others in behalf of Jonathan Walker, imprisoned in Pensacola..." Serving with Reed were Councilors R. G. Daniels, A. D. Foster, and George Morey.

As *The Liberator* announced, the committee "reported [the following day, October 2] that the Executive [branch of the state government] has no jurisdiction in the matter, and no authority to provide counsel, or in any manner to use the funds of the State for the purpose asked in the memorial [petition]." The council's minutes quote the report: "As this in the opinion of the Committee disposes of the subject, we deem it wholly unnecessary to express any opinion in relation to the case further than to say we cannot advise the Governor to provide the said Jonathan Walker with Counsel or afford him any pecuniary aid."

The Council, in fact, did indirectly express an opinion and did advise Governor Briggs. In something like a "however," the report added:

> The Committee are not insensible to the misfortunes of their fellow-citizens, and sincerely sympathize with the said Walker and his afflicted family. As it is believed by the Memorialists [that is, the petitioners] and others entitled to our respect and consideration that the said Jonathan Walker is treated in prison with cruelty, and that he is

sick, and that he may be called to trial wholly unprepared for defense, we do advise and recommend to his Excellency the Governor to instruct the Secretary of the Commonwealth to write to the Governor of Florida to obtain for him relief from all unnecessary severity in the execution of their laws, and a delay of the trial, if the said Walker be unprepared, and we are not aware that anything more can be done by the Executive in the case.

That seemed to satisfy Governor Briggs, whose home in Pittsfield was at the opposite end of the state from Cape Cod. He sent a message to the Massachusetts Senate, enclosing the council report. Any funds to help Walker would have to come from the General Court, as Massachusetts calls its legislature. None were provided, as Briggs no doubt anticipated. Briggs, however, followed the council's advice and directed John G. Palfrey, the state secretary, to write to the governor of the Territory of Florida on Walker's behalf.

Like Reed's committee and Governor Briggs, Palfrey wasted no time. On October 2, the same day that the council committee headed by Reed had reported, Palfrey addressed Florida's Governor John Branch, requesting a delay of trial in order "to obtain a mitigation of the hardships which he is said to be enduring, and such a delay of proceedings as may afford opportunity for securing that highest object of justice, safety to the innocent."

Palfrey's letter was regarded in the South as both unwelcome interference by one state in the affairs of another and, perhaps equally unacceptable, as a breach of etiquette. Didn't Massachusetts know that correspondence to the Florida governor should not originate with an official lower on the political ladder than the governor, even if the second governor's jurisdiction had not yet gained statehood?

Palfrey concluded his lengthy letter: "Assured that your Excellency will estimate justly the solicitude on the part of the Governor of this Commonwealth [Massachusetts], for the safety of its helpless citizens..."

Palfrey was falsely "assured." By October 25, 1844, Governor Branch had decided how to handle this breach of conduct. He dispatched a letter to Walker Anderson. He chose well; Anderson had two roles appropriate to this impudence from the Bay State. As the United States attorney for West Florida, Anderson would prosecute Jonathan Walker. Further, as a state senator, he headed the Florida legislative committee considering a proposal to raise to death the punishment for assisting runaway slaves.

Underlining key words for emphasis, the governor wrote:

I herewith transmit to you a copy of a somewhat extraordinary communication which I have received from the Secretary of the Commonwealth of Massachusetts. I have not, and probably may not, take any official notice of it, for reasons which will readily occur to you. You are, however, at liberty to make such use of it as you may think proper; as I have entire confidence in your discretion and ability to do justice to a subject which seems to excite the <u>sensibility</u> of the <u>good people</u> of that Commonwealth, and which cannot be one of indifference to the southern slaveholder....

[Massachusetts] had tried to interpose and stay the proceedings of a coordinate department of this government, to gratify the morbid feelings of Northern fanatics, thereby impeaching the impartiality and purity of our highest judicial tribunals.

U.S. Attorney Anderson responded to Governor Branch on November 9 – a few days after returning from a court assignment outside Pensacola and only two days before the Walker trial was scheduled. He wrote as a court official not inconsiderate of Walker's needs, yet his somewhat playful style – spiced with a dash of superciliousness and a touch of obsequiousness – would have pleased the ceremonious sensibilities of Governor Branch.

One by one, Anderson addressed the points Palfrey made in his letter. First, he took up Walker's health: "I am happy to inform your Excellency that the Governor of Massachusetts has been entirely misled..." Walker had been ill from exposure in an open boat but "he informs me, and as he looks to be, he is in perfect health."

Anderson then considered Palfrey's claim that Walker's leg chain was a "circumstance of unusual hardship." Anderson wrote: "The crime with which he is charged is characterized by our law as a very grave one, and the executive officers of our court have looked to that law for their guidance, rather than to the opinions of those to whom they at least owe no accountability."

Regarding Palfrey's suggestion that the court date should be delayed, Anderson wrote: "There is no disposition, I am sure, in any of the officers of this court to press this trial with unusual precipitancy, but on the contrary, there is a sincere desire to do... no more than justice." In fact, the federal attorney wrote: "[Walker] has a right to demand his immediate trial, and I have been assured by him only today that he is anxious that his case should be disposed of during the present term of the court. This desire of his, so natural in itself, we shall feel bound to regard as paramount in its claim upon us... I trust, therefore, that his Excellency of Massachusetts will perceive that we are prevented from complying with his request by the superior duty of yielding to the wishes of the prisoner in this regard."

Moreover, Anderson wrote, Walker had requested a modest delay – "to as late a period of the *term* as practicable, and it has accordingly been fixed for the second week of the term, and I doubt not it will be put off to a still later period of the term if the prisoner should show good cause therefor."

Finally, Anderson took on the Massachusetts official's concern that Walker should have adequate legal representation. He wrote Governor Branch: "Counsel is within his reach here, fully competent to the task of maintaining his rights anywhere, and your Excellency, I am sure, anticipates me in the assurance that his poverty will oppose [sic] no obstacle to his procuring the aid of such counsel."

Governor Branch, in language equally elaborate and florid, commended Anderson's response as "full of instructive admonition to those deluded victims of a vicious credulity; and it is hoped that their incendiary and disorganizing intermeddling with our domestic institutions will stand rebuked by his calm and dignified refutation of their unfounded calumnies."

The governor concluded: "Death is the punishment provided by law for such offenses in the slaveholding states generally, and it ought to be so in Florida."

The governor's statements are recorded in the *Florida Senate Journal* for 1845. *The Liberator*, on January 3, 1845, reported that "no answer has been returned" to the Massachusetts middleman, John Palfrey. No record has been found that Branch ever deigned to answer the Massachusetts appeal.

As it developed, an even more significant result could be assigned to the correspondence, and that is the decision by Florida in 1845 to impose the death penalty on anyone convicted of helping slaves attempting escape. For now, far from assisting Walker, Massachusetts was helping to create an environment that would lead, only a few months later, to authorizing the ultimate punishment for helping runaway slaves.

    *   *   *   *

Jonathan Walker had attempted to acquire a lawyer to represent him, although he was not certain of success until the day of his trial. He had written a veteran Pensacola lawyer, Benjamin Drake Wright, on July 25, "requesting an interview." That he was anxious for help is indicated by his having contacted the lawyer four days before he wrote his first letter to "Dear Wife and Children."

Walker explained: "The reason for my requesting an interview with B. D. Wright was knowing that he was a candid man and experienced in his profession, and that I should be likely to obtain correct information from him."

Wright was indeed "a candid man." He had not answered sooner, he suggested in a response to Walker, because he considered Walker's offense an insult to "the community" – the white community, of course. His delayed response reflected an attorney's professionalism slowly overcoming personal dislike for a client's crime in order to provide the defendant with proper legal representation. Dated August 30, 1844, some five weeks after Walker's invitation, the lawyer's letter explained:

> I have for some time thought I ought to answer your note... I have not called for reasons which I will frankly state. In common with all who know you as a citizen here, I was very indignant, not so much at the *injury* which your offense occasioned, as at the *insult* which it implied to the whole community. This feeling is still strong in me, but I feel that it is gradually giving way to gentler impulses.
>
> It is the indignant feeling above mentioned that has hitherto prevented me from seeing you. If the object of your note was to avail

91

yourself of my professional services, I can only say that after thinking the matter over, I do not see how I can refuse them, nor do I think that by the time the November court comes, I should desire to refuse, so that if you cannot do better, I will *then* attend to your defense.

Walker still held out hope of legal help from a more sympathetic lawyer. Without explanation, he noted in his log for November 7, "Received a letter from A. B. Merrill, of Boston, counselor at law." The contents of that letter have never been made public. It is known, however, that the Walker Committee in Boston did not hire Amos B. Merrill to conduct Walker's defense in Florida. The assignment – and the fee – went to Florida lawyer T. M. Blount. Perhaps that was the message that Merrill sent Walker. Uncertain that Wright would appear on his behalf in court on November 11, Walker would have been heartened to have a letter revealing that legal help was on the way.

*   *   *   *

While the Walker case stirred abolitionist groups to his legal defense and to his family's aid, Walker himself seemed to be looking to his life beyond the court trial. As much as he must have dreaded the need to stand accused of an act he believed was justified, Walker welcomed the trial, even knowing that it would produce an order for his punishment. At least he would then have a specific period of confinement. He had spent four months simply awaiting trial. A sentence, no matter how severe, would represent an end to his anxiety – perhaps even his feeling of guilt – because of his long absence from home. A sentence would permit him to start counting the days – or weeks, or months – until his release.

Both the prisoner and the prosecuting attorney noted that they met together just before the court trial. Attorney Anderson's letter to Governor Branch put the date as Saturday, November 9, 1844. Walker logged the visit on Sunday, November 10, the eve of the fall court session's second week.

Anderson's weekend visit in November was good news for the prisoner. Jonathan Walker did not care about the delicate, deft parrying of political fencing taking place in Boston and Tallahassee. Had he been asked, he would not have supported the Massachusetts attempt to delay his trial. And so, when the U.S. attorney stopped by to inform Walker that his long wait for a court hearing was nearly over, the prisoner would have been relieved. After all these months of torture, he was going to trial.

While waiting through the dark hours of Sunday night and early Monday for his time of reckoning, perhaps Walker recalled a letter he had received in late summer in which his friend Elkanah Nickerson, Jr., had solemnly advised: "My dear brother, you have a glorious trial; make a right use of it."

Walker would do no less than that.

> I consider trial by jury as the only anchor yet
> imagined by man, by which a government can be
> held to the principles of its constitution.
>
> **Thomas Jefferson**

CHAPTER 7   Trial and Imprisonment

Jonathan Walker had time that Monday morning, November 11, 1844, to consider how he might present himself for "a glorious trial" at the Superior Court of Escambia County in Pensacola, Florida. Despite his own efforts, and the assurance that United States Attorney Walker Anderson had given Florida Governor John Branch, the Massachusetts sea captain still had no lawyer to consult.

When finally he was taken, under guard, the few blocks from the jail to the courthouse, sometime after ten o'clock, he was walking outside his jail cell for the first time in four months. "[C]onducted to the courthouse and placed in the prisoner's box," he wrote,

> ...[I] was asked by the judge if I had counsel. I replied that I had not, and that my means were too limited to provide counsel; but that I was daily expecting advice from friends in regard to that point; and I requested that my trial might be put off a few days. The judge informed me that if I was not able to provide counsel for myself, he would furnish me with counsel, and that I could have anyone from the bar that I chose to defend me (there being three, besides the prosecuting attorney). I said that I would be glad to have my trial deferred a few days; and that if I was not then provided with counsel, I would avail myself of his honor's proffer. So the trial was postponed until the 14th and I was again placed in jail.

While Walker longed to have the legalities ended, he understandably would seek the most supportive lawyer he could get. He could not be blamed if he hoped to have a New England abolitionist lawyer by his side. His defense was based on a theme that abolitionists supported, legally and morally. Walker did not believe he was guilty of the crime of stealing a property for the simple reason that he did not believe anyone could own another person; therefore "ownership" was illegal, and a person who, as he had done, helped another human being to escape from illegal bondage was not guilty of a crime. He would, nevertheless, want legal help.

Walker could recall the candid note from Benjamin Drake Wright. The Pensacola attorney had had to overcome his own "indignation," but he offered to defend Walker – if he could not "do better." This defendant would want his lawyer to help with his heart as well as with his head. Walker, "not having any more information from my friends" during the next seventy-two hours, was back in court soon after ten o'clock on Thursday morning, November 14. He chose attorney Wright to defend him.

Walker Anderson began the proceedings as U.S. attorney for West Florida and prosecuting officer for the Territory of Florida. He presented four indictments handed up by the Superior Court Grand Jury for Escambia County. The indictments were not written in exactly the same language for a reason that later would bring praise to the district attorney. In summary, they alleged that "Jonathan Walker, late of the County of Escambia, laborer, on the first day of July":

1. Concerning "one Negro man slave, named Silas Scott, of the value of six hundred dollars of the goods and chattel of one Robert C. Caldwell": "with force and arms... feloniously and unlawfully did aid and assist to run away, thereby willfully causing a loss of labor of the said slave to the said Robert C. Caldwell, against the dignity of the Territory of Florida, and against the form of the statute in such case made and provided."

2. Concerning "one Negro man slave, known by the name of Anthony Catlett, of the value of six hundred dollars, of the goods and chattels of one Byrd C. Willis": "feloniously, unlawfully, and with force and arms, did steal, take, and carry away [Anthony Catlett] against the peace of dignity of the Territory of Florida..."

3. Concerning "a certain Negro slave, named Moses Johnson, of the goods and chattels of one Robert C. Caldwell, then and there being found, of the value of six hundred dollars... feloniously, unlawfully, and with force and arms, did steal, take, and carry away [Moses Johnson] against the peace and dignity of the Territory of Florida..."

4. Concerning "one Negro man slave, named Charles Johnson, of the value of six hundred dollars, of the goods and chattels of one George Willis, then and there being found, feloniously and unlawfully did entice to run away, thereby willfully causing the loss of the labor of the said slave to the said

94

George Willis; to the great damage of the said Willis, against the peace and the dignity of the Territory..."

In the strict sense of the law, none of the eight men, when apprehended near Cape Florida four months earlier, denied that they had violated federal law. Walker and the slaves had said, when apprehended near the Florida Keys in July, that Walker had agreed to help them. Walker admitted that. So, in the view of the law, Florida had in custody a man who did not deny that he had violated territorial law.

The indictments were as notable for what they did *not* do as for what they did. The charges, for example, did not name the other three men who had accompanied Walker. Nor was there an indictment against any of the seven slaves. By November, one had died, having committed suicide on September 1, after being jailed for stealing an object later found to have been misplaced. The other six had been returned to the "goods and chattels" of the white men who claimed to own the slaves. No matter what punishment awaited Walker, these seven, through death and continued enslavement, had fared worse.

The four indictments, then, covered one of the two Scott brothers who had run away from slavery at the farm of R. C. Caldwell; one of the four Johnson brothers claimed by Caldwell and a second Johnson claimed by George Willis; and Catlett, the only slave claimed by Byrd Willis. Not named were Harry Scott, who was claimed by Caldwell, and Leonard and Phillip Johnson, who were claimed by George Willis.

The indictments had slightly different wordings, and as a result the crimes alleged were not the same. The legal language seemed to imply three different levels of criminality. Walker was charged, in reverse order of relative severity, with *aiding and assisting* Silas Scott to run away, with *enticing* Charles Johnson to leave, and with *stealing* Anthony Catlett and Moses Johnson. Why? Possibly District Attorney Anderson had sought indictments for "aiding" and "assisting" the men he believed had first asked Walker's help, and for "stealing" two men who simply showed up on the getaway night, apparently to Walker's surprise. If this conjecture is accurate, perhaps Anderson reasoned that Walker could have refused passage to the late arrivals and, because he did not, he had stolen them.

However the prosecutor had determined the reasons for the Grand Jury to hand down indictments, spite or meanness had nothing to do with it. Walker later wrote that Anderson...

> is entitled to my thanks for his kindness and humanity towards me, both in his private and official capacity. He is a mild, considerate, and intelligent man; and were he not surrounded by a powerful slavery influence, any society might be proud of such a member. I have for a number of years known him, and can say that he is of the most amiable disposition of any person I ever knew in Pensacola...

Nor was Jonathan Walker going to be tried without a perceptive and sensitive defense. Benjamin Wright had delayed accepting Walker's invitation to represent him, but once appointed, he offered an instant and stout defense. Walker wrote: "My counsel objected to four indictments being arrayed against me for one act of offense, if it was an act at all."

This was a major legal point. If the judge upheld the defense attorney's objection, the prosecutor may have elected, or been required, to return to the Grand Jury to seek a single indictment. "On this point," Walker reported, "a discussion of some length took place between [Wright] and the prosecuting attorney..."

The judge may have had some reservation about ruling against the defense objection. The announced intention of Walker's Northern supporters to carry the case to the United States Supreme Court had been widely reported. If the judge knew that, it is possible that he chose to act cautiously, at least at the trial's beginning. Walker wrote: "[T]he judge decided that in order to come at the subject properly, one case should be tried. Accordingly, the jury were selected and sworn, and took their seats."

*   *   *   *

The hearing that was to make of Jonathan Walker a martyred hero in the abolitionist movement would take no more than an hour. The judge ordered trial on the first indictment, "aiding and assisting Silas Scott." The prosecution called two witnesses; the defense, none.

Robert C. Caldwell, who claimed to own Silas Scott and Moses Johnson, testified that he had accompanied the U. S. marshal, Ebenezer Dorr, to the U.S. Navy Yard outside Pensacola when Walker was returned for trial. Caldwell was, at that time, a Navy lieutenant stationed there. Dorr was going to the Navy base to meet the U.S. steamer *General Taylor* and to take Walker into custody.

Walker wrote later that Caldwell's testimony concerned a conversation he had had with Walker. Referring to himself in the third person, Walker wrote: "[P]risoner said that Silas came to his boat a little below the city, and got in with some others, but that he did not know him, and did not recollect ever seeing him before. This he (witness) believed to be correct, for it agreed with what the boy (Silas) had told him..."

Caldwell's purpose in testifying was to establish Walker's admission of guilt. To support his first statement, he offered another: "[P]risoner also said that he had for a long time been of the opinion that he would aid slaves to secure their liberty, if opportunity offered."

Walker never clarified this testimony by confirmation or denial. Walker may have told Caldwell what he thought would be most helpful to Silas Scott's future, just as he had made up a story about transporting slaves for their owners when stopped off Carysfort Reef on July 8. If Caldwell could conclude that Silas Scott had left without having planned an escape, had perhaps acted on a whim, Caldwell might not treat him so badly upon his return to Pensacola. As it developed, Caldwell later in July had promised Walker he would not punish his two runaways, and he kept his word.

Walker had heard that Caldwell, an Ohioan, had studied for the ministry before joining the Navy. Because of his own firm religious tenets, Walker would have given Caldwell courteous attention even as he wondered how a man claiming to be a Christian also could be, in good conscience, a slaveholder. Caldwell, said Walker, had married "a wealthy young woman in Pensacola who had a number of slaves, and in this way... is year after year receiving pay from the United States government for overseeing his own, or his wife's, slaves." Walker was apparently linking Caldwell's being somewhat permanently stationed at the Pensacola Navy Yard with his living at home and supervising slaves.

Recalling the July incident in which Caldwell had persuaded Walker to give Caldwell the rights to his boat, Walker wrote:

> He visited me several times soon after my committal, appeared very friendly, and seemed disposed to urge upon my mind some religious considerations, and had the politeness to bring me some pound-cake, as he called it; but no sooner had he succeeded in getting possession of what little I had in the shape of property than every friendly and social consideration was abandoned, and he spared no pains to persecute me to the extend of his ability; and was still anxious to gratify his malignant appetite on the victim of his rage, to the very last.

There was another echo from the Navy lieutenant's visit with Walker in jail in July. When Caldwell suggested that Walker give up any claim to his boat, Walker had thought about the possible outcome: "a refusal might excite a spirit of revenge, and that if disposed, he could make my situation more desperate than it was already..."

As Caldwell stepped down from the witness stand, Walker may have wondered if Caldwell's testimony, were it given in a spirit of revenge, could have been any worse.

The other witness in the November 14 trial of Jonathan Walker was Richard Roberts, the captain of the sloop *Eliza Catherine*. His testimony was to show that some of the slaves admitted they had run away. Roberts had stopped Walker and his passengers south of Cape Florida on July 8, ending their flight. "He was suspicious that the black men were runaway slaves," Walker quoted Roberts as testifying, "[H]e found out, by some of the black men, that they were runaway slaves; consequently, he took them all to Key West... The prisoner was very sick at the time, but requested that he might be allowed to have his boat and proceed on, saying that he had a family that were dependent on him for support, and, if deprived of his services, would suffer in consequence."

That was the end of the testimony, as Walker recorded it.

From the first reading of his autobiographical account when it was submitted for publication in 1845, to present day historians' study, Walker has been praised for his attempt to present an objective report of his adventure. Roberts' testimony is an excellent example of how he did that. In this case, he presented it without comment, even though it must have troubled him to do so. In the last statement, the man who captured him and the seven black men had left the impression with those in the court that day, and with all who would read Walker's uncorrecting account, that Walker's main concern was to get away from Florida and back to his family.

Walker, of course, may have felt that way, and may have told that to Captain Roberts. If so, he took on the cloak of a runaway himself. There were, however, other incidents to suggest that Walker would not have tried to leave the seven men behind. For one, he was an honest and loyal friend, and he had promised to "I "share the risk with them." For another, there was his statement to Captain Roberts, soon after capture, that he had persuaded the slaves to run away.

The depth of Walker's character is displayed by his not disputing or, apparently, altering, in his account of the trial, Roberts' depicting him as pleading for help in leaving behind the men he had promised to share the risk with.

In fact, Walker continued in his reportorial shorthand: "The jury were charged, in a few formal words, and the first indictment handed to them. They retired to their room..."

Walker and his lawyer did not have much time to discuss strategy for the other indictments. The jury, Walker wrote, returned "in about a half an hour... with the verdict, that they had found the prisoner guilty, and awarded him to be branded on the right hand with the letters SS."

*   *   *   *

The judge, apparently satisfied that a defendant pleading guilty could be fairly tried in his court, ordered the hearing to continue with the three remaining indictments. If Walker and Wright offered new argument that a single crime should not evoke multiple trials, Walker did not record it. He wrote: "The same jury was sworn again, and by the judge charged on the other three indictments. They withdrew, and were out between two and three hours, and returned with the following verdict: that they had found the prisoner guilty of all the charges preferred against him in the other three indictments, and awarded him to stand in the pillory one hour, to be imprisoned fifteen days, and to pay a fine of $150."

The jury had acted under territorial law. Section 14 read: "Be it further enacted, That any person convicted of stealing a slave, or of enticing, or of giving a pass, or of doing any other means of inducement to any slave to run away, or of aiding, assisting, or abetting any runaway slave or otherwise willfully causing a loss of labor of such slave to his or her owner or owners, shall be fined not exceeding one thousand dollars or stand in the pillory one hour, or be branded on the right hand with the letters S.S., or imprisoned for a term not exceeding six months, at the discretion of the Jury."

Trial and Imprisonment

Because Walker had been found guilty on four counts, it was in the jury's discretion that he should suffer all four of the legal penalties.

Walker provided no comment on the relatively long time the jury had spent on reaching a second verdict. Court having begun in mid-morning, the jurors probably took time for lunch. But, having already reviewed the legal basics as outlined in the judge's charge, the jurors had nothing new to discuss in their second sitting on Walker's indictments. Possibly some of them were reluctant to support any new punishment, having already recommended the unusual act of branding.

Over the decades since, the Walker story has included the claim that in all of the history of federal jurisprudence only he was ever ordered branded in a federal court. James S. Rush, Jr., assistant chief of the Civil Reference Branch of the National Archives, Washington, D. C., wrote the author on March 8, 1993: "The Department of Justice did not maintain records concerning the various types of punishments ordered by the courts and therefore we cannot determine if Jonathan Walker's punishment was unique."

Branding was the major penalty inflicted on Walker. By comparison, the pillory, fifteen days in jail already served, and a fine were minor penalties. Perhaps they were recommended as a result of a jury compromise between those who were distressed at the crime of slave stealing – Walker's attorney had reacted in that manner – and those who favored a gesture of compassion.

In any event, Jonathan Walker had had a day in court, and now he was taken back to the two-room jail to await the judge's decision on the jury's recommended punishment.

*　　　　*　　　　*　　　　*

Walker didn't have long to wait. The itinerant judge was at the end of his two-week sitting in Pensacola and, no doubt, anxious to be on his way. He scheduled a court session on Saturday, November 16, 1844, two days after the trial. It didn't take long, either, for Walker to learn how quickly justice could be carried out. He wrote: "[O]n arriving at the courthouse (in front of which was the pillory), the marshal proceeded to place me in the pillory. I told him that I had not yet received sentence. The marshal replied that this was sentence enough -- referring to the pillory. But before I was properly secured, the deputy marshal ordered me to be brought into court. This order was obeyed; and I was again arraigned before the court..."

Marshal Eben Dorr had yielded under intervention from his deputy, James Gonzalez. As it developed, Dorr would soon lock the prisoner's head and arms in the pillory's wooden yoke.

If Walker had hoped that the judge might reject, or reduce, some of the jury's recommended punishment, he would have been disappointed. The judge simply set the order in which the four penalties were to be carried out: "To be placed in the pillory for one hour; then brought into court, and branded in the right hand with the letters SS; and then remanded to prison for fifteen days, and remain there until the fine ($150) and the costs of prosecution should be made."

Jonathan Walker The Man with the Branded Hand

By November 18, 1844, Jonathan Walker had been imprisoned since July 8. Of those 132 days, 121 had been spent in the Pensacola jail. Now he was to begin serving "fifteen days, and remain there" until paying the fine and costs. But first, he was taken outdoors. An artist's rendition, "The author confined in the pillory," appeared in Walker's 1845 account. It shows a man standing with his head and both hands projecting from holes in two heavy boards erected between two large pillars in the front of the courthouse.

Walker continued: "[W]hen I had been there about half an hour, George Willis, mentioned in the fourth indictment, stepped from the crowd of spectators, who were standing by (quietly beholding the inhuman administration of the laws of Florida) and snatched from my head a handkerchief, which had been placed there by the deputy marshal [Gonzalez], to screen me from the sun; saying that he had offered a dollar to any person that would do it; but as no one else would, he would do it himself."

An anonymous spectator wrote the following day, in a letter to *The Liberator* in Boston:

> [Willis] took from his pocket two rotten eggs, and hurled them at the prisoner's head, which took effect. This excited a burst of indignation from many present. I was satisfactorily informed that [Willis] had been very solicitous among the boys, offering them a great price for some rotten eggs, and any persons who would throw those he had at the prisoner; but he could not bribe or find anyone inhuman or vile enough to do the deed but himself. The prisoner remained silent throughout, except to the officers who had him in charge.

Dorr, Walker wrote later, permitted Willis' assault "without interfering other than saying, 'Don't, Mr. Willis, for we have got to take him into court,' as much as to say, 'he would appear indecent,' or 'someone's senses will be offended.'" Unimpeded by these limp admonitions, Willis committed the assault and later was taken to account for it in a courtroom.

The 1845 illustration shows the prisoner with the putrid yolk and albumen running onto his face as Willis, arm raised, is about to release another egg. Willis is in black tails and he and a dozen spectators are all wearing high hats and formal clothing. Nearby stands a hatless man wearing work clothes. The artist may have intended this figure to represent the deputy marshal, James Gonzalez.

*   *   *   *

The officials who had Walker in custody – Marshal Dorr and Deputy Gonzalez – came from vastly different backgrounds. Eben Dorr's family had emigrated to the colonies from England about 1670. Dorrs had participated in the Revolution. James Gonzalez, on the other hand, was a first generation American, son of former citizens of Spain.

Ebenezer's father, William Dorr, was a soldier in the American Revolutionary War, serving with Benedict Arnold at Quebec in 1775. His uncle

Illustration from *Trial and Imprisonment of Jonathan Walker* (1845)

"The author confined in the pillory." So Walker identified this drawing. George Willis, one of three slaveholders who claimed that Walker had stolen their chattel property, is about to heave a second rotten egg at the prisoner. Willis later was fined for this action.

was the Revolutionary hero Ebenezer Dorr, for whom the marshal probably was named. His uncle was born in 1739 and participated in the "ride of Paul Revere." According to *William Dawes and His Ride with Paul Revere*, by Henry W. Holland, "The intelligence that the British intended to go out to Lexington was conveyed over Boston Neck to Roxbury by Ebenezer Dorr of Boston, a leather dresser by trade who was mounted on a slow jogging horse, with saddle bags behind him and a large flopped hat upon his head, to resemble a countryman on a journey."

The younger "Eben" was born in Hallowell, Maine, in 1787, and was a twenty-five-year old sailor when the War of 1812 was begun. He was the first of his family to settle in Pensacola, arriving in 1827. He did well over the next decade, acquiring Florida real estate and a Gulf trade vessel. He was appointed the United States marshal for West Florida in 1841, during the time that Jane and Jonathan Walker were living in Pensacola with their children. During the 1844 Walker trial, Dorr was fifty-six years old, compared to Walker's forty-five. At 5-foot-7 ½, the marshal was nearly a head shorter than his prisoner.

Dorr was himself a slaveholder, Linda Ellsworth wrote in a paper for the Historic Pensacola Preservation Board. That would have influenced his attitude towards Walker's violation of the Florida laws. In contrast, Walker Anderson was a letter-of-the-law district attorney. He maintained a manner of civility that included both respect and an occasional lightness bordering on humor. This was in sharp contrast to Eben Dorr's no-nonsense approach to carrying out the law. Eben's brother, William, was to write in that same "guilt is guilt" manner: "It is not a matter for the court to consider whether the criminal enticed the slaves from their homes to sell them, for say five hundred dollars a head, at some port on the Spanish Main, or to sell out at about the same price to some abolition association – the wages of his crime being termed 'passage money,' 'traveling expenses,' or what not. He worked for money..."

Walker, the Dorr brothers clearly believed, deserved punishment.

There was legal justification on Dorr's side. As United States marshal, he was the chief law enforcement officer in the district. The Constitution and federal law left to the states and territories the choice of legalizing slavery, or not. Florida's territorial law protected slaveholders in recognizing slaves as chattel property; therefore anyone who helped a slave to escape was breaking the law.

Jonathan Walker could have had it worse. He could have been in the custody of George Willis. That slaveholder had been the West Florida district marshal prior to Eben Dorr's tenure. He had served during Jonathan and Jane's residence in Pensacola, "during which time," Walker had commented wryly, "he had the honor of hanging three or four colored men."

The character of James Gonzalez could be placed somewhere between that of the marshal, who took an impersonal approach to his role in enforcing these laws, and that of the district attorney, who carried out his duties with equal faithfulness but also with courtesy and kindness. On this painful day for Walker,

Trial and Imprisonment

Gonzalez seemed to be the only court official showing understanding, even compassion. This was the same deputy who four months earlier had escorted the collapsing Walker from the Navy Yard to the courthouse, protecting him through a crowd.

James Gonzalez had been born in Escambia County to one of the first families of Spanish descent in the Pensacola region. He was the seventh of ten children born to Don Manuel Gonzalez, a native of Spain, and Mary Louise Bonifay, who was born in Martinique. When only in his twenties, James was the city's tax collector, and one of Pensacola's most respected citizens. He owned a brick-making business. He had supervised construction of the first road across northern Florida to St. Augustine. In 1838, when he was only twenty-five years old, he purchased the home of Don Francisco Moreno, who had been the Spanish consul in Florida since 1821. Soon after, he married Petronilla de la Rua, a member of another first family of Spanish descent. Historian Leora Sutton wrote that Gonzalez "repaired the chimney of the [consul's] house with bricks carrying his name. The bricks in the pillars of the house were manufactured at his grandmother's kiln and marked 'M. Bonifay.'"

In 1844, when he was assigned to guard Walker, Gonzalez was thirty-one years old and had been married for ten years. His father had died in 1839. It is likely that James and Petronilla had several children, and perhaps the deputy marshal, on long, boring duty tours, enjoyed discussing family life with a man like Walker who also had a large family.

In her book, *Florida: The Long Frontier*, Marjory Stoneman Douglas, noted: "A few Spanish residents expressed sympathy for him." James Gonzalez, as deputy marshal, could not have done so openly. When he countermanded Marshal Dorr's order to lock Walker in the pillory before Walker had been sentenced, however, he had at least displayed a sense of fairness within the law, as well as courage in rebelling against a superior officer's orders.

Later, Walker wrote:

Although this officer had but little to do with me, yet so far as he had anything to do with me, he manifested a kind and friendly feeling. Those who have never been in critical circumstances cannot tell how [sensitively] every look, action, and word is felt by one in my situation... James Gonzalez... is entitled to my thanks for his humane deportment towards me.

Gonzalez' "deportment," as Walker put it, contrasted also with that of the slaveholder who pelted the pilloried prisoner with rotten eggs. George Willis, nevertheless, more nearly reflected the attitude of many West Floridians in his anger at Walker's role in his servants' escape.

Who was this George Willis? He was, apparently, one of Pensacola's wealthiest residents. In her study, *Blacks and Slavery in Pensacola*, Leora Sutton identified forty-two "slaves associated with George Willis," including twenty-seven men, eleven woman, three children, and one person whose name is incomplete. After listing many of them, including Leonard, Charles, and Phillip Johnson and Anthony Catlett, who were among the escapees with Walker, she remarked: "[A]ll had last names!" Catlett, apparently, had at one time been held by George Willis, although Byrd Willis claimed ownership in 1844.

Sutton wrote:

The Willis family had dealt with runaway slaves before. In one ad of the Pensacola *Gazette*, a $500 reward was offered by William Willis when a Negro 'boy,' age about thirty-five, named Jerry, escaped. He was five feet and some inches high, dark complexion, high forehead, quick spoken, had one of his foreteeth out, the rest very long. George was also missing. He was about twenty-five years old, yellow caste, with a down look when he talked, hanging his head. He had one or two large bunches of flesh on his back between his shoulders (significant of brutal beatings). And [also missing was] John, about twenty, who had an injured eye. It was believed the three traveled with forged papers.

George Willis, in Walker's opinion, was "a haughty, overbearing, and cruel man... [T]he manner in which he displayed his feelings at the courthouse, when undergoing the penalties of my first trial, may be considered a specimen of the man."

In this time in the pillory, Jonathan Walker had encountered two men who represented the dissimilar personalities of those who had prominent roles in 19th Century slavery.

*　　　　*　　　　*　　　　*

"After the expiration of the hour, I was taken back of the courthouse, and water given me to wash with, and then conducted into court again, to receive the remainder of my [physical punishment]."

Jonathan Walker was about to be branded on his right hand with the letters SS.

> Walker has not only been sentenced to imprisonment
> and to be fined for aiding the oppressed,
> but BRANDED IN THE HAND...
> And this in democratic, Christian America!
> Horrible, horrible beyond all expression.
> **William Lloyd Garrison,** *The Liberator*

CHAPTER 8   The Branding

The jury – and, by their acquiescence, the judge and other court officials – had determined that Jonathan Walker, the tall, strong, abolitionist from Massachusetts, should forever carry the mark of "slave stealer."

The branding iron had been made for this occasion during the forty-eight hours between the jury verdict that Thursday and the act of branding on Saturday. Getting an iron was not accomplished easily for the court. No one had ever been marked with the letters "SS," and so no branding iron existed. The *National Anti-Slavery Standard*, the New York-based newspaper for which Sydney A. Gay had become editor earlier in 1844, reported that the first blacksmith approached by court authorities declined the assignment. This man, who ran the blacksmith shop closest to the courthouse, was quoted as refusing because branding was for animals and not human beings. According to Elmer Koppelmann's account, "Another blacksmith designed the iron; however, he refused the use of his forge to heat it just prior to the branding." In the end, Marshal Dorr apparently had a fire made in the courtroom.

Pedro Yniestra has been identified as the man who made the SS branding device. Illustrative of how small Pensacola's population was then, and of how intertwined were the principals in Walker's life during this episode, Leora Sutton's monograph, "The Quina House 1800-1870," includes a genealogy showing Pedro Yniestra as the uncle of Manuella S. Bonifay. She was married to Constantine F. Quina, who was Maria Quina Torward's brother and a son of Desiderio Quina, who had been Francis Torward's court-appointed

Illustration from *Trial and Imprisonment of Jonathan Walker* (1845)

The original caption read, "United States Marshal branding the author." Ebenezer Dorr, holding the smoking branding iron, is labeled "Maine" (he was a native of that state's city of Hallowell). "Mass." for his home state is on Walker's chest. The branding took place in the Pensacola courtroom where Walker was tried before a judge and jury on four charges. The two men wearing dark clothing, left and right of Marshal Dorr, may represent principals in the drama. Figure at left probably represents George Willis, who Walker said stood close by him. Figure at right may represent Deputy James Gonzalez, stationed in front of spectators for security purposes.

The Branding

guardian. Constantine was himself a tinsmith, although there is no record to indicate that he was invited to prepare Walker's branding iron.

Walker described the scene inside the courtroom:

When about to be branded, I was placed in the prisoner's box. [Marshal] Dorr... proceeded to tie my hand to a part of the railing in front. I remarked that there was no need of tying it, for I would hold still. He observed that it was best to make sure, and tied it firmly to the post, in fair view; he then took from the fire the branding- iron, of a slight red heat, and applied it to the ball of my hand, and pressed it on firmly, for fifteen or twenty seconds. It made a spattering noise, like a handful of salt in the fire, as the skin seared and gave way to the hot iron. The pain was severe while the iron was on, and for some time afterwards.

A second illustration published with Walker's autobiography was identified as "United States Marshal branding the author." In the drawing, Eben Dorr is marked "Maine" and Jonathan Walker "Mass." The judge is seated at the bench, high above the group of men crowding the prisoner's box. A grim-faced Walker has his right hand tied to a post. Smoke is rising from the branding iron, which Dorr is holding against Walker's flesh. There is no danger of Dorr's being harmed. The branding iron has a foot-long handle. The letter S is visible near the palm as the iron applies a second S on the hand's heel. Off to one side of the gathering is a balding, short man wearing plain clothing; a figure similar to the one that may have represented James Gonzalez in the pillory illustration. In the drawing of the branding, standing close to Dorr is a man wearing tails, apparently the unnamed artist's representation of George Willis.

"There appeared to be but few that wished to witness the scene," Walker wrote, "but my friend, George Willis, placed himself where he could have a fair view, and feasted his eyes upon it, apparently with great delight."

*　　　　*　　　　*　　　　*

Branding was seldom committed on white men in early America. One of the rare, and famous, cases emanating from a courtroom occurred after the Boston Massacre. On March 5, 1770, British troops were goaded by a small, vocal group of Bostonians angry with the royal decrees and royal troops clogging their efforts at freedom. The troops, under command of Captain Thomas Preston, fired into the unruly crowd. They killed three men outright and mortally wounded two others. The first American shot dead was, ironically, Crispus Attucks, a former slave who had run away twenty years before from Deacon William Brown of Middlesex County, Massachusetts. Attucks was descended from Indians, blacks, and whites. He was, at 6-foot-2, a huge man for his time. Attucks was a sailor, in Boston that day awaiting a berth.

Fair trials, and strong representation for the accused, were already being practiced in the spawning nation's jurisprudence. No less than a future president of the United States, John Adams, defended the nine accused British soldiers at two week-long trials, October 24-30 and November 27-December 5, 1770. While Captain Preston and six of his men were acquitted of murder, Privates Matthew Kilroy and Hugh Montgomery were found guilty of manslaughter.

The branding resulted from something like an early version of today's plea bargaining. At the sentencing on December 14, 1770, the two British soldiers were asked if either had any reason why the death penalty should not be carried out. Each promptly 'prayed clergy.' Still claiming innocence, Kilroy and Montgomery held out their right thumbs for Sheriff Stephen Greenleaf to brand. The barbaric ceremony completed, the prisoners were released.

The privilege known as "benefit of clergy" had originated in Great Britain and by the 14th Century had been extended to all people who could read. People found guilty in secular courts of any crimes less than treason could qualify for hearings at bishop's courts by declaring their innocence.

*   *   *   *

Now, his own branding completed, Jonathan Walker was returned to the jail cell where he had already spent four months. He was perhaps enjoying a feeling something like relief. Possibly due to the prisoner's physical distress, Jailer Francis Torward did not lock the chains on his legs and arms. For the first time in four months, he could walk about this room. And, at last, he knew the outcome of his trial. He would be relieved also, perhaps, in thinking he could, finally, measure the remainder of his sentence in days and dollars.

For the court appearance, and the punishments, Walker had been away from his cell less than three hours. Returned about one o'clock in the afternoon, or a bit later, he may have been accorded a late lunch by Maria Torward. Perhaps he lay down on his straw sack bed. Weary from the tension and the unaccustomed exercise, he may have lain still as the events of that demanding morning at the courthouse went through his mind, like waves crashing against a weakened dock bracing. Now, again, he was having his head and hands locked in the pillory, his head and face were being covered with the sticky drip of rotten eggs, and then the stench of his own skin burning while he endured the early sizzle, then the deep pain –

...one second, two seconds, three, four, five;

as many as twenty.

A man of Walker's strong religious inclination also would have prayed: giving thanks that the punishment was no worse; pleading for strength to survive and to remain strong.

Whatever reverie may have come over Walker in his exhaustion, the spell was soon shattered. The worse was not, after all, over. Having been punished for helping four of the seven slaves, Walker was now being called to account for his actions on behalf of the other three men.

"A few hours after my recommitment," Walker wrote, "the marshal called and served three writs upon me, for trespass and damage, to the amount of $106,000, on the property of Robert C. Caldwell, Byrd C. Willis, and George

The Branding

Willis." Damages had been alleged by Caldwell and Byrd Willis at $3,000 each, and by chief tormentor George Willis at $100,000.

Walker was informed that he was to stand trial during the next Superior Court session – now six months away in May 1845. When he and attorney Wright had failed to convince the judge that only a single indictment should cover Walker's involvement with seven runaway slaves, Walker apparently decided to accept the punishment and be done with it. But now, here was the marshal – the man who only a few hours before had marked Walker for life with a hot branding iron – here was Ebenezer Dorr formally announcing that the law was still after Walker for his crime in helping the three slaves not covered by previous indictments.

*   *   *   *

Eben Dorr's business-like serving of the papers ordering Jonathan Walker to another court hearing presented the kind of calamity that no one ever becomes accustomed to receiving. More than six months later, Walker was still smarting over this new grief. Writing about the shattering setback of November 16, 1844, he began calmly:

> The Territory of Florida was established by a law of the *United States*, passed March 30, 1822. The fifth section of this act provided 'that the legislative power shall be vested in the governor, and in thirteen of the most fit and discreet persons of the territory, to be called the Legislative Council,' etc.; that 'their legislative powers shall also extend to all the *rightful* subjects of legislation; *but no law shall be valid which is inconsistent with the Constitution and laws of the United States*, or which shall lay any person under restraint, burden, or disability, on account of his religious opinions, profession, or worship, in all which he shall be free to maintain his own and not burthened with those of another.'
>
> The tenth section of the same act provides, 'That... all fines shall be moderate and proportioned to the offense, and excessive bail shall not be required, *nor cruel nor unusual punishments inflicted.*'
>
> ...The law under which I was indicted was enacted by the territorial government, and provides as the punishment for the crime therein recited imprisonment not exceeding six months; standing in the pillory; *branding*, or a fine not exceeding one thousand dollars, at the discretion of the jury.

As he continued, Walker's calm had been replaced by clenched-teeth control:

> It seems plain that the law of the United States having prohibited *cruel and unusual punishments*, and having declared that no law of the territorial government, inconsistent with the United States laws, shall ever be *valid*; this territorial law, under which I was punished, is void.

Jonathan Walker The Man with the Branded Hand

So declared Jonathan Walker, prisoner of Pensacola. No one who had anything to do with the law in West Florida, Territory of Florida, openly agreed with him. The law was quite alive and actionable. And the thirteen "most fit and discreet persons of the territory" who made up the Legislative Council were soon to decide that the very law which Walker had denounced was not, in fact, tough enough.

*   *   *   *

The law, and how it was going to sway his life in the months ahead, was on Walker's mind in the weeks following his court appearance. He would, of course, have been wondering what happened to his helpful Harwich friends. They had formed a committee, and had conducted fund-raising activities back in Massachusetts, not only to help Jane and the youngsters but also to help Jonathan develop and execute a legal defense and, if unsuccessful, to pay any fine. He had been forced to accept the reluctant, although not unmeritorious, assistance of local lawyer Benjamin D. Wright. And he had no money to pay the fine of $150. So he sat and lay in his jail cell, and walked more often, and more strongly, as he recovered from the experiences of being pilloried and branded in mid-November.

December began with a surprise. On Monday, December 2, 1844, Walker "received a visit from T. M. Blount, of New York," Walker wrote, misspelling his name "Blunt." This was the same Thomas M. Blount who was a charter member of the Alabama, Florida, & Georgia Railroad's Board of Directors in the early years after its founding in 1833. Walker had worked for the railroad in the early 1840s, while living in Pensacola with Jane and the children.

Not only did he remember Blount from his railroad years; he had no respect for the man. When Walker wrote about Blount a half-year after this incident, he could not hide his agitation:

> I was sufficiently well acquainted with the man, and his course of behavior and conduct, for seven or eight years and knew him to be void of any good principle, and pro-slavery to the backbone; bred and practiced in the hot-bed of that soul- destroying system, which is one of the greatest scourges arranged against the well-being and happiness of man, and one of the highest insults against the authority and government of God, who has provided ample means for the happiness and welfare of the great human family...

> Thomas M. Blount was also looked upon by the inhabitants [of Pensacola] as a very corrupt-minded man, and a base and common swindler.

Questions must have rushed to Walker's mind. Foremost was: How did such a man come to be chosen? Blount "was employed in New York to manage my defense at the November court, in Pensacola – or to take an appeal to the United States Supreme Court, and have the case presented there. I have not attempted to give any account of him, other than noting his visits to me at the prison in December... feeling that his being sent was nearly the greatest insult that friends at the north could impose on me."

Walker had not known that Blount had been retained in his behalf until that Monday in December. "He then called at the prison, and talked with me a few minutes through the window, without offering to come in. He stated to me that he had seen Amos B. Merrill before he left New York..."

Merrill served as secretary of the Boston abolitionists working to help Walker gain freedom. Apparently Merrill had made the arrangements for Blount's trip to Pensacola.

Why was Blount late in arriving to "attend" Walker's case? Walker's use of exclamation points indicates how he felt about the lawyer's explanation: "...[I]n consequence of the high (!) or low (!) stage of the water in some of the rivers near there [Pensacola], he was prevented from being in the place in time to attend to my trial. [Yet Blount] had been in the place twelve or thirteen days." That meant that the lawyer had arrived about November 19, two or three days after Walker's courthouse punishment had been carried out.

Here on Walker's behalf? For nearly two weeks? Why had Blount not reported to Walker immediately on his arrival? Walker had no explanation.

"[Blount] said he had told people there that he was paid two hundred dollars to manage my case, and that my friends wished to take an appeal to the Supreme Court of the United States, and wanted to know if I would consent to an appeal. I told him that I would, in case I could be bailed out, and not be subjected to illegal treatment. He said he would try to get an appeal on the case."

Sometime over the next few weeks, when it became apparent to Walker that he would not be released on bail, he took a stand against appealing his case to the nation's highest court. He took a fundamentalist view of the Constitution and his rights: if he could not be found innocent for the "right reason" – that he could not have stolen what was unstealable – he was willing to pay the penalty established by Florida law.

During Blount's first visit, Walker wrote, "He wanted to know what the expense amounted to; I told him that I had not yet been able to ascertain what it was."

The judge's sentence included paying the city and district for the expenses of maintaining Walker as a prisoner, in addition to the fine of $150. When Blount left that day, Walker would have wondered if the lawyer had enough money to cover his fine and costs, and possibly to meet bail so he could be released until his next trial. No new sitting was scheduled for the Superior Court in Pensacola until May of 1845 – a half-year away. Despite his dislike for Thomas Blount, Walker must have harbored the hope that he might help him in some way when he returned.

*　　　　*　　　　*　　　　*

On December 6, four days after Blount's visit, Marshal Dorr brought Walker his "bill of costs." It amounted to $421.45, including the $150 fine. The itemization shocked Walker. He was being charged for "paid witness from Key West, $57.75," plus $3.75 for testimony – against him – by one of the three plaintiffs, R. C. Caldwell. The bill also included three dollars to cover the expense of Deputy Gonzalez "for traveling to Navy-yard to arrest" Walker, and, presumably, help push him in a cart to the courthouse because he was too weak to walk.

The stunned Walker wrote, "It may not be improper to remark here that I had no witness, nor asked for any," "and those whose fees are charged in the bill are Richard Roberts, of Key West, master of the vessel that took me, near Cape Florida, and the other, Robert C. Caldwell, who claimed to be an owner of three of the slaves that left Pensacola in my boat."

When Blount returned a few days later, Walker gave him a copy of the bills. After nearly five months in jail, Walker's desire to leave surely provided sufficient motivation to join forces with a man whom he barely tolerated. He wrote:

> I informed [Blount] that the 'fine $150' could be paid in Territorial scrip, which could be bought at a large discount, and that a sum of less than $400 would be sufficient to effect my release. I asked him if he could not make some arrangement to satisfy the demand, so that I might leave the place. He said he was going to the next county, where he had some money owing him, and if he could get that, he would release me; but that he could not get an appeal on the case, for the bail would be so high that it could not be given...

The situation remained grim. Back in his cell, Walker would have mulled over the money needs. He had figured $400 would cover what he owed, as well as meet bail. Blount apparently thought the bail would be higher than Walker thought it would be. Or, perhaps Blount knew he would not be able to put together $400 and was simply stalling Walker.

The best that Jonathan Walker could hope for was that Thomas Blount would bring good news on the day he promised to return – Christmas Day of 1844. "[W]hen he called again," Walker recounted, "[he] said he was then going to New York, and would stir up my friends about the matter, and urge them to have the means necessary to my release forthcoming."

There was, then, little hope for immediate help, and none was to come. Later, Walker was to learn that the Boston committee had given Blount $750. Assuming that Blount was accurate when he claimed he was given $200 for his fee, and that his expenses to and from New York amounted to $150, Blount still should have had enough to pay the fine and court costs. Walker no longer wrote of Blount with agitation. With the equanimity of the Quakers whom he admired, he finally wrote him off: "This is the substance of my positive knowledge of the doings of Thomas M. Blount in regards to my case." Blount never returned, nor communicated with Walker.

The Branding

The *National Anti-Slavery Standard* remarked: "[P]ocketing the fee was the only part of the business that [Blount] thought it worth his while to attend to."

Because he was not vindictive by nature, Jonathan Walker probably was not cheered to learn that a court had ordered George Willis to pay a fine for throwing eggs at Walker as he dangled in the pillory. Richardson reported: Willis was indicted as an offender "against good order" in Escambia County, where the incident took place. This probably was an action initiated by District Attorney Anderson. Granted his request for a hearing in adjoining Santa Rosa County – probably because he did not believe he could get a fair trial in his home county – Willis "was there tried, and fined six and a quarter cents," Walker reported without comment.

*   *   *   *

Word of Walker's punishment was spread slowly across the nation, the news traveling frequently from one newspaper to another. It would be a month before Walker's conviction and punishment were reported widely. Being nearest, the Pensacola *Gazette* was able to print the trial's result in its edition of Saturday, November 23, 1844, exactly one week after the branding. Not many Pensacolans would be awaiting the newspaper's report to learn the outcome; that information would have been spread quickly in the small community. The details, and how editor John McKinlay reported them, however, would be of interest to local readers.

As was the fashion for newspapers of the time, the *Gazette* categorized the news. Under the general title of Pensacola, the paper had a subtitle "Naval," and the first item there on November 23 was a two-line, single sentence: "The U.S. ship *Falmouth*, Com'r Sande, sailed from this port on Monday last." The item that followed took up about a column and a third; it was headed: "The case of Jonathan Walker."

Editor McKinlay's report began with a "plain statement":

As the case of this malefactor has occupied the attention of this community for the last few months more or less, and as many representations and misrepresentations (innocently no doubt) have been made by some of the northern papers on the subject, and especially as we have been roundly accused of endeavoring to forestall public opinion and excite prejudice against Walker, we purpose (sic) giving a plain statement of what has been done and of how stands the matter now.

The account that followed began with a brief, and adjective- free, resume of Walker's capture with the seven slaves and the Grand Jury's returning "four true bills." The newspaper story at this point takes a different view from that reported by Walker in his biography. Wrote the *Gazette*:

On the first of those indictments, the prisoner was arraigned and plead not guilty, but before proceeding to offer his testimony, the District

Attorney, with a frankness which cannot be too highly commended, disclosed to the Jury, the prisoner's counsel, and the public, that he held in hand four indictments against the prisoner, embracing as many distinct offenses which had been committed by the act of carrying off these Negroes, and then invited the discussion and settlement of the preliminary question of law, if whether or not more than one indictment would be against the prisoner under the circumstances of the case. Several hours were spent in the discussion of this question during which a host of authorities were arrayed on the part of the prosecution to justify the course taken by the District Attorney, while on the other hand many long arguments of great force and ingenuity was advanced by the opposite counsel to show that the cases cited were not parallel and that the authorities referred to though very good gave no warrant for the proceedings at bar. The court held the matter under advisement until next day, and after sleeping on the point give it clearly in favor of the District Attorney, compli- menting him on the masterful skill "with which the indict- ments were framed so as to obviate any just or technical exception to their multiplicity.

The *Gazette* reported the conclusion of the case in a few "plain" sentences, and printed the section of the law under which Walker had been convicted.

Walker later cited five errors in the story:
* District Attorney Anderson made "no disclosures or allusions" to the public or to the jury, which in fact had not yet been impaneled.
* Not "a host of authorities" were cited; only two.
* "Several hours" were not required. "Not more than forty minutes were consumed in discussion."
* Walker disagreed that the judge considered a point overnight; "for the whole trial... did not exceed five hours."
* Walker was returned to court for punishment two days later, not the following day.

The *Gazette* continued to address the issue of one crime-one indictment in a later edition. On December 21, the newspaper noted the conviction of the Reverend Charles Torrey on charges of "abducting three slaves (a mother and her two children) belonging to a gentleman in Baltimore." Torrey died before completing the seven years imprisonment to which he was sentenced. The newspaper argued:

It appears that three indictments were returned against him and that he was tried and convicted upon each, notwithstanding there was one act of aspertation, and the slaves all belonged to one individual... In the case of Walker it was ruled that four different indictments might be sustained for the abduction of different Negroes – this position was controverted by defendant's counsel. If the decision in Torrey's case be good law, then the decision in Walker's case is evidently so, for in the latter case a different Negro was the subject of each indictment belonging to different individuals, and the offense was different in each indictment – one [each] for aiding and assisting him to run away and two for stealing the slaves.

The *Gazette*'s report of the Walker trial concluded:
And now... we will venture to assert that the action of the Jury on these bills of indictments presents an instance of forbearance and humanity unparalleled in the history of judicial proceedings. In the face of all the vituperation and malignant abuse that has been showered upon us at abolition meetings at Boston and elsewhere at the North and with the broad sanction of the act before them, instead of assessing a fine of $1,000 and imposing six months imprisonment, they have fined $150 and imprisoned 15 days.

*   *   *   *

When word reached Boston, editor William Lloyd Garrison found no such words to praise the jury. In print, he wrung his hands: "Horrible, horrible..."
Garrison displayed an extra large headline at the top of the front page in his December 6, 1844, *Liberator*:

JONATHAN WALKER SENTENCED, AND BRANDED!!

Amid a forest of exclamation points, Garrison wrote:
It appears [from an anonymous but reliable letter writer] that the amiable, noble-hearted Walker has not only been sentenced to imprisonment and to be fined for aiding the oppressed, but BRANDED IN THE HAND with the letters S.S. (Slave Stealer is meant, we suppose!) made with a red hot iron! And this in democratic, christian America! Horrible, horrible, beyond all expression. This is not all. Suits for damages have been brought against him to the amount of $106,000! And for all this, the American people and the American Congress are responsible.

The Liberator's first informant was the "anonymous but reliable" writer, identified in the printed account as "An Eye-witness." The letter was dated Sunday, November 17, the day after Walker's courthouse punishment and the serving of additional charges against Walker. This anonymous writer obviously was close to the scene. Indeed, some argument could be made for a theory that the writer actually was Walker himself, although his writing hand, the limb that had been branded, would have been difficult to use.

In the account of the egg-throwing by George Willis, "Eye-witness" used the phrase, "I was satisfactorily informed..." In two other instances, his writing suggested special access to information. "Eye-witness" reported that

Jonathan Walker The Man with the Branded Hand

Walker, upon his return to the jail, "was not put in irons, as before, greatly to his relief." Not many people would have had that information within twenty-four hours. And "Eye-witness," noting Walker was assessed a fine "and cost of prosecution," added: "which cost I have not been able to ascertain." Few people would have dared inquire, again indicating that the writer, if it was not Walker, was a person close to the scene, perhaps even one who regularly appeared in the jail building.

Two other points hint at Walker's involvement:

- The writer would have had to be sensitive to the news needs of people in the North. He wrote, "Being under the impression that there are some persons in your section of the country who are anxious to learn the result of Jonathan Walker's trial in Pensacola, I hasten to inform you..."
- The letter was addressed to Henry W. Williams ("Respected Friend"). Not many Southern people would have a "respected friend" in the North. Williams got the letter quickly to Garrison; it appeared in *The Liberator's* December 6 edition.

Reaction in the Massachusetts press was swift, and almost unanimously in support of Walker. In New Bedford, where Walker had many supporters, the *Bulletin* decried "the heartless, cold-blooded wretches who inflicted the inhuman outrage."

The *Christian Citizen* considered Walker among "a new order of knighthood in this heroic age of philanthropy... his hand daguerreotyped in the chancery of heaven..."

Shouted Garrison's editorial comment:

If Walker can only be suffered to return to the North, THAT BRANDED HAND must be held up in the presence of all the people; and the effect will be to fill their bosoms with indignation and horror, and to unite them for the overthrow of the diabolical slave system. Northern Freemen! swell the cry – "NO UNION WITH SLAVEHOLDERS!"

Garrison had invented the "No Union" phrase in May of 1844 after the American Anti-Slavery Society adopted Wendell Phillips' resolution, proclaiming that "secession from the present U.S. government is the duty of every abolitionist." Garrison's phrase became the society's motto. Some abolitionists took the sentiment literally, and, long before Southern states moved to secede from the Union, they were willing to work for the withdrawal of "free states" from the Union.

Abby Kelley and others took a more moderate attitude, a sort of isolationism against Southern states by Northerners ignoring them. Those who supported this movement were called "Come-Outers," a phrase used earlier in reference to those who withdrew their support from the established church in America. Kelley explained, "The 'come-outer' ground is the genius of our enterprise. No communion with anything that sustains slavery." Kelley, a native of Pelham, Massachusetts, was then only thirty-four years old and perhaps the leading American female voice for equality. Dorothy Sterling, in *Ahead of Her Time*, added: "Disunion... offered Northern states a way to abolish slavery unilaterally. If they withdrew from the Union, they would peacefully bring about a collapse of the slave system."

Kelley's husband, Stephen Foster, rejected disunion with a motto of his own: "Revolution, Not Dissolution."

Jonathan Walker never failed of indignation when informed that his motives were considered suspect. Walker singled out a Cape Cod weekly newspaper to answer: "Some editorials of the Barnstable *Patriot* have gone forth to prejudice the people's minds against every reasonable measure calculated to aid the abolition of slavery and to cherish a pro-slavery feeling, and a most unsocial and unchristian spirit. I lament the depravity and lack of dignity which seem to preside over the genius of its editor."

Despite occasional criticisms, he made clear in the strength of his writing that, as he neared his forty-sixth birthday, he was stout of heart and spirit. *The Liberator's* "Eye-witness" correspondent gave a glimpse of that stalwartness in words that resonate with Walker's message to his parents a few months earlier: "I shall weather the storm." "Eye-witness" – who almost surely had to be Walker himself – wrote the Boston newspaper: "He is in good spirits, and thinks that, if it is for the best, he shall weather the storm by and by."

Jonathan Walker did, indeed, weather that storm, and others that he could not have predicted were to make his predicament far worse over the next few months.

The Nation As Jonathan Walker Knew It in the 1840s

The United States in which Jonathan Walker lived in the mid-1840s was a nation divided – in several ways. The older, settled regions were "slave states" and "free states." Free territories were in the Old Northwest. To the south and west lay half a continent still under controversial control. Native Americans controlled much of "Indian Country," even as entire tribes were being relocated there from such newly developing territories/states as Florida. Mexico extended into areas that were to become California, Arizona, New Mexico, and Nevada. And Oregon Country, a vast area reaching northward to present-day Alaska, was claimed by both the United States and Great Britain.

It is to be regretted that the punishment for such flagrant crimes
should fall... upon the less responsible agent,
who is induced by a desire of gain or by an ignorant fanaticism
to come among us on his unholy crusade...
and still more is it to be regretted that we are constrained, in self-defense
to cut off some of those indulgences to our SLAVES,
which has made their situation hitherto one of happy contentedness.
1845 Florida Legislative Committee Report

CHAPTER 9   The Unholy Crusade Denounced

J onathan Walker left no record of gratitude for what the Pensacola newspaper called the "unparalleled humanity" demonstrated by an Escambia County jury on his behalf. He was far more pleased with learning in December of 1844, about a month after his branding, that he had been commended in London by the British and Foreign Anti-Slavery Society. The late-arriving lawyer, Thomas Blount, had delivered the news: "He handed me a paper in which was enclosed a letter, and resolution..." In *Trial and Imprisonment*, Walker reported on this matter, obviously ignoring Blount's role as messenger: Through the kindness of a friend in New York, I received the following resolution and the annexed epistle, just two months after its adoption...

At a meeting [in London] on Friday, October 4, 1844, George Stacy, Esq., in the chair, it was resolved unanimously:

That, considering the enormous wickedness of American Slavery, whether viewed in relation to the iniquity of its principle, which deprives nearly three millions of human beings of their personal rights, or to the atrocity of its practice, which subjects them to the deepest degradation and misery; this committee feel it to be their duty, publicly and warmly, to express their sympathy with those devoted friends of humanity, the Rev. Charles T. Torrey and Captain Jonathan Walker – who are now incarcerated in the prisons of Maryland and West Florida... and the laws under which they are to be arraigned, as utterly disgraceful to a civilized community, and in the highest degree repugnant to the spirit and precepts of the gospel.

The resolution was signed by Thomas Clarkson, president, and sent on October 8 by John Scoble, the society's president. Scoble, Walker continued, sent along a personal note:

The painful circumstances in which you have been placed by your humane and Christian attempt to deliver some of your fellow-men from the sufferings and degradation of slavery, are not, as you will perceive by the accompanying resolution, unknown to the abolitionists in Great Britain.

They truly sympathize with you in your affliction, and they trust that the efforts which are to be made for your deliverance from the power of evil men and evil laws will be succeeded by the divine blessing.

The letter and the British society's document were, Walker wrote, "wrested by force from me, and laid before a committee of the Legislative Council of the Territory of Florida for their action." As a result, Walker felt unable to respond to Scoble's letter until his release the following summer. But the consequences of his British support were to come much sooner from the Florida legislators.

Governor Branch, who only a few weeks earlier had bristled at Massachusetts Governor Briggs' breach of courtesy, was now fully aroused. After reading the papers seized from Walker, he sent them to a joint select committee of the Legislative Council. He wrote:

From their perusal you will see that the "British and Foreign Anti-Slavery Society for the Abolition of Slavery and the Slave Trade throughout the World" has been clandestinely cooperating with the authorities of Massachusetts in fiendish machinations against our domestic institutions. Under such circumstances, further forbearance on our part not only ceases to be a virtue, but would be, in effect, an abandonment of our vital interests. I therefore recommend the subject to your dispassionate investigation with a decided opinion on my own part that the time has arrived when Florida has a right -- nay, would be false to herself, were she not to demand from the Federal Government a prompt enforcement of the Federal Constitution.

That committee's report, issued early in 1845, began as if the bitter Branch himself had written it. But after the opening, the phrasing and terminology changed, suggesting an understanding of how the issue of slavery affected the growing crisis within the new American coalition of states. This report was signed by the heads of the council's two branches: I. Ferguson, Jr., who chaired the House committee, and Walker Anderson as chairman of the

The Unholy Crusade Denounced

Senate committee. This was the same Anderson who, as U.S. attorney for the district of West Florida, had prosecuted Jonathan Walker, and who had earned Walker's esteem for his personal courtesy. The legislative consideration began barely a month after Walker's conviction, and long before conflict-of-interest laws were created. Given Jonathan Walker's regard for his prosecutor, it's possible to infer that Anderson – the kind, courteous upholder of Southern values – may have brought his personal style to the committee's written report.

The Ferguson-Anderson report must have pleased Governor Branch by expressing the same kind of resentment against outside involvement in Florida affairs that Branch had displayed in his earlier bout with Massachusetts. The West Floridians were telling the British to mind their own business. The committee members, the report said, "regard... the interference of foreign states... as insulting and unwarrantable, and that it should be repelled promptly and indignantly."

Their resentment next took on the repeated references to the acts of "Christian philanthropists" in the resolution and in Scoble's letter:

> A vicious fanaticism, clothed in the garb of religion, is prowling around our borders, and by means of its more reckless and abandoned instruments, invading our inmost sanctuaries, whose direct purposes, scarcely concealed, are to deluge our very hearthstones in blood, and to rear an altar to its false principles upon the ruin of all that is precious to us as freeman and dear to us as men.

The report then sounded an alarm for Southern alertness, one remarkable for its clarity in defining the philosophy of the "slavocracy" while showing fear for "disunion." Here's what the West Florida legislative report said:

> The most sanguine and forbearing among us must long since have been painfully convinced of the existence of this unfriendly feeling towards us among some of our own countrymen; and the public mind throughout the whole of the Southern States has been roused to a state of distrust and watchfulness, which augurs ill for that harmony which is becoming [sic] between members of the same great family. The South has no cause for self-reproach, growing out of this feeling of estrangement. Their position has been eminently that of self-defense; and they are prompted to maintain that position by every consideration of duty and self-interest. They would be recreant to themselves, and unworthy of the rank which they hold among the nations, if they were to falter in the assertion of their rights and their resistance of this foul injustice.
>
> In the unhappy dissentions which have grown up between ourselves and our countrymen of the North, there are, however, considerations prompting us to still longer forbearance. It is not easy to forget that we are brothers, enjoying the same great heritage of liberty which was purchased by the blood of our common sires. We are

reluctant to let go our confidence in the returning sense of justice of those who are bound to us by such endearing ties, and we will not willingly dissever from our soil the blood-honored fields of Lexington, of Bunker Hill, and of Saratoga – we will "suffer long and be kind" – will bear many things, hope many things, and endure many things. And we do this the more readily because there is no hesitation amongst us as to the limits of their endurance. Among the millions of bosoms that are throbbing under a sense of the injury and outrage which have been so wantonly inflicted upon us by our Northern brethren, though there are many that plead for longer forbearance and forgiveness, there is probably not one that does not feel that there is a point beyond which forbearance would be ruin and dishonor – there is not one that would not unhesitatingly fling to the winds all the cherished recollections of the past, and all the exulting hopes of the future, rather than bow down in slavish abasement to the demands of those who seek to sacrifice us upon the shrine of their unholy fanaticism.

While Southerners could be patient with their Northern countrymen's misunderstandings, they need not be so with foreigners, the Ferguson-Anderson report went on. "We regard their false and intrusive philanthropy with unmingled resentment, and it becomes us to resist at once, and in the most effectual manner, all their efforts to control us in our internal police."

What could the Legislative Council and the governor of the Territory of Florida do by way of punishment to what the report called "foreign incendiaries who intermeddle with our domestic institutions and seek to interfere with the administration of our laws"?

Certainly, Florida could not successfully wage war with Great Britain, or even with the British anti-slavery society members. That left only the abolitionists who came to Florida and involved themselves in attempts to help slaves; and, of course, the slaves themselves. At this point, the committee report seems to have been written with Walker in mind, if not directly at least for his illegal act:

The committee regret that the only means which are within our reach to counteract their hostile designs, and to avert danger from ourselves, consist of increased penalties for the violation of our laws, and in stricter police arrangements in regard to the Negro population. It is to be regretted that the punishment for such flagrant crimes should fall rather upon the less responsible agent, who is induced by a desire of gain or by an ignorant fanaticism to come among us on his unholy crusade, than on the more wicked and intelligent felon, who plots his cowardly schemes of mischief in the security of a foreign country, and still more is it to be regretted that we are constrained, in self-defense, to cut off some of those indulgences to our SLAVES, which has made their situation hitherto one of happy contentedness.

The Unholy Crusade Denounced

This paragraph of the report carries two major philosophies of the pro-slavery faction. The first is in the suggestion that American abolitionists from the North – Walker was not considered an untypical anti-slavery activist even though he had resided in Pensacola for five years earlier – were either out to steal slaves for later resale at profit, or were acting simply on a principle sincerely believed but nonetheless misguided.

The second philosophy comes with the decision that if the troublesome aliens were out of reach for punishment, then the penalties would be imposed on those under control and nearest at hand, the slaves.

People like Walker, the legislators were saying, were not nearly so "wicked" as the foreign cowards who schemed to carry their "unholy crusade" to America to interfere in the local policies of a free people. The committee seemed, however, to suspect that more than the British were involved. The committee report said:

> Some of the circumstances developed in this case of Jonathan Walker have satisfied the committee that there are evil-disposed persons amongst us who permit themselves to be made channels of intercourse between the convicted felons in our prisons and their accomplices abroad, and in other ways lend their aid to the dissemination of unsound and dangerous doctrines on the subject of slavery. Towards such offenders the law should be unsparing in its penalties. To punish such of this class as are found among us with sufficient severity, and exclude those who may be officiously intruded upon us, its most solemn sanction should be invoked...

The committee may have overestimated Walker's influence and connections, both in Pensacola and abroad. Walker claimed he had no knowledge of the British society's action until two months after it took place, and we have no reason to disbelieve him. Nor did Walker ever give any indication that he was corresponding with anyone abroad, or giving information to anyone in Pensacola who could send the information abroad. In fact, he complained that his mail was censored severely.

Given the determination of intruding troublemakers, there was no recourse, the committee said, except to step up police security to catch slave stealers and to lift the favors the white slaveholders claimed they were giving to make the slaves "happy" and "contented."

But don't blame the committee for these necessary changes in local practices, the report said. "Heavy is the accountability of the abolitionist, both in Europe and at the North, not so much for the happiness and harmony of a great nation, which he has disturbed and periled by his ignorant and wicked intermeddling with the affairs of which he knows but little, as for the new burdens which he has imposed on the slave, and the new obstacles which he has interposed to the gradual amelioration and improvement of his condition."

123

Beyond stepping up police action and clamping down on the slaves, what could Florida do to discourage interference with the way it handled slavery? The committee now turned its attention to Jonathan Walker:

The crime of Negro-stealing has heretofore been punished by our laws with exceeding lenience, and in the very striking case to which the attention of the committee is now directed, where the offense was flagrant, and the evidence conclusive, the [November] punishment of the guilty man was so slight as to prove that, heretofore, in punishing this crime, we have not in any degree been moved by undue resentment. Henceforth, we are compelled to regard Negro-stealing, by the instruments of the abolitionists, as a crime of a different character. It is no longer a mere larceny, but a species of treason against the State – a direct assault upon the very existence of our institutions...

In obedience, then, to the rule which requires that the punishment of an offense should be commensurate with the difficulty of preventing it, as well as its enormity, the committee feel constrained to recommend that the crime of Negro-stealing, and of aiding and abetting Negro-stealing, be made punishable hereafter by death. They make this recommendation not lightly, but with a deep and impressive sense of the responsibility which they assume; but they feel that the responsibility in its heaviest extent rests elsewhere. They believe that such a law is necessary to the safety of the country in the new aspect in which this crime must now be regarded; and if blood be the penalty, which the Negro-stealer has to pay for his crime, it will be upon the skirts of those whose excitement and applause have driven him to his doom.

The select joint committee then went on record as supporting a bill already before the Senate establishing death as the penalty for stealing slaves in the Territory of Florida. The Legislative Council followed the committee's recommendation and waited until the territory was admitted to the Union. Florida became the 27th state on March 3, 1845. Exactly one week later, on March 10, the new state had a new law: "Any person convicted of stealing a slave shall suffer death." The law, fortunately for Walker, was not retroactive.

*   *   *   *

Floridians' reaction to British support for Jonathan Walker brought strong outcry in the press of the North. The Ohio newspaper, Cincinnati *Philanthropist*, wrote with heavy sarcasm under an all-capitals headline: "A HORRIBLE PLOT --- TO ARMS! TO ARMS!" The story said: "Governor Branch, of Florida, has just discovered a horrible plot, the disclosure of which calls for a prompt and decisive action on the part of the General Government. We submit to President Polk whether an extra sessions of Congress may not become necessary."

The Unholy Crusade Denounced

After quoting the British society's resolution, and John Scoble's letter to Walker, the Ohio newspaper wrote:

To us this looks very Christian-like, but the choleric Governor Branch smells rank treason in it. The letter is found on Captain Walker's person – hence it must have been conveyed to him. This is shocking – not to be tolerated. The marshal of the United States (the United States, remember, is the sleepless bodyguard of slavery), with trembling haste, forwarded the dread missile to the governor, and the governor lays it before their high mightinesses, the Senate and House of Representatives of that illustrious territory... Whew! What shall be done for our little sister? She must throw herself upon her reserved rights. A Pensacola jury must find true bills against John Scoble and Thomas Clarkson [of the British society], as fugitives from justice. John Branch must transmit the requisite documents to President Polk, demanding the prompt enforcement of the guarantees of the federal Constitution; Secretary Buchanan must make the formal demand on Lord Aberdeen, for these vile incendiaries and fugitives from justice, Messrs. Scoble and Clarkson, charged with fiendish machinations against the domestic institution of Pensacola; and don't you think they would be given up? Ah! how the British Lion would crouch, and smooth its mane, and still its roar, when it heard the voice of John Branch saying, "Forbearance on our part has ceased to be a virtue."

"Try it, Governor!" taunted the *Philanthropist*, ending its comment. As it and other newspapers frequently did, *The Liberator* reprinted the Ohio challenge.

Walker himself saw irony in being supported from abroad. He wrote later to the British and Foreign Anti-Slavery Society:

I am an American-born citizen, and have lived forty-five years under this republican form of government, but I am ashamed to acknowledge that, while enjoying the greatest social and religious privileges of any nation upon the earth, boasting of our liberal and free institutions, of the inherent right of all men to 'life, liberty, and the pursuit of happiness,' of our arts and sciences, civilizations, and the dispensation of the gospel; yet we cherish in our midst the most heinous, unjust, oppressive, and God-provoking system that ever cursed the dwellers of earth, nourishing jealousy and discord through the land, poisoning the life-streams of our Union, corroding the vitals of this young and growing nation, and destroying the mental and moral faculties of one portion of its inhabitants to corrupt and debase the other; and if anyone is found among her sons whose humane feelings prompt him to extend an act of sympathy towards his deeply injured fellow-subjects – who have nowhere to look with any earthly hope for the mitigation of their wretchedness but in the hearts of the few, and are denied the privilege of seeking redress from the laws and counsels of their country – such a one is sought out and hunted like a beast of prey, and dealt with as a traitor to his country, and as a slayer of his fellow-men; and this, notwithstanding every precaution, has been used to prevent any act of violence on the part of the truly wronged, and none but pacific means are countenanced to obtain relief.

    *   *   *   *

During the early days of Winter 1844-45, Jonathan Walker settled into the familiar routine of life in the old calaboza. As if it were a job, he continued his daily journal entries. Navy sailors were still being picked up and jailed, even on Christmas Day. Here are some of the entries Walker made after his court appearance and through the long winter:

December 25 - Two seamen committed from brig *Hazard*, of Portland, for attempting to obtain their discharge. They had refused to do duty on board.

December 28 - [O]ne of the seamen put in on the 25th was discharged.

January 24 - The other seaman put in from brig *Hazard* on the 25th ult. was discharged. A deserting soldier caught, committed, taken out, and sent to the Navy-yard.

The entries for African-Americans were more numerous:

November 19 - Slave man committed for being out too late.

November 20 - [The same man] flogged twenty-four blows with paddle and discharged.

December 5 - A slave woman committed for not staying at home enough, and taken out next day.

December 16 - A slave man committed for disobedience; whipped ten blows with a paddle, and let out next day.

January 10 - A slave man committed for going out of town at Christmas, and staying too long. A slave boy put in with me. He had played truant. He was let out next morning.

January 13 - A white man committed on suspicion of plotting to rob the mail. [Discharged January 20.]

January 15 - A white man put in with me, to get sober, to use in evidence. He was taken out next day.

January 21 - A slave boy committed for running away.

January 26 - The slave man put in on the 10th taken out and sent to New Orleans to be sold.

January 27 - A slave woman committed for attempting to defend herself when about to be whipped by her mistress. The next day, she was flogged twenty-four blows with the paddle, and twelve with the cow-hide, and sent home.

The Unholy Crusade Denounced

Walker had written earlier that Jailer Francis Torward

...also inflicts punishment upon slaves sent there by their masters or mistresses to be punished. I know not whether he is under any official obligation to perform this task, or whether custom has made it a rule. For this service, I believe he is entitled to extra pay from the persons who employ him for that purpose. It is by no means a general rule for masters or mistresses to have their slaves flogged by the city marshal, for it frequently costs them some loss of their service or time, besides what they have to pay the marshal; so that but few are disposed to incur the expense, when they save it by a few minutes' exertion of their own muscular powers, and at the same time feed their rapacious revenge upon their helpless slaves.

*　　　　　*　　　　　*　　　　　*

Jonathan Walker was, by now, what the 1990s call a "media celebrity." The abolitionist press was filled with information and opinions about him and his punishment. So celebrated was he that the Rhode Island Anti-Slavery Society announced plans to publish a monthly newspaper, costing fifty cents a year. "Its title and motto will be – THE BRANDED HAND!" Garrison trumpeted in a Page 1 story on January 10, 1845.

While *The Liberator* was foremost among the abolitionist press, its circulation never exceeded 2,500 a week. One reason was the slowness of transportation; it took two weeks for the paper to reach Ohio, for example. As a result, anti-slavery papers were founded in most Northern cities and even in growing Western areas by hard-working abolitionists such as Abby Kelley.

Almost weekly, in New England at least, reports were printed of the work of Loring Moody, the Cape Cod man who had taken over active direction of the local Walker committee. Moody was working full-time now as an agent of the Boston and Harwich conventions of the Massachusetts Anti-Slavery Society.

A typical appearance occurred on December 10, 1844, when Moody appeared in Hubbardston, a small Massachusetts town, and told Jonathan Walker's story to citizens assembled in the Unitarian vestry. *The Liberator's* correspondent, H. W. Carter, reported January 3, 1845, that Moody spoke "with a power and earnestness of manner which showed he had the 'virtue to be moved;' which could spring only from a strong and lively sense of the goodness and greatness of the cause he was advocating. Would that his narrative and appeal might be listened to by every man and woman in the Commonwealth!"

The gathering adopted resolutions, including one asserting "that Walker, in the humane attempt to set the bondman free, did no more than it was his duty to do..." A collection brought $9.16 in donations, "delivered over to Mr. Moody for the benefit of Mr. Walker." Carter added: "The sum of $4.20 has since been paid in for the benefit of Mr. Walker." The total, $13.26, represented an average of nearly a dime from each of the 150 attending, and probably as much as Walker was ever able to provide his family in a month.

Another front page offering was an unsigned letter criticizing the clergymen of East Abington, Massachusetts. Only one of seven "has opened his lips or his purse in aid of Jonathan Walker, and his afflicted family. Yes, out of seven men, set apart from the world to be a guide to others in matters of faith and *practice*, but *one* can be found to say or do anything to aid an unfortunate brother who is suffering the horrors of a Southern dungeon..."

After another typical meeting – in Andover on November 29, 1844 – a report was sent to four Massachusetts abolitionist newspapers: *The Liberator, Emancipator*, Boston *Recorder*, and Massachusetts *Ploughman*. The meeting, ten days earlier at the Baptist Meetinghouse, was reported by Garrison's newspaper under the headline, "Sympathy Meeting at Andover." Moody told about Walker's experiences, resolutions were adopted, and a collection ($17.10) taken. "After which," J. M. H. Dow wrote the newspapers, "a committee of seven was appointed, to be called the 'Walker Committee,' to solicit aid for Captain Walker and all who might be brought into similar circumstances."

The abolitionist press was, of course, preaching to the converted. A different view came from some of the general community press. The two genres could not even agree on a description of Walker. To the Pensacola *Gazette*, Walker had "a suspicious countenance, slouchy person, stooping shoulders." Two Massachusetts newspapers, the Essex *Transcript* and New Bedford *Bulletin*, used phrases such as "a tall, stout, fine-looking specimen of a Cape Cod skipper with a countenance expressive of good sense and benevolence," "just such a man as would be likely to have his sympathies awaked in behalf of the oppressed and downtrodden." A family history describes Walker's appearance at age forty-four this way: "sailor, father, adventurer, and abolitionist... tall, dark, loosely built with a rolling gait of a man of the sea, and one arm that was a little lame from the bullet of the Mexican robbers."

A photograph taken of Walker about that time shows a strong, erect man with sloping shoulders, his black hair thinning at the front of his head and worn long enough on the sides and back to cover his ears and his shirt collar. Deep-set eyes, a long, sharp nose, sunken cheeks, and deep lines around his mouth suggest an alert but weary countenance. Despite his limited jail diet, he appeared in the photo, which was taken within a year of his release, to be slightly overweight.

The anti-abolitionist press was often more concerned about the potential for violence in the struggles over slavery. The pro-slavery New York *Herald* warned, in January 1845, that "trials and convictions [such as Walker's] ought to teach the wild enthusiasts who are operated on by the abolitionists of the North to take care and conduct themselves with [restraint] when they go to the Southern states. But we rather fear that no advice will be taken in that quarter."

And the Tuscaloosa (Alabama) *State Journal* wrote, under the heading, "The Fanaticism of Slavery":

The Unholy Crusade Denounced

A statute similar to that of South Carolina, of which Massachusetts complains, is now in force in Alabama; and it may soon become our turn to meet a like effort to tamper with the slave interest. With all their philanthropy, the citizens of Massachusetts, generally, are very chary of their dollars – and perhaps it would be well for our legislature to enact a law at its present session imposing a heavy penalty, *in dollars and cents*, with imprisonment at hard labor... on any agent, attorney, or other person who may visit Alabama on the same business...

Walker undoubtedly knew of some of these newspaper reports through correspondence from Harwich friends and his wife. From his place in a world where jailkeepers were paid to whip runaway slaves, and where those who, like him, attempted to help were stripped of possessions and dignity, the debate must have seemed interesting but the debaters more involved with theory than reality.

      *   *   *   *

As winter brought gray day after dreary day, Walker had settled into a routine made only slightly less rigorous by the Spartan courtesy shown by the Torward family. Walker wrote:

[A]fter being there for some time, by some cause or other, I seemed to get partly in to their good grace, and was treated by [Maria] with perfect civility and some degree of kindness; and frequently found in my dish some little luxuries, unusual, I presume, for prisoners to receive except at their own expense, or by the kindness of friends. But if I had had no means to provide anything for myself, I should much of the time have gone hungry, as the portion given me which I could eat was insufficient. My food consisted mostly of bread and fish for breakfast, and bread and a dish of soup or some calavance beans for dinner. The bread was generally good, made of flour, and most of the time raised; and the rest was mixed up and baked in thin cakes without raising. I had the curiosity to weigh it for two weeks, and the result was ten pounds seven ounces for fourteen successive days, two pounds thirteen and one half ounces of which was Johnny-cake, or flour and water kneaded up and baked by the fire as above. Some days I had but little other than bread given me.

...It was for my benefit to make as little complaint as possible, and therefore, having a little money, I supplied at my own expense what was lacking on their part, which amounted to little more than a dollar per week during my imprisonment, for food, washing, and a little clothing.

Perhaps this combination of jailer's trust and personal discontent – spurred by a threat of immediate and new court-ordered punishment – led Jonathan Walker in early February to undertake a daring adventure that was to

Jonathan Walker The Man with the Branded Hand

earn the only criticism some of his friends were to make of his conduct in Pensacola. He tried to escape on Wednesday, February 5, 1845 – and failed.

The Pensacola *Gazette* reported the action February 8 in a story only two sentences in length. The first sentence read: "On Wednesday evening last, Jonathan Walker, who is still in prison here under his conviction of November last, for Negro stealing, attempted to escape, and so far succeeded as to get the jail door open, having been supplied by some friend with a pick-ax for the purpose."

Here's how Walker told the story:

While eating my dinner, I was informed, by what I thought good authority, that the marshal would take me, at 4 p.m., before a magistrate, to be examined on other charges – what, my informant would not, or could not, tell; but said that he heard the marshal say he was coming for me at four o'clock. I was somewhat apprehensive that it was a device of some persons ill-disposed towards me and not satisfied with the course which the law had taken, and who were disposed to make use of other than legal means. I hinted this to my informant. His reply was, "They are going to play the devil with you." My suspicion was strengthened by the district attorney and judge being abroad at the time, and by the lateness of the hour selected for taking me from prison; so I did not think it prudent for me to leave the prison, except I could be convinced that I should be subject to no illegal dealings.

At [four o'clock], the marshal called, and requested me to go with him before a magistrate. I declined going, and gave him some reasons why; and told him that whatever examination I was to undergo I preferred it should take place where I was. The marshal left, and some time after returned, saying that the magistrate refused to come to the jail; and again requested me to go with him. I still declined. He then started to leave, when the jailer spoke to him a few minutes. He then returned, and read to me a letter from the district judge, who was then at Tallahassee (Middle Florida), with instructions to take me before a magistrate for examination on a charge of inducing three slaves to leave the service of their masters. The marshal then left me; and the reader may picture to his mind my feelings, as well as he can; for I have no faculty to express them on paper.

Walker had drawn a scene in which Marshal Dorr had simply summonsed him; and of Jailer Francis Torward convincing Dorr, in whispers, that he should inform Walker of the district judge's order to have Walker finally arraigned on the three new charges revealed to him on the November day he had been returned to the jail after his branding.

Walker claimed he had "no faculty to express" his depression, but he did:

The Unholy Crusade Denounced

I had for several weeks been expecting to be liberated from my disagreeable situation, through the liberality of friends who had been imposed upon in regard to my true situation, and prevented from doing for me what they had attempted, by supplying the pecuniary means to satisfy the demands of the court; and had been twice disappointed; but now it seemed that the most favorable issue which I could expect was to be chained up for three or four months longer in that woman-whipping shop, and go through another trial for the same offense, with the continual accumulation of obstacles to my release; and for my family to remain objects of charity; my aged parents and other near friends, suffering affliction; and all to gratify a few God- and man-haters who were feasting their rage upon one helpless object whom Providence had in some measure placed where they could wreak their vengeance on him. These were some of the most favorable considerations which occurred to my mind, and which have since been realized.

Walker, in citing his being "twice disappointed," apparently referred to Thomas Blount's receiving $750 from the Walker committee in Boston and using all of it for his own fee and expenses. The prisoner's account of his attempted escape continued:

Seeing that it required but little effort or ingenuity to open the doors myself, I gave way to the impulse of present feeling, and without any difficulty succeeded in opening the doors without doing them one dollar's worth of injury... But, as a very slight noise could be heard in the rooms above, the family took the alarm and prevented my departure. I was made secure until the next day, when the marshal called and, without any ceremony, took me before three magistrates. Satisfactory evidence against me was produced to insure my committal until the next term of court in May, unless I give bail in the sum of $3,000. So I was remanded to prison again and put in irons to await the result of what might follow.

What followed, almost within hours, was the *Gazette*'s brief report, apparently prepared at deadline for the weekly newspaper. The account said Walker had used a "pick-ax" to pry open the jail door lock. That could have been accurate; a sympathizer daring enough to tell Walker of the marshal's impending visit would have been competent enough to provide a tool that could be used to force open the lock on the cell door.

Who would have told Walker? Certainly not Ebenezer Dorr. He and Walker had had too many conflicts, from Dorr's aggressive conduct at the pillory to reprimanding Walker "for one or two words in a private letter to my wife."

Nor is it likely that Francis Torward, or Maria, his wife, would have informed Walker, despite what seemed to be a quiet respect if not outright trust between the prisoner and the jailer's family. If the Torwards had warned Walker of the marshal's coming visit, why would they have stopped the attempted escape when one or more of them heard Walker making "a very slight noise"? Ironically, the Torward family moved to another home in Pensacola from their two-room apartment on thin boards above the jail cells on February 19, exactly two weeks later.

The most probable conspirator would be James Gonzalez, the deputy marshal. He would have had opportunity to hear Marshal Dorr discussing his plans to visit Walker in jail, and Gonzalez's presence at the jail, even if arranged only to warn Walker, would not have seemed suspicious. Additionally, Gonzalez was disposed to kindness to Walker, earning the Massachusetts man's praise.

Maria Weston Chapman, in the introduction to Walker's *Trial and Imprisonment*, gave the definitive explanation for Walker's not revealing the name of his informant: "It is to be lamented that many interesting and illustrative incidents must be suppressed, out of regard to the safety of individuals whose liberties and lives their publication would endanger..."

*   *   *   *

Other questions about the escape attempt also have gone unanswered.

Motivated by fear "to use some pacific means" to avoid a trip to the court, did Walker really think he could escape? He knew it was possible, surely recalling that "a white man committed for being noisy" had "broke out and went off." Walker had logged that October escape, and never noted the man's recapture.

Should Walker have attempted the escape? He never expressed regret; in fact, he suggested justification when he noted that some of his fears for further punishment were afterward realized. Nor did he regret upsetting or angering newspaper writers and others who disapproved of his action. His only comment was this: "I have been almost censured by warm friends."

The *Gazette*'s first sentence in the February 8, 1845, edition told of the escape. The second sentence, in Walker's words, "belches forth" the editor's opinion: "It is a subject of no little wonder here that the zeal and benevolence of W's abolition friends abroad have not yet led to his being supplied with the funds necessary for his release."

In early February, Walker may have agreed with that. His bitterness and disappointment were to deepen. "In a short time after this," he wrote, "the proprietor of the same paper writes to a friend of mine in Boston, who made the inquiry through him, to know on what conditions I could be released; and his reply was that 'it was impossible for anything to be done until after my trial at May court.'"

Joe Richardson wrote: "Such a comment from Florida, widely reprinted in Northern papers, irritated abolitionists, and they began to ask the same question of each other and in newspapers... As a result of the aborted escape, Walker's friends were spurred to greater activity, and large numbers of Floridians were greatly angered."

The editors of two abolitionist newspapers published a thousand miles away in Boston did not share Walker's despair. Wrote *The Liberator*'s Garrison, "We are sorry that such a hopeless attempt should have been made when arrangement had been made to free him at the earliest practical period." The *Emancipator* said, "Mr. W. must have been aware of the efforts of his friends to supply him with the funds necessary for his release." The editor, however, was prepared to forgive him for trying to evade "the fangs of the slaveholder, or his merciless bloodhounds."

$$* \qquad * \qquad * \qquad *$$

In mid-winter, Walker's friends were, indeed, making an effort towards his release. By now, the story of the blundering Blount's taking the Boston committee's $750 and accomplishing nothing had reached the North. And Walker had informed his friends that he did not wish to fight this case to the United States Supreme Court. It's likely that, having now spent more than six months in jail, and still facing three more charges, he feared an appeal might require even more jail time beyond the impending May 1845 Pensacola court hearing.

This time, the initiative towards freeing the Massachusetts captain was to come from the Harwich committee. The Cape group seemed to accept without protest Walker's decision to forego an appeal. They had perhaps concluded that Walker, by attempting to escape jail, had ruined any efforts in a higher court to prove his noble motivations in helping the runaway slaves. J. P. Nickerson reported that Harwich neighbors, aware that the fine and court costs through November amounted to $423, decided to seek Walker's release through the simple procedure of having a local man pay the fine in Florida. They sent a letter to Captain Samuel Smith, Jr., of Harwich, who was then in Florida with his ship. They authorized him to pay as much as $500, provided Walker could accompany Smith home. It is not likely that the Pensacola authorities would have agreed to such a bargain, but as it developed they never had a choice. When Smith received word from Harwich, he agreed to provide the money in Pensacola and accept repayment when he returned to Cape Cod. He was, however, unable even to discuss Walker's release with Pensacola officials. Marshal Ebenezer Dorr was away for several days, and only Dorr could arrange for Walker's freedom, Smith was told. Meantime, Smith's ship was loaded and ready to sail. He left.

In fact, Captain Smith could not have brought Walker back to Harwich with him. The well-meaning Harwich friends, and Captain Smith, did not know that Walker, in the meantime, had attempted to escape, motivating the authorities to indict him on the three late-filed charges and setting bail at $3,000. Now there was no hope for Walker's being set free before the May hearings.

The Only Photo Image of Walker's Branded Hand

Courtesy of the Massachusetts Historial Society

The Unholy Crusade Denounced

American Heritage magazine reported in a 1976 edition: "Sometime shortly after his release, Walker met Albert Southworth, a pioneer photographer who had learned the daguerreotype process from Samuel Morse and had recently gone into partnership with Josiah Hawes. Southworth and Hawes produced some of the finest early daguerrean images, and their skill and imagination are evident in [the] stark likeness of Walker's hand. The image is among the earliest 'conceptual' portraits ever made – that is, one in which a part of the body is made to symbolize the personality of the subject. Ironically, no full portrait of Walker is known to exist, but his memory is well enough served by the image of his strong, scarred hand. The initials are here reversed, since the daguerrean process produced a mirror image."

In fact, the polished plate was known as "a mirror with a memory," according to Chris Steele, curator of photographs at the Massachusetts Historical Society. The original plate is a treasure at the society's collections in Boston, a "gift of Nathaniel Bowditch through his mother, Mrs. H. I. Bowditch of Jamaica Plain, in March 1930." Mr. Steele describes it as "a sixth plate which measures 2¾ x 3¼ inches and is housed in a half case with the leather removed on the back of the case..." From it over the past one and a half centuries have repeatedly come excellent photographic prints reproduced in such publications as *The American Heritage, National Geographic*, and *Yankee* magazine.

How was Walker able to keep his hand immobile for a period of time while Southworth made the image? Chris Steele points to the edge of a table visible beneath Walker's hand as indicative of the firm surface on which the wounded hand was rested

From the daguerreotype image, historians generally acknowledge, an artist made a line drawing. That ubiquitous icon has been reprinted countless times in newspapers, magazines, and books, and even on signs. The original printer's plate, mounted on a small (1½ x 2¼ inches) wooden

block as it was used by *The Liberator* in 1845, is in the historic collection of the Boston Public Library. This is among "gifts from the family of William Lloyd Garrison," made August 31, 1899, more than thirty years after Garrison, and his newspaper with him, retired, having accomplished their goals of seeing an end to slavery in the United States.

Jonathan Walker The Man with the Branded Hand

> What great masses of men wish done, will be done...
> There are now other energies than force...
> which no man in the future can allow himself to disregard.
> **Ralph Waldo Emerson, "Emancipation in the British West Indies"**

CHAPTER 10   Freedom At Last

That Christmas of 1844 would have been a lonely period for prisoner Jonathan Walker. Although the day had not yet taken on the luster of the current gift-giving holiday celebration, the sailor was, after all, the Christian father of eight children during the most sacred day on the Christian calendar. His wife, children, parents, and brothers were more than a thousand miles away in Massachusetts. And here was he, fighting through the boredom and uncertainty of a winter in jail and the physical and emotional pain that came with living in chains in a small prison cell.

He was a faithful correspondent and journal-keeper, and no doubt he had a lively exchange of mail to help keep up his spirits. Despite his weary familiarity with slavery's cruelties, he continued to record some of the life around him. He never learned to overlook the many floggings taking place in the jail building almost daily. Indeed, Walker was able to write evocatively about such events even after months of witnessing them; specifically, about the beatings that Maria Torward administered to the family slave-cook:

> It may be thought that those whippings were of no great severity, and merely administered as a parent would correct a child; but to test the quality let a person be covered only with a thin cotton frock, and let a woman, excited to uncontrolled passion, apply a rawhide switch to the back of the other with her greatest strength from twenty to fifty blows, and they would not need a repetition of it to ascertain its mildness. But some of those floggings were applied by a more

powerful arm than that of the mistress; and the marks and scars were visible upon the slave's neck and face from the time I was first committed to the day of my release. My senses have conveyed to my heart inexpressible feelings of disgust and abhorrence for such a mode of discipline or punishment upon rational human beings. Often when these exhibitions have taken place have I thought of the following lines:

> Hate's quivering lip, the fix'd, the staring eye,
> The grin of vengeance, and the forehead pale,
> The deep drawn breath, the short hyena cry,
> All in connection tell the dreadful tale,
> Where cowhide, paddle, chains, and slavery does prevail.

If any parents, guardians, or masters wish their child, minor, or servant to hate them with a perfect hatred, let them flog them!

*　　　　　*　　　　　*　　　　　*

With much time on his hands, Walker even figured out what it would have cost Mrs. Torward if she had had to pay a fee the jailer charged white slaveholders for flogging their slaves. Walker wrote:

Suppose the slave... had cost her master 75 cents for each whipping, the amount would have been about $30 from the 19th July, when I was committed, to the 19th February, when the family moved from the jail. The reader will have perceived that those whippings were much more frequent in the warm weather than in the cold, and also before her mistress' confinement, than afterwards. The reader is at liberty to make his or her comments or conjectures as to the cause of this.

Day by day in the cold months of 1845, Jonathan Walker logged the cruel punishment of slaves, and the comings and goings of prisoners. Excerpts from his journal give the raw material of slavery's bleak drama:

February 9 - A slave man and woman were committed for being out too late, but discharged the next day.

February 10 - The slave boy committed the 21st of last month taken out and sent to New Orleans to sell. None but myself now in jail.

February 17 - Two slave women and one man brought to jail and whipped ten blows each, on the bare back, and discharged. They were accused of using some of their master's money without his permission.

February 25 - A slave boy committed, who received twenty blows with the paddle, and was then sent home. He had played truant.

March 16 - A slave man brought to jail and flogged twenty-five blows with a paddle and twenty with a cowhide. He was charged with not doing work enough.

April 1 - A slave man committed; he had been sent to New Orleans for sale, but was returned.

Freedom at Last

April 12 - A slave woman brought to jail and flogged severely. The slave man committed on the lst flogged twenty-four blows with the paddle and thirty with the cowhide, to gratify his drunken mistress, as they could not sell him [at a price satisfactory] to their mind in New Orleans. The flogging made him quite sick for several days.

April 19 - The slave man flogged on the 12th was taken from jail and sent to Mobile to be sold. This was the slave that was committed on the 10th of January for staying too long with his wife and children at Christmas. His master had a plantation thirty or forty miles from Pensacola, where he had lived for a number of years, but had lately moved to Pensacola and offered his plantation for sale; and, not having employment for his slaves, was desirous to convert some of them into other property. And although this slave was permitted at Christmas to go and see his family, who still lived in the neighborhood he had formerly lived in, and were claimed as property by another man, yet his staying over his time gave sufficient cause (as per slave code) for removing him forever from them, notwithstanding he offered to produce the proof of his inability to return at the time appointed, on account of sickness. Nevertheless, he was kept in jail sixteen days, and then sent to New Orleans. But being too old to meet with a ready sale in that market, he was returned again the lst of April, and lodged in jail until the 12th, when his mistress came there in a rage, under the influence of liquor, and caused him to be flogged as mentioned above; and during the performance, she stood by and gave directions to the operator, yelping all the while at the mangled victim of her anger. A few days after, he was sent to Mobile for sale. He did not meet with a market, and was sent back; but soon after his return escaped from his tormentors, and I have since heard no more of him.

May 1 - A fugitive slave apprehended and committed; he had straight hair, and looked more like an Indian than a Negro, and tried to pass himself for one.

From time to time, the grim monotony of Walker's life in the Pensacola jail was broken up by outside developments of interest. On March 3, 1845, Florida became the 27th state in the Union. Its motto: "In God we trust." Soon after, Ebenezer Dorr was elected the first sheriff of Escambia County. He apparently resigned his position as United States marshal but continued serving until a successor replaced him many months later.

On March 27, "I received a letter from B. D. Wright, counselor at law, enclosing a letter to him from H. I. Bowditch of Boston, relating to my circumstances." Walker did not explain, but other records indicate that Dr. Bowditch probably was assuring Walker, through the prisoner's last-known attorney of record, that funds to pay for his fine would be available by the May session of court. How relieved such a message would have made Walker feel.

Bowditch, a professor of clinical medicine at Harvard, was perhaps better known as a Garrisonian and member of the Board of Managers of the Massachusetts Anti-Slavery Society.

*   *   *   *

Abolitionists, meantime, were marching across New England in a second series of "100 Conventions" sponsored by the Massachusetts Anti-Slavery Society. The first series had been carried out across New York, Ohio, and Michigan in 1843. One of the tour stops in February, 1845, was in Harwich, Massachusetts, Jonathan Walker's hometown. On February 28, *The Liberator* devoted nearly two full columns to Charles C. Burleigh's account, "Tour of the Cape." He wrote that he and Charles Remond, a free-born black abolitionist, had begun the week-long Cape visit with discouragement: "[W]e were almost persuaded that the hearts of the people were as barren, and desolate, as were the fields and sand-hills which surround [them]. But we succeeded better than we anticipated."

The tour included Harwich for two days. Burleigh wrote of Walker's hometown: "We learned before we went there that the Congregational Meetinghouse was bolted hard against the cause of Freedom, and before our meetings had concluded we found strong evidence that the report had not belied that church."

In early New England, each community was responsible for erecting and, through self-taxation, maintaining a meetinghouse to be used for town business and religious gatherings. Such worship for generations was carried on in "the Congregational Way." As new sectarian groups in the 19th Century raised their own buildings, those who remained with the original group became identified as Congregationalists. In 1834, this town-church relationship was "disestablished" in Massachusetts. Now the Congregationalists were free to decide when, and if, their building could be used for non-religious gatherings. In 1845, abolitionists were not welcome to use the "new" meetinghouse, erected in 1832, by the Harwich Congregational parish.

The abolitionists' first-day gatherings were held in the Methodist Church, but that building had been reserved earlier by another group for the second day. A new effort was made to use the Congregational Church. Burleigh wrote that

> a committee man [present] had personally no objections to our going in, "if it wouldn't make a *touse*;" but if it was going to "make a *touse*," he didn't want us to go in. Another thought that if we would say nothing only about anti-slavery, that there would be no objection to our going in: which meant that if we would talk of the slavery of the South, and have nothing to say of the partnerships of the North in its guilt – and would not expose the lurking places of pro-slavery, that we might enter their holy house. Another thought that the opposition made to our going in had been made under the supposition that [Stephen Symonds]

Freedom at Last

Foster was coming, and if we were going to talk as Foster did, he didn't want us in their house.

Foster, one of abolitionism's most forceful speakers, was considered radical even among those working to abolish slavery. He urged whites to sit in the church seats assigned to the blacks as a sign of support. He proposed impeachment of President Tyler because he was a slaveholder. Sterling wrote in *Ahead of Her Time* that "steeple-house troubler" Foster claimed he was ejected from churches twenty-four times and jailed four times in only a four-month period in 1841. In fiery speeches throughout the Northeast, he urged audiences to quit their churches and denounce the federal government. Among the critics of Foster was Maria Child, whose book, *An Appeal in Favor of That Class of Americans Called Africans*, was the first to call for immediate emancipation. She once said: "I could scarcely find words to express my disapprobation of that man's way of doing things." By early 1845, Foster was generally considered to have moved slightly towards a more conservative abolitionist attitude, although he had become a leading supporter of "disunion."

As it happened, Foster did not attend the 1845 convention on Cape Cod. But conservative Harwich residents were not wrong in anticipating trouble whenever he did appear. Three years later, and then only thirty-five years old, Foster was a prominent participant in what has come to be known as the "Harwich mob" and the "Harwich riot."

But even assuring Harwich folks that Foster was not on the list of speakers did not, Burleigh said, appease reticent Harwich Congregationalists: "It was truly ludicrous to see how anxious they were to keep an anti-slavery reputation while gagging the defenders of Freedom by shutting their church against them."

Making their trip worthwhile, however, Burleigh and Remond found "noble spirits there" in support of Jonathan Walker. Burleigh wrote: "[H]earts spontaneously leap up at the call of enthralled man, and gird themselves for the conflict; and they have not been slumbering while one of our old band has been imprisoned, and ignominiously branded, for an act of the purest love. They have run the trumpet-blast of agitation through their town, and wakened many who were asleep, and roused many stupid souls."

Not all souls had been roused. Burleigh continued:

There is a good deal of feeling in Harwich against Jonathan Walker's imprisonment and barbarous treatment; but I was surprised to find so much indifference among the Cape Cod people generally, in reference to his case. Many of them heartlessly say, "He went to steal the slaveholders' property, and it is good enough for him"; and others think he was very imprudent, and not worthy of any sympathy. I cannot express the deep loathing and abhorrence of my soul for that inhuman sentiment and soul-hardened feeling. I pity the men whose spirits are so base, and whose moral principles are so dead, that they can feel and talk thus of that noble and generous man. They dwindle into pigmy insignificance, compared with his great-hearted example.

  *   *   *   *

Denied a church hall, the 1845 convention held its final Harwich meeting at the new Pine Grove Seminary, which had been opened only a few months earlier almost directly across Main Street from the high-steepled Congregational Meetinghouse. The church, and criticism of its general failure to support actively the abolition of slavery, remained the center of controversy. This brought into action two Harwich natives who spoke out against the critics of their churches from quite dissimilar backgrounds. One was "Captain Weeks," as *The Liberator* identified him. This was probably the forty-four-year-old Cyrus Weekes (the name was spelled almost interchangeably "Weeks" and "Weekes" in early records). The other was Sidney Brooks, at age thirty-one the founder, principal, and head teacher at Pine Grove Academy.

Weekes and Brooks were in the crowd that packed the largest room in the new seminary that cold February evening. The meeting, Burleigh wrote,

> ...was interrupted by the noisy bluster and threats of an old sea captain, who came forward in rage and wrath to defend the Church. Remond had been commenting pretty severely, and with great justice, upon the conduct of that pro-slavery church in shutting up their house to us, as the humble representatives of the anti-slavery cause. He had spoken a short time when this redoubtable champion of the Church, a Captain Weeks, came forward with great valor, and standing in front of Remond he doubled up his fist, and, looking as though he would annihilate us both in the millionth part of a second, he said, "I'm not going to hear this stuff any longer. I came here to hear an anti-slavery lecture, and I won't sit still and hear the Church abused in this style. Now, sir, you stop, or you'll go down over the stairs head first, quicker than you would like to. If you'll go on the right track, you may go, but if you don't wish to be pitched headlong down stairs, you had better stop your abuse of the Church, and your talk about politics."
>
> Through all this raging tempest in a teapot, friend Remond stood calmly before the bully, who was trying to work up his courage sufficiently to strike him. A young man came down the aisle just at this time, saying that "if Remond went down stairs, he should go, too" – and another stepped out from another part of the hall and faced the fury-filled captain in a very un-non-resistant manner; and though the whole scene seemed rather ludicrous to me, I half feared, for a few moments, that we were to have a regular fight in the meetinghouse. Mr. Remond's perfect self-possession seemed to act powerfully upon the whole company, to calm down the disturbed and excited feelings of the audience.

Freedom at Last

Sidney Brooks, who was to become one of Harwich's civic and church leaders through the years, stepped forward, not to challenge Captain Weekes but to apologize for permitting abolitionists to use his schoolhouse. Burleigh wrote:

...Mr. Brooks... was evidently much frightened, and made a most unmanly apology for opening the hall to us. I was grieved that any man, claiming to be a freeman, should thus cowardly yield the right of free speech to the dictate of some blustering aristocrat. I hope Mr. Brooks will learn yet that Freedom is worth more than bread and butter, or the smiles and flattery of tyrants and doughfaces.

While Captain Weekes was complaining so bitterly of Remond's rebukes against the [Harwich Congregational] Church, a prominent man who had formerly been a member of it rose and remarked that he had been thoroughly acquainted with that Church, and could assure the audience that nothing too severe had been said, but rather the half was not told. After some other discussion and conversation, in which Mr. [Loring] Moody and Elkanah Nickerson, Jr., and others took part, defending free speech... the angry Captain... kept quiet during the remainder of the evening, and listened to a faithful application of truth to the pro-slavery Church...

Mr. Brooks came to the defense of the Church, and argued that we should not judge of the Northern Church by the Southern action, but by the opinions of the leading organs of the Church at the North – such papers as the *Puritan* and the Boston *Recorder*. I think, if he had known their character as well as abolitionists know them, he would hardly have quoted them as the proof of the anti-slavery character of the Northern Orthodoxy. I apprehend slaveholders would never fear any influence which those papers, and others like them, exert at the North.

The position of any religious community in respect to slavery was among the most debated topics during the mid-19th Century. At times, it seemed that there was no middle ground. Not all abolitionists proposed that people should abandon membership in a church that did not take a strong anti-slavery stand. Maria Child had said in 1843: "To push everybody off the anti-slavery platform who would not leave their religious associations seems to me narrow and prospective. I resist their effort to coerce the free will of individuals."

*   *   *   *

Despite Captain Weekes' outburst, the Harwich meeting was successful, in Burleigh's view, because much support was demonstrated for Jonathan Walker:

A good impression was evidently made upon those present. Before the close of the meeting, a subscription was taken up in behalf of Walker – to pay his fine, or bail him out of prison. One man subscribed $100, another $25, and many others $10 or $15 each. This shows the feeling toward that good man. My respect for him is much increased since I have heard his character from the lips of his neighbors. He is, on all hands, represented as a courageous and generous man, whose whole character is fairly represented in that glorious act for which he now suffers. He is withal a pretty thorough reformer, and on Christian grounds objects to any legal proceedings in his own behalf, choosing rather to suffer wrong than use the bloody sword of this government to obtain release, and therefore, as I was informed, the efforts to carry his case into the Supreme Court were without his consent.

We were glad to meet Loring Moody in his own town, and to receive his hearty assistance in our labor to arouse that people. I trust that Mr. Moody, whose labors in behalf of Walker have been alike honorable to himself and serviceable to the cause of Freedom, will continue to agitate this community for the deliverance of the millions whose fate is even worse than that of the noble Cape Cod philanthropist.

*   *   *   *

Among the many debates over semantics that took place between pro-slavery and anti-slavery forces was one over the term "slave stealer." Since those supporting slavery regarded slaves as the kind of property called chattel, and not as human beings, theft of a slave was seen as theft of property; hence, the terms "slave-stealer" and "Negro-stealer" carried the same weight of condemnation, for example, as the charge of being a "cattle thief." Those who opposed slavery often used the term "man-stealer," intending a non-gender generality. The distinction they suggested was that the person being taken into custody was not a slave until put into those conditions; such a person was free until captured and forced to endure bondage. They argued that enslavement of a person was the end result of a kidnapping, a "man stealing."

Walker, then, could admit that he helped men to escape from what he regarded as an illegal bondage. But slave-stealing? No one could be bound to another person, especially in a nation dedicated to freedom and equality, he argued. Walker considered "slave stealing" a charge "to which... I did, and do still, plead not guilty... [N]either was it ever my intention to commit it, and God forbid it ever should be."

In his second book, *A Brief View of American Chattelized Humanity, and Its Supports*, Walker claimed that church members would deny friendship to a sheep stealer while embracing "to their communion a *man*-stealer." For all of organized religion, he had harsh words: "...devils dressed in angel's robes, and hell presenting the semblance of paradise."

In *Trial and Imprisonment*, Walker freely underscored key words as he argued his innocence:

> Have not the fathers of our nation proclaimed to the world, by the Declaration of Independence, that 'all men are born <u>free</u> and <u>equal</u>'? and that they 'are endowed by their <u>creator</u> "with an inalienable (sic)

right to <u>life</u>, <u>liberty</u>, and the <u>pursuit of happiness</u>"? And is peaceably assisting those who have been robbed of these rights, without in any way infringing upon the rights of others, slave stealing? Was the benevolent and humane conduct of the Samaritan, in assisting the man who had fallen among thieves and was robbed, to get to the inn where he could be provided for, stealing? Is practicing that invaluable rule, of doing to others as we would they should do unto us under similar circumstances – enjoined upon all Christians, by Jesus Christ himself – slave stealing?

As to my infringing upon any man's rights, or trespassing upon any man's property, I deny it in toto. Neither Byrd C. Willis, George Willis, nor Robert C. Caldwell had any more right to Anthony Catlett, Charles Johnson, or Silas Scott than I or any other person had; nor did they ever have a right to those men. Under God, they had a right to themselves, which they had never forfeited; and those who claim them as property or chattels assume authority over the ALMIGHTY CREATOR of all things...

I know that many are ready to say [that slaves] are guaranteed to their holders by the laws of this government, and so are held by right. But neither this government nor these States have the right to guarantee one part of the home-born citizen to become the property of another party, nor to delegate the inherent rights and liberties of one portion to the absolute control and disposal of another portion. From whence do rights proceed? I repeat again that they never had such rights.

Walker in this plea cleared himself of suspicions initiated at the time of his departure from Pensacola and his capture near Cape Florida. He did not carry out his mission for personal gain, he explained. He wrote:

Be it known to all people that I made no bargain, contract, or agreement with any of those persons for any pecuniary remuneration for the aid and expense which I devoted to their escape from bondage, other than this: that I remarked to one or two of the men that if they succeeded in getting where they could be free, and accumulate something for themselves, they might give me what they felt able or disposed to in payment of the expense of their passage, as it might suit their convenience or circumstances; and when we arrived at New Providence they would be at liberty to go where they pleased, or remain there...

I wish to be distinctly understood, that no one but myself and those who were with me in the boat, had any knowledge of the undertaking; and I never gave the hint to any other person... It seems to have been a matter of wonder to many here at the North to know what I expected to gain by aiding those slaves to escape from their masters. In reply, I will also ask what did the Good Samaritan expect to gain by helping the man who had fallen among thieves, and was robbed and wounded, to a place of refuge and health? In Pensacola, and in the South generally, I believe there is but one opinion in regard to my motive – that it was to aid the slaves in obtaining their freedom, because I considered it their right.

      *   *   *   *

During that winter of 1844-45, Walker no doubt was anxious to have the Spring court term begin so he could get on with his life outside the jail.

"On May the 8th, soon after 10 a.m., I was conducted to the courthouse by the marshal and constable," Walker wrote. At last, ten months to the day since his capture, he was in court for what would be his final move towards freedom.

His appearance was on Thursday, the fourth day of the first 1845 session of the Escambia County Superior Court, and it started for him in much the same way as the November trial. "The judge inquired if I had counsel. I replied that I had not." In fact, Walker did not wish a lawyer. He explained later: "I had no desire to have counsel to manage my defense, not thinking it would be to my advantage, but [I preferred] to submit the case to the magnanimity of the jury; but as the judge had appointed counsel, I did not deem it advisable to reject it – confident that it would excite his displeasure, which would be likely to have an unfavorable effect on my case."

The judge appointed Alfred L. Woodward to defend Walker. He also named W. W. J. Kelly, assistant counsel. Walker apparently was being represented by the only other practicing lawyers in Pensacola besides Benjamin Wright. He never explained why Wright did not represent him in May. In November, Walker had said that he had a choice of three, and selected Wright.

Again, the hearing was postponed. "As Mr. Woodward was not duly informed in the case, we thought it best to have the trial put off until the next day... I remarked to my counsel that I consented to a present trial only on condition that all relating to the charges preferred against me should be placed before the court for final action; and that no part or section be kept back or reserved for a future consideration." No one could blame Walker. Only hours after being pilloried and branded in November, he had been informed of these new charges.

Walker met in his cell that Thursday afternoon with lawyer Woodward to discuss the legal conditions facing them. Walker would be tried on three criminal charges involving the runaway slaves; the suits for damages by the three slaveholders had been dropped. Such claims, Caldwell and the two Willises surely recognized, would never be paid even if upheld in a court. Jonathan Walker didn't have six dollars, let alone one hundred six thousand dollars.

The following morning, the jurors, one of whom was Pensacola's mayor, were called and seated. "The district attorney produced three indictments against me," Walker wrote, "charging me with assisting as many slaves to escape from their masters, etc." The slaves involved were Leonard and Phillip Johnson, both claimed by George Willis, and Harry Scott, a servant of Caldwell.

At this point in his narrative, written two months later, Walker began referring to himself in both the first person and the third person:

> A short discussion followed between the district attorney and counsel for the defendant, respecting the validity of the law in the multiplication of punishments for the same offense, and at different periods; but the court decided that I was liable to be tried separately for each charge alleged against me, although there was but one act in the commission.

As in November, Caldwell testified about accompanying Deputy Gonzalez to the Pensacola Navy Yard to meet Walker as he arrived, under arrest, from Key West. Caldwell told the court, Walker wrote, "that defendant told him that he had been for a long time of the opinion that whenever an opportunity offered, he would assist slaves to obtain their freedom."

There were no other prosecution witnesses. George Willis, perhaps chastened by his own court appearance the previous December for having pelted the pilloried Walker with rotten eggs, did not appear.

The defense called no witnesses. Walker was pleading not guilty to stealing slaves, but he did not contest charges that he broke Florida's law.

"The district attorney addressed the jury for a few minutes," Walker reported, "portraying the magnitude of the offense, the abuse of rights, etc., stating the results of the trials of Charles T. Torrey and Calvin Fairbanks, in Maryland and Kentucky – not forgetting to direct a few shot at the Northern 'fanatical abolitionists.'"

Now, at last, a jury was to hear persuasion on Walker's behalf. The assistant defense counsel, Kelly,

> ...next made some very appropriate and feeling remarks upon the administration and severity of the law already inflicted on the prisoner for the same offense, and his long confinement in prison and in chains, and the deprivation entailed upon his deeply afflicted family, etc. He was followed by A. L. Woodward, commenting on the multiplicity of punishments for the same offense when no act of an incendiary, or violent, character had appeared to aggravate the case, but the prisoner had quietly submitted, without a murmur, to the heaviest punishments the law could inflict upon him. He appealed to the magnanimity and humanity of the jury to put a stop to this persecution; neither the law nor the interest and welfare of the country demanded more; even common sense forbade it. He requested them to render a verdict which their conscience would approve, and not to heap vengeance on the head of their helpless fellow-being, etc. etc.

As Walker reported it, Woodward's final argument could be taken as providing an adequate defense by a Southern lawyer in a Southern community. He never suggested that Walker was not guilty. Rather, he simply suggested that sufficient punishment had been carried out. Even so, he did not ask for acquittal, only "a verdict which [the jury's] conscience would approve." When his attorneys sat, Walker must have felt that they had done their best. As well, he surely would have hoped that the lawyers had struck a responsive part of the jurors' hearts.

The judge did not encourage that. Walker reported that the judge

...charged the jury to find the prisoner guilty, and not to allow any sympathy for the accused to sway them from inflicting strict justice on him, for it was not the accused who had the right to complain of the severity of the law, or demand their sympathy; but those that were dead and their friends. The rights, safety, and honor of the country demanded justice from its courts.

A little over an hour after his arrival at the courthouse, Walker was led back to the jail while this second jury considered his punishment. During the few minutes' trip, he had time to ponder the judge's meaning in seeking sympathy for "those who were dead and their friends." Walker concluded: "I know not what he meant by this expression, except he had his eye on that old St. Domingo hobby horse, so often backed by the advocates of slavery." The judge was apparently reminding jurors of a slave uprising in the island nation of San Domingo only two years before. This was another of the times' frequent suggestions that the black majority was capable of insurrection, of taking over the white population and their possessions in America. The people of color in the Caribbean nation, now called the Dominican Republic, had declared their independence. The island that Columbus called Hispaniola, and which also includes Haiti, had been claimed over the centuries by the French and Spanish, and even by Haitians. Despite the 1843 uprising, border disputes, and even a final submission to Spanish invaders, were to continue until Dominicans gained permanent independence in 1865.

Returning once more to the jail building on Intedencia Street, Walker had no doubt in his mind about the finding; he had, after all, admitted guilt. His fear was that new punishment would be administered. He probably enjoyed the two brief walks outdoors; he had not been away from the brick prison in nearly six months. It would have been a special relief because he had been shackled in iron since his attempted escape in February.

No word came that Friday, May 10, and Walker was again secured in chains. The next day, he was given a note from attorney Kelly. The jury had reported. The magistrate apparently did not consider it necessary, or courteous, to have the defendant present when the verdict was read. Nor did Kelly and the chief defender, Albert Woodward, deem it important to speak with their client.

Freedom at Last

The jury had returned that morning, Kelly wrote, and had, as expected, found Walker guilty on all counts. For punishment, the jury's recommendations were surprisingly pleasing. The jurors had "assessed me a fine of five dollars in each case; and that I was to remain in custody until the fines and costs were paid."

Having been fined $150 on the earlier charges, Walker now owed $165 in fines, plus court costs. He had many times over served the fifteen days ordered in November. Now, to gain his freedom, he had to come up with the $165 in fines, plus costs, which had been put at $208.05 until early December. That figure must have doubled by May.

How much money did the levy against Walker represent? More than a man could earn from working for five months – for each one hundred dollars. In *A History of Cape Cod*, Henry Kittredge reported: "The Honorable Zeno Scudder, of Osterville, has calculated that a fisherman's earnings for four months for the decade between 1841 and 1851 were sixty-three dollars. The government bonus brought the figure up to seventy-seven dollars." That averaged out to about nineteen dollars a month. In Florida, wages were not much different for a jail guard. The bills charged Walker included a guard pay of $87.50 for four months' work, averaging a little over twenty dollars a month. By comparison, Walker had possessed fifteen dollars when he arrived at the Pensacola Jail, and had been doling it out, along with incoming gifts of money, for food and other small needs. So he had virtually nothing. The amount of the fine alone would have been impossible to raise without help for a man in Jonathan Walker's situation .

*   *   *   *

Once more, Jonathan Walker was in the familiar jail cell with no known prospects for immediate help. He easily would have slipped back into jail routine. Writing was part of that routine, and he pulled together his thoughts on the newest trial:

> The judge, district attorney, and my counsel were slaveholders, and some of the jury also. Surrounded by slaveholders, and in a section of the country where slavery is held to be one of their most sacred rights, what had I to expect at their hands; [I who was] well known, and thoroughly proved to be hostile in the highest degree to the system of American slavery, and placed in their power, subject to their will, for the commission of an act which is now held to be a capital offense, and punishable with death?

Given those conditions, Walker was bound to appreciate the relative leniency of the punishment. In fact, he wrote later, he was satisfied that humanity had won a small victory in Pensacola that day:

> In consideration of these, and some other things which might be brought into the account, it shows that vengeance has not yet buried humanity, nor destroyed all the sympathy existing between men and

those whose opinion differs from their own upon subjects of great importance. The jury was an intelligent one... and I submitted my case cheerfully to their decision, confident that the verdict would be as mild as their responsible situation would admit of; and my expectations were more than realized; for which mild and humane verdict they are entitled to my grateful thanks and high consideration, for they have shown themselves to be untrammeled by prejudice, or actuated by revenge toward their helpless fellow-being.

I thought the judge manifested a considerable degree of prejudice against me, especially in this last trial; "Surely oppression maketh a wise man mad." But I saw no display of any unkind feelings from any other person, in or out of court, except by those who considered themselves so grievously injured and imposed upon by my allowing some of their two-legged chattels to walk off in company with me; or rather, to allow the wind to blow them away from that mill which is constantly grinding the faces of the poor, and whose owner, like the greedy horseleech, thirsts for more, "and saith, it is not enough."

    *   *   *   *

Jonathan Walker's court costs, fines, and jail expenses were marked paid by Marshal Ebenezer Dorr on Tuesday, May 20, 1845. The count of calendar days is impressive:

It had been **ten days** since Walker's second trial,
105 days since his attempted escape from jail,
186 days since the conclusion of his first trial on November 16, 1844,
306 days since he had been brought in chains to Pensacola on July 19
317 days since his capture on July 8 off Carysfort Reef.
256 days had been spent alone, "in solitary confinement"
173 days bound with irons and chains.

Walker had waited six months, following the fruitless visit by Thomas M. Blount, for someone to arrive with money to release him. The receipt signed by Dorr – now the sheriff but apparently still carrying out some of the marshal's duties – was made out to "C. C. Keyser, Esq.," indicating Keyser was an attorney hired to deliver the money.

Walker wrote only that "a friend" provided the funds. It is likely that he did not know the details, and mistakenly may even have thought that a Harwich sea captain had put up all the money. It is easy to imagine such a misunderstanding taking place during the confusing period in which Walker prepared to leave the jail. For days, he had persisted again in efforts to get a detailed billing from the various authorities.

In fact, the money was raised by the Walker Committee in Massachusetts. In all, it appears that nine hundred dollars was needed, nearly six hundred to gain Walker's release and the rest, apparently, to pay Keyser's fee and to provide Walker with some money for the trip home to Cape Cod. An explanation of the sources was not to come for another year.

The bill came to $597.055. (Between 1793 and 1857, the United States minted a copper half-cent.) The total, just under $600, represented perhaps as much as three years' work for a man of Walker's skills.

The itemization of Walker's bill was in two parts. The first totaled $385.05 and included the following: cost of court and fines in seven suits, $291.05; paid witness [Captain Richard Roberts] from Key West, $57.75; paid witness R. C. Caldwell, $3.75 and $2.50 [he testified in both November and May]; and Deputy Marshal Gonzalez "for travelling to Navy Yard, to arrest," $3. The second part of the bill totaled $238 and one-half penny, as follows: lock for jail, 87 1/2 cents; blacksmith, repairing jail, $9.13; D. Quina, for guarding jail, etc., $87.50; City of Pensacola for use of jail, $25; and city jailer for board up to May 23, 1845, $115.50.

Again, no explanation was offered for differences in mathematics. The charge for Walker's meals figures out to 308 days at 37.5 cents per day, making the final meal on May 23, although the receipt is dated May 20. Moreover, Walker wrote in July: "I have been detained in prison until the 16th of June, when, after having undergone a second trial... I was released by the liberality of friends in paying the fines and costs of prosecution, which were charged against me."

It is possible, in a time when arranging transportation and getting sufficient funds for travel were not accomplished quickly, that Walker stayed in jail until mid-June as an unshackled "guest," being permitted to leave at will to find a northbound ship on which he might work his way home.

*   *   *   *

Walker took time to check the bills, noting particularly the ten-dollar charge for buying (87.5 cents) and installing ($9.13) a jail lock after his attempted February escape. Walker wrote: "A slave man came to the jail one day and worked on the doors about two hours, and fastened a piece of iron athwart an aperture in the door, through which I had been in the habit of receiving my food; and I do not know what the 'etc.' is for, except for riveting the irons on my leg, and making the branding iron."

By underlining "branding iron," Walker seemed to be calling attention to an unspeakable spite, as if the hangman were to charge the victim the cost of the rope. It is doubtful that he thought the slave had actually forged the iron fashioned with the letter "S."

Walker added: "For what purpose the lock was used I know not. I am sure it was not used on any of the jail doors, for the same locks that were on the doors when I went there were on the doors when I left."

His penalty for attempted escape, then, included more than a hundred additional days in chains – and ten dollars in costs.

And just as there appears to be no record of the use of the new lock, history has not left us any information about the "S" branding iron made especially for Jonathan Walker.

Here are some of Walker's other comments on the bills:

"City of Pensacola, to use of Jail, $25." This to me, I confess, is rather a singular charge to bring against a prisoner.

"City marshal's bill for board," was at the rate of 37 1/2 cents per day; but a small part of which was expended for me, as I was under the necessity of using about forty dollars to provide myself with food, which consisted mostly of bread and molasses.

"Cost of court and fines, in seven suits, $291.05." The fines were one hundred and sixty-five dollars, and the cost of court consisted of the district attorney's, marshal's, and clerk's fees, and the evidence before the grand jury. There were other charges in the case, and I suppose they were brought against the United States; and the whole cost and expense would have been charged to the United States if my friends had not paid it in order to [gain] my release...

A special guard had been hired at the jail for approximately four months, from Walker's arrival in July until his first court trial. Walker's book lists the guard as "D. Quina," which is possibly a typographical error. Quina was a common name in Pensacola and the family of Desiderio Juan Quina was especially close to jailkeeper Francis Torward. Desiderio Quina, Jr., born about 1817, was a doctor, according to Sutton, so it is unlikely he was a prison guard. He had a son, Desiderio the third, who would have been too young to serve as a guard in 1844-1845. It is possible, then, that Torward hired the elder Quina, who had been Torward's guardian when Torward was a boy. Quina would have been about sixty-nine years old at the time.

Of the guard, Walker wrote: "The charge for guarding the jail, $87.50, is a mooted point with me; at one time I was told that it was guarded to prevent people without from molesting me, and at another time that it was guarded to prevent my escape from prison; but I think, probably, more to make a show than anything else."

During most of the four months under guard, Walker was ill, at times too weak to stand, and locked in foot chains. Walker's comment illustrates his keen awareness of the importance that authorities may have placed on demonstrating to pro-slavery citizens – and the Pensacola *Gazette*'s editor – that the strictest security was being applied against this slave-stealer from Massachusetts.

*　　　　*　　　　*　　　　*

But here, at last, his bills paid, Jonathan Walker was free to follow his own will. His life had been interrupted by his attempt to help seven slaves escape. He had not gone to Florida for this adventure, at least not knowingly. The instincts that had led him to agree to help the seven men, and had carried

Freedom at Last

NEW-YORK, July 12, 1845.

WM. LLOYD GARRISON:

DEAR FRIEND—You will be rejoiced to hear of the safe arrival in New-York of that noble, devoted and suffering friend of the slave, JONATHAN WALKER. I have just had the pleasure of taking him by the hand, in the Anti-Slavery Office. He arrived yesterday, in the brig Lowber, from Pensacola, and will leave here on Monday, for his home in Harwich, Mass. His health has evidently suffered some during his long and painful confinement in the dungeon of Pensacola; but in despite of these sufferings, he is one of the noblest specimens of that daring and hardy race of 'Massachusetts men' that I have ever seen. His apparel, however, indicates the hardships through which he has passed, and the consequent poverty to which these human (?) harpies have reduced him.

On the palm and ball of his right hand, the letters

S S

of about double this size and rudely formed, are distinctly visible, burnt in with the red-hot branding iron of the Slave Court—THE UNITED STATES SLAVE COURT IN FLORIDA. I need not say, give him a warm reception in Boston.

Truly yours,   ELIAS SMITH.

A correspondent for The Liberator relayed word quickly in 1845 that Jonathan Walker had set foot in a non-slave state after a year in the Pensacola jail. Elias Smith and many others – Walker included – served as unpaid, voluntary reporters for the abolitionist newspaper. Editor William Lloyd Garrison caught his readers' attention by setting the letters "SS" in one inch high black type. For a time, Garrison referred to the Cape Cod sailor as "the Pensacola hero." The admiration was mutual. Jonathan and Jane named their twin son Lloyd Garrison Walker in honor of the editor.

him through the year-long punishment in Pensacola, were with him now as he walked out the door of the jail for the last time. The fateful event that kept him in Pensacola for nearly a year had changed his life – forever.

As he headed away from Intedencia Street towards the docks and a trip home, Walker may not yet have decided that abolitionism was where he belonged. But the same instincts that had served him this past year were to guide him in a new undertaking as he sailed north. Jonathan Walker probably was unaware of how well known he had become, and he certainly did not know how that fame would determine his destiny for the next years of his life. He knew only that he was free, and that more than two million of his countrymen were still enslaved. On these two conditions would rest Jonathan Walker's destiny.

I had scarcely returned to my family when I received pressing invitations
from various quarters, and numerous friends of the slave,
to come among them, or go forth and preach the anti-slavery gospel.
Jonathan Walker, *National Anti-Slavery Standard*

CHAPTER 11   To Cast in My Mite for God's Poor

If being in jail for stealing slaves had put Jonathan Walker in the proverbial frying pan, he was about to land in the fire of abolitionism with his departure in June 1845 from the Pensacola Jail.

His long journey home to Massachusetts began quietly enough. He had to ask around about outbound ships from the Pensacola wharf. Arranging the trip would have taken a few days. He may have been allowed to stay at the city jail, a kind of prison alumnus guest. Or, he might have had somewhere in the city a friend brave enough to be host to the erstwhile prisoner. It's not unlikely that he would have had to work aboard the ship carrying him home. He may have had a few dollars from the friends who had paid his court fine, but not enough to be a paying passenger. Somewhere near June 20, he would have walked the few blocks to the town's wharf; the Navy Yard eight miles away was reserved for government vessels.

Walker boarded the brig *Lowellan*, sailing first southward around Florida's long peninsula. This must have evoked memories of his trip a year earlier, especially sailing the Straits of Florida and towards Biscayne Bay and Cape Florida, where his own small boat had been confiscated and he and his seven passengers taken prisoners. But he was not long detracted, if at all. As the *Lowellan* edged northward along the Atlantic coastline through the last days of June and the first two weeks in July, Walker filled hundreds of pages, writing probably all of his account of his *Trial and Imprisonment* and perhaps some of his smaller book on the slave as property – chattelization.

155

Jonathan Walker The Man with the Branded Hand

New Englanders knew that Walker had been released, and they were being exhorted in *The Liberator* by Garrison "to see this Christian martyr, face to face, that we may thank him for what he has done, and bless him for what he has suffered in the cause of God and Liberty." The Boston *Emancipator and Weekly Chronicle* declared, "His branded hand must be seen all over Massachusetts."

When Walker stepped off the brig in New York City, he brought with him the bundle of paper he had covered with his sweeping, clear handwriting. Besides authoring the autobiography and educational pamphlet, he would have continued his mission as a confirmed letter writer. Long before carbon paper and photocopy machines, he carefully replicated much of what he wrote. Some copies were made for his own records, many to be distributed to other sources for publication.

His first action, probably even before looking for transportation to Massachusetts and his family at home, was to post a letter he had written in response to the support given him the previous fall by the British and Foreign Anti-Slavery Society. A copy was sent to Garrison's *Liberator*. Dated July 12, 1845, the letter to London began: "I heartily respond, gentlemen, to the declaration in the last clause of the resolution which you adopted, that 'the laws under which we were to be arraigned are utterly disgraceful to a civilized community, and in the highest degree repugnant to the *spirit* and *precepts* of the *gospel*.'" He enclosed a copy of the Florida Legislative Council's select joint committee report recommending death for those who violated Florida's law against stealing slaves.

That same Saturday, Elias Smith hurried off a note to "Dear Friend" Garrison. Six days later, it was printed in the July 18 *Liberator*:

> You will be rejoiced to hear of the safe arrival in New York of that noble, devoted, and suffering friend of the slave, Jonathan Walker. I have just had the pleasure of taking him by the hand, in the Anti-Slavery Office. He... will leave here on Monday for his home in Harwich, Massachusetts. His health has evidently suffered some during his long and painful confinement in the dungeon of Pensacola; but in spite of these sufferings, he is one of the noblest specimens of that daring and hardy race of "Massachusetts men" that I have ever seen. His apparel, however, indicates the hardships through which he has passed, and the consequent poverty to which these human (?) harpies have reduced him. On the palm and ball of his right hand, the letters SS of about this size [printed by Garrison in letters almost three-fourths of an inch high] and rudely formed, are distinctly visible, burnt in with the red-hot branding iron of the Slave Court – THE UNITED STATES SLAVE COURT IN FLORIDA. I need not say, give him a warm reception in Boston.

To Cast in My Mite for God's Poor

Before sailing to New England, Walker stopped by the office of the *National Anti-Slavery Standard*. This weekly newspaper had been established by the American Anti-Slavery Society in May, 1840, to replace the *Emancipator*. He left with Sydney H. Gay a copy of the letter he had posted to London. He probably thanked the newspaper for its reports on his experiences. Editor Gay was not one to miss the opportunity to keep readers informed of abolitionists' activities, especially of one as newsworthy as Jonathan Walker. He asked Walker to "furnish an occasional article." Walker made no promises to Gay, a youthful lawyer who had a year earlier assumed the New York editorship after lecturing against slavery in New England. "My objection," Walker recalled later, "was my inability in consequence of not having the benefit of an education. Were it otherwise with me, I should have been glad to have contributed something to the columns of the *Standard*."

Garrison, meantime, editorialized: "[Walker's arrival] will create a thrilling sensation in the breasts of thousands who have deplored the imprisonment of the noble Walker as among the blackest atrocities of the age. We presume he is now with his long bereaved family – and what a meeting it must have been to them all!"

*   *   *   *

The family's reunion in Massachusetts, indeed, must have been pleasant but, typical of Jonathan Walker, it would have been busy, involved, and relatively short for a man who had spent most of the last eight years living in Florida. During his first week or so back home, he undoubtedly made the rounds of his many friends and relatives, thanking the Nickersons, the Underwoods, Loring Moody, and others for their efforts to help Jane and the children during his recent nineteen months' absence.

He must have been jolted the first time he was told, "We never expected to see you here again." He reported that he also often heard the question, "How is it that they let you come so soon?"

His answer was driven by his charitable and considerate disposition:

> Although what they term the laws of Florida could have been executed with greater severity, and I subjected to more cost and longer imprisonment, yet there was a strong abhorrence on the part of the citizens of Pensacola, generally, to any further infliction of punishment; and many were opposed to its execution thus far. During my residence in Pensacola, I had formed an acquaintance with most of the people of that place, and was on social and friendly terms with all; never having any difficulty or misunderstanding with any.

> Another reason is that there was, as I believe I have before stated, but one opinion as to the motives which induced me to commit the act for which I was called to suffer; all seeing that I was acting upon the principle which I believed to be true, just, and right... All the people saw that I was not influenced by pecuniary considerations, and that I

had no intention of trespass or fraud upon the rights of property of anyone.

There was less indignant feeling towards me on another account. A large part of the inhabitants were Creoles (descendants of French and Spanish parents), and not generally so irresistibly devoted to the system of slavery as the American-born and bred citizens were; and this Creole population manifested more sympathy for me than the rest of the community did.

On Cape Cod, the Yarmouth *Register*, which had not reported on Walker's activities since recording his arrest a year earlier, gave an account of his release in its July 24, 1845, edition. That news story included, without attribution, a comment probably copied from the New York *Tribune* of a few days earlier. The New York editor's reasoning, as repeated in *The Liberator*, was as follows:

If the slaves had been *white*, and Capt. Walker had endangered his life in taking them away from the Arabs, the brand would have been deemed a mark of honor in every part of the country, and Congress would have hastened to testify the respect and gratitude of the nation for his services. But the slaves were black and held in bondage under the authority of U.S. law, and we suppose there can be no doubt that he was a rogue! Hail, Columbia!

The *Register*'s version lacked the wit of the *Tribune* in asserting: "If the slaves had been white and he had freed them from Arabs, then he would have been a hero; because they were black and protected by U.S. law, he is therefore a rogue."

*   *   *   *

On his Cape Cod return, Walker may have spent time going over his writings, preparing to offer more of them for publication. "Having never been favored with an education, and laboring under the disadvantage of writing hastily on my passage home, as I found opportunity," Walker wrote, "the narrative will not be so attractive as it otherwise might be."

It was not long before he undertook a trip to Boston. Eighty miles overland, in a coach or a saddle, would have required two days' travel. More likely, Walker would have gone by the popular packet trip through Cape Cod Bay to Boston Harbor. Such a trip could take from six hours to as much as thirty hours. Twenty-five to fifty passengers would be charged $1.50 each for the round trip – including meals.

We can wonder how Jane responded when Jonathan told her, having been home perhaps a week, that he was leaving for a few days. Jane would not have been surprised had anyone been able to tell her that Jonathan's trip was, in fact, the start of what would become a long journey in behalf of emancipation for the slaves, one that would take him away from his family more often than

To Cast in My Mite for God's Poor

not over the next six years, over uncounted miles through a dozen states while giving hundreds of lectures before thousands of men and women.

Nor would Jane Walker have been unnerved to know that her husband's arrival in Boston was to begin his career as an abolitionist lecturer, "more like a dream than reality," as her husband would say later. Walker described this new beginning as an accident, in a letter that Garrison published in *The Liberator*:

> On arriving in [Boston] the evening of [July] the 24th, I saw in *The Liberator* a notice of a meeting to be held in Lynn on the evening of the 27th, to receive Jonathan Walker, etc. This to me was somewhat unexpected, and I thought rather strange... [I]n a few days I found myself, for the first time, in that place – warmly greeted by many friends of humanity... I went to the Lyceum Hall, which was soon filled to overflowing with a delightful audience. The meeting was addressed by several able speakers, who were listened to with attention throughout.

MASS MEETING IN LYNN!

A MASS MEETING will be held in Lynn, on Sunday ext, at 6 o'clock, P. M. in the open air, if pleasant, receive Capt. JONATHAN WALKER, the Here Pensacola. An immense gathering is expected om Lynn and the neighboring towns. Several able eakers will be present.

The Liberator item that attracted Walker into a public mission.

Music often played a part in abolitionist programs, and the Lynn audience was to hear the four singing Hutchinson brothers, Jesse, Judson, Asa, and John. From a New Hampshire Baptist church choir, they had begun a long career as anti-slavery advocates by singing in Lynn in 1841.

Later, a Boston newspaper reported in 1901, "With original songs written in the heat of the anti-slavery excitement, they went about the country, and became famous as a sort of band of secular revivalists. Sometimes they appeared with Wendell Phillips, William Lloyd Garrison, Theodore Parker, N. P. Rogers, Parker Pillsbury, and other great advocates of abolition, supplying the music for these occasions..."

Walker was buoyed by his Lynn experience in more ways than one. He wrote:

> A collection was taken up to pay for the use of the hall, the surplus to be presented to me as a token of sympathy for myself and family; and with sincere gratitude I acknowledge the receipt of twenty dollars from the kind-hearted people of Lynn. The best feeling seemed to pervade

the whole audience, which numbered 1,000 to 1,500. My having been chained up in solitary cell so long, excluded from society, and looked upon as an outcast among men – and from thence ushered into a spacious hall, among New England's pride and beauty – completely unhinged the mind, and almost prevented the power of utterance. It seemed more like a dream than reality.

Not long after, Walker attended a "First of August" rally in Waltham, south of Boston. *The Liberator* reported:

MIDDLESEX AND SUFFOLK COUNTIES.

The abolitionists of Middlesex and Suffolk Counties, and the people generally, will unite in the celebration of the anniversary of West India Emancipation by a Festival in HARRINGTON'S GROVE, WALTHAM, on the 1st of August.

Among the distinguished friends of emancipation who will be present, are Ralph Waldo Emerson, Capt. Jonathan Walker, S. S., (Slave Savior,) the Hero of Pensacola, Loring Moody, Wm. I. Bowditch, Esq., of Boston, James N. Buffum, and Hon. Henry Wilson of Natick.

Walker could not help himself. The magnetism of such gatherings – the power of exhortative speech-making, the music, the applause of hundreds of supporters, perhaps even the admiration – was drawing him directly away from the home hearth. Perhaps he felt about being away so often from his wife and children the way another developing abolitionist did. Writing from the other end of Massachusetts, John Brown was managing Perkins & Brown, a wool marketing cooperative in Springfield. When, in October 1846, the Browns' daughter, Ruth, accidentally caused the fatal scalding of her year-old sister, Amelia, John Brown wrote home:

My Dear Afflicted Wife and Children:

Providence seems to lay a heavy burden and responsibility on you, my dear Mary, but I trust you will be enabled to bear it in some measure as you ought. I exceedingly regret that I am unable to return and be present to share your trials with you... If I had a real sense of my habitual neglect of my family's eternal interests, I should probably go crazy.

*   *   *   *

Jonathan Walker had been temporarily sidetracked to Lynn and the abolitionist gathering when he went to Boston only two weeks after returning to Cape Cod. The purpose of the trip was to see about the publication of his account of his Florida adventure. Possibly on Sydney Gay's recommendation, he made one of his first stops at the Cornhill office of the American Anti-Slavery

To Cast in My Mite for God's Poor

Society, which, two years earlier, had decided to relocate its national headquarters to Boston from New York City. Because most executive committee members lived in Massachusetts, having a Boston office made it convenient for them to meet frequently.

Walker received immediate encouragement from Maria Weston Chapman. She was, Sterling wrote, "the dominant figure in the Boston Female Anti-Slavery Society as well as a powerful force in the Massachusetts and American Anti-Slavery societies." She was probably also the best person Walker could have talked to about his Pensacola report. Educated in England, she was a former principal of Boston's Young Ladies High School. Now thirty-nine years old, she was known also for writing editorials published in *The Liberator*. A year earlier, she had served as co-editor of the *Standard* along with Sydney Gay and Edmund Quincy.

Chapman recalled Walker's visit in a preface that she wrote to introduce his book:

> On his return from Florida, after his release, Captain Walker called on me with the manuscript narrative of his trial and imprisonment. In common with very many of the members of the American Anti-Slavery Society, I had long known his character as a man of the strictest veracity and the highest conscientiousness; and his narrative seemed to me to cast so strong a light upon the religion, the moral, and the political condition of the United States, from the practical workings of their great organic law – the Constitution – down to the minutest of the territorial usages and enactments which result from that law; and to exhibit in so clear a view the contrast between the principles and ideas which at present govern the public mind, and those which are beginning to struggle for the mastery, that I could not but warmly urge this publication.

Walker had prepared the manuscript, she said, "for the action of his friends." But a wider audience would benefit, she wrote. Chapman cited

> ...those who doubt whether the North is as guilty as the South with respect to slavery; ...those who, while they condemn slavery, at the same time assert that its extinction may be best promoted by studied silence, and... those, too, who believe the abolitionists to be instigated by a bitter, unkind, fanatical and insurrectionary spirit... And there are others who, honoring the holy cause and respecting the disinterestedness of abolitionists, yet justify themselves in standing aloof from the movement under the idea of being better able to befriend the cause by refusing to be numbered among its adherents...

> It was for the sake of all these classes that I most earnestly urged Captain Walker to give to the public, whose great majority these compose, the manuscript...

Walker, despite his protestations of being uneducated, was a prolific writer and needed no urging. Walker, Chapman noted,

> ...had not been able to provide a completely detailed account, out of regard to the safety of individuals whose liberties and lives their publication would endanger; yet what could, better than such a fact, illustrate the condition of slaves and freemen in the United States of North America; or better plead the cause of those few of the inhabitants who are pronounced by the rest to be over-zealous, because they have been the first to perceive what all will soon be obliged to acknowledge – that the liberties of our land are gone?
>
> ...This is a painful tale for an American to read, and think, meanwhile, that it is circulating through the civilized world... It will be a painful tale for all to whom the carefully concealed features and inevitable consequences of the slave system have never before been exhibited.

Walker had determined to write a clear, factual account of his adventure. When he abandoned his reportorial writing to express an opinion, he usually made clear that that was what he was doing. On a few occasions, he resorted to mild parody and satire to express his disrespect for an attitude or an action. Walker wrote:

> As to the persons whose names I have here been using, I have no inclination to misrepresent or abuse them, for I delight not in vilifying my fellow-creatures, but would far rather speak well of them; and what I have here said has been under a sense of deep moral feeling, and I have suppressed much that might have been said with propriety, and in strict accordance with truth. But if any... can show in any instance where I have misused them, I will hasten to make public confession and beg their pardon.

*   *   *   *

Soon after Walker's Boston visit, Maria Chapman sent the handwritten manuscript – 119 printed pages including Chapman's homilic preface and Walker's rambling appendix – to George A. Curtis with instructions to begin the stereotype work. Curtis' New England Type and Stereotype Foundry delivered the metal forms for printing to Dow & Jackson's Power Press.

The first page carried the sentence-length title on nine lines. The author's name was in the largest type – all capital letters. It read:

Trial and Imprisonment of
JONATHAN WALKER
at Pensacola, Florida,
for Aiding Slaves to Escape from Bondage.
With an Appendix, Containing a Sketch of His Life.

To Cast in My Mite for God's Poor

Walker's book was published in the fall of 1845, and sold well enough that a second edition was published in 1846, including his photograph. His background was still not well known. Even in a fifteen-page appendix, he gave very little detail of his early life.

While the manuscript was still at the printer's, Parker Pillsbury used expansive rhetoric before a Massachusetts abolitionist gathering to predict the popularity of Walker's book: "A full account of the diabolical transactions is in press, and will in a few days be given to the public. It will startle the deeps. It will be quoted in the British Parliament, in the Mexican Congress, in every council chamber where slavery is despised, to the disgrace and execration of this infamous nation."

With the publication of Walker's sometimes dry, sometimes charged reportage, his story was now broadcast throughout the land. As Buckmaster put it, Walker's story "sizzled through the North like the branding iron on his skin."

*   *   *   *

Walker was entitled to a few weeks, or even months, for rehabilitation. There is no record that he took any time for him and Jane alone together. Perhaps his charitable friends had provided enough money for Jonathan to delay the inevitable decision about the future. Ultimately, of course, he would head into his future with the boldness he had brought to sailing into the wind. What would he do to support his family?

As she may have done nearly a decade before, Jane Walker could well have attempted to get her husband to settle down – finally – in Massachusetts. These were boom times on Cape Cod. As early as 1837, according to local historian Paul Mangelinkx, six hundred sixty-eight salt works were counted. On more than thirteen million feet of flats, ocean salt was dried to produce 626,364 bushels a year, not including byproducts such as Epsom and Glauber salts. This huge industry along the Cape's shores had grown from a little solar heat experiment to evaporate sea water begun by John Sears of Dennis in 1776. By 1840, Mangelinkx wrote, a census attributed to little Cape Cod ten tanneries, fifty-one gristmills, eight ironworks, two ropeworks, three cotton mills, two woolen mills, two glass factories, three hat factories producing twenty-two thousand palm leaf hats a year, several shoe factories making nearly twenty-five thousand pairs in 1837, and eight hundred forty shops and other commercial businesses.

Farming had an exciting success unique to Harwich. Sea Captain Alvan Cahoon in 1845 was promoting the use of a new bog crop for commercial sales. Now that sugar was more readily available, the Cape's extensive acres of the tart cranberry were being made into a tasty sauce. Zebina Small and Nathaniel Robbins were among the leading growers. Cape Cod and Massachusetts were to become the nation's top producer.

Jonathan Walker The Man with the Branded Hand

Perhaps, aware of all this activity, Walker was tempted to return to the plant and harvest cycle on which he had spent the first sixteen years of his life on his father's farm. And only just below the surface lay his hope of pioneering a western region.

For men with Jonathan's skills, there was even greater excitement in New England with the burgeoning ship building industry. Anthony Thacher laid the keels for a small fleet of vessels in Harwich and Chatham. Such activity was common around the Cape's harbors. In East Dennis, the Shiverick boatyard had been earning national fame, and a fortune, in constructing the famous clipper ships. Other Barnstable County boatyards were building the smaller packet ships that carried passengers and salt between coastal communities.

Jonathan Walker, now at the age of forty-six, was barely able to feed his family, even when employed. But he was an excellent boatwright. He would have had no difficulty getting employment with Thacher or Shiverick. Tutored in carpentry on the home farm and at the mill his grandfather and father had operated in Harwich, Jonathan had honed his skills in shipyards throughout the South. He had built a twelve-ton vessel in Fairhaven in 1835, a small boat in Mexico in 1836 for his runs to New Orleans, and apparently another in Mobile, Alabama, during the winter of 1843-44. Such a man would have been drawn to visit these busy yards on Cape Cod, even without his wife's encouragement. Walker would have followed his sense of curiosity, and perhaps even have respected Jane's request that he at least check into the possibilities of working on the Cape.

When it came down to deciding his future, Jonathan would follow his heart. And Jane, as she had done during the more than twenty years of their marriage, would not have pressed him to act otherwise. Her contribution to the cause of freedom for the slaves was made by keeping the home and supporting, probably even encouraging, her husband. Even had she wanted to join Jonathan in an active role, Jane would have had difficulty. Women were not welcomed in public affairs.

Meantime, Jonathan was being invited to anti-slavery meetings. Five days after the flattering Lynn gathering, he was in Waltham for the picnic celebrating the West Indian Emancipation. People came from fifty miles around to see and hear him. Jonathan knew, almost without reflection, that his future did not lie in a boatyard. From correspondence received during his stay in Pensacola, from conversations with people on the trip home and on the Cape, and now at the Lynn and Waltham meetings, Walker knew he had become a celebrity. An incident soon after his return to New England illustrates that.

In its September 26, 1845, edition, Garrison's *Liberator* reprinted from the *Christian World* newspaper a story written by "a clergyman" recounting the plight of a little boy wearing rags on a train between Boston and Fall River. When the boy declined to ask passengers for donations,

> ...a fine, benevolent looking individual arose in a seat near me and unostentatiously offered to plead for him, who would not prefer his

own claim. Most successful was the warm-hearted appeal which he made to the passengers, and ten dollars were collected. [The man was Jonathan Walker] and the branded hand well attested the fact...Yes, on this man, so benevolent, with a heart so tender, had the friends of slavery wreaked their shameful vengeance.

 *   *   *   *

Such recognition, and the acclaim he was being given at anti-slavery conventions, were like hooks pulling Walker into the tent of abolitionist lecture tours. Garrison seemed to be leading the campaign:

As soon as practicable, we hope he will make his appearance before thronging multitudes in this Commonwealth and elsewhere, and lift up THAT BRANDED HAND in their presence, that thus a fire may be kindled against slavery that shall not cease to burn till the shackles of every slave be melted, and the trump of jubilee sounded throughout the land. We long to see this Christian martyr, face to face, that we may thank him for what he has done, and bless him for what he has suffered, in the cause of God and liberty.

Equally stirring words had been formed into poetry within six weeks of Walker's returning to Cape Cod by John Greenleaf Whittier, thirty-seven years old and perhaps America's best-known anti-slavery poet. The fifty-two lines of his poem, "The Branded Hand," first appeared on August 6, 1845, in the Boston *Emancipator and Weekly Chronicle* with "an exact representation" of the branded hand. The drawing was copied from a daguerreotype image made by Albert Southworth. *The Liberator* introduced Whittier's poem that August 15, and soon it was being reprinted in newspapers throughout the country. Another poet's work, "March! Here Comes the Branded Hand!," was offered in the *Emancipator* on August 25, and was soon forgotten.

During those first weeks of Walker's return to Massachusetts, the historic photograph had been made of the branded hand. This was achieved by the early process known as daguerreotype, a form of etching on silver-coated copper plates that was transferred to paper. The photography was arranged by H. I. Bowditch, the Harvard physician-professor who had headed one of Walker's support committees. The original work, now in the collection of the Massachusetts Historical Society, is attributed to the firm of Southworth and Hawes, but generally acknowledged as the work of Albert Southworth

 *   *   *   *

Now, the time had come for Jonathan Walker to move into his future. Would a man who had already invested so much of his life on behalf of slaves; would a man who believed so strongly in equality; would a man so encouraged; would Jonathan Walker now turn his back on the plight of the African American?

In a letter to Sydney Gay at the *National Anti-Slavery Standard*, Walker described how he made his choice:

Jonathan Walker The Man with the Branded Hand

I had scarcely returned to my family when I received pressing invitations from various quarters, and numerous friends of the slave, to come among them, or go forth and preach the anti-slavery gospel. Feeling that my experience, and a simple statement of the facts that came under my knowledge, might prevail with some well-disposed persons to take a deeper interest in behalf of our down-trodden and brutalized brothers and sisters, I went forth to cast in my mite for God's poor, and from that time...

Jonathan Walker had decided. His sailing career was behind him now. He would put aside his dream of returning to the soil out West. For now, he had a calling. He had a ministry. He *was* an abolitionist.

*   *   *   *

Walker was quickly dedicated to his new life as a lecturer. A typical notice of a visit follows:

Jonathan Walker is now free and will be in Philadelphia at the time of the Fair. A public meeting will be called, which he has consented to address. His history is deeply interesting. It is published in a book of 119 pages, and for sale, price 25 cents, at the Anti-Slavery Office, 31 North Fifth Street. As he is not expected to remain long with us, those who wish to see his BRANDED HAND and to hear the tale of his wrongs and persecutions ought to be in the city at the time. Remember the 18th, 19th, and 20th days of December! Let them be devoted to the slave, whether you come to the city or not.

By deciding to dedicate the next years to standing for equality, Jonathan Walker was aware that he was placing a major responsibility on others. He could not hope to earn enough money to travel extensively while maintaining his large family. Those who had helped Jane with living expenses, and had helped Jonathan with funds to meet his Pensacola obligations, now would be called upon for new pledges. Walker may have been attempting to help sustain that aid by taking care to acknowledge all gifts. His doing so in *The Liberator* helped contribute to the New Englanders's record of charity. The newspaper ran such an acknowledgement on December 19, 1845, for "the reception of twelve dollars, forwarded by Sophia Little, from Newport (Rhode Island) last spring, to my wife, as a donation from sympathetic friends of that place..." Making clear that this public recognition followed private confirmation, he added: "The same was acknowledged by letter..."

At the same time, efforts were being made to clarify the bookkeeping for the money raised to free Walker in Pensacola. Walker apparently sent Garrison a copy of a note he had received from a Harwich sponsor, "Binny" Small. Under the title "Acknowledgement," *The Liberator* in that December edition carried this report:

To Cast in My Mite for God's Poor

Captain Zebina H. Small, of Harwich, who so generously periled his little property in sending on the means for the release of Jonathan Walker (in connection with the Walker Committee), in a letter to Captain W. dated [November 23, 1845] says: 'I have received your favor of the 20th, enclosing ten dollars from our friend, Wendell Phillips, which is placed to the credit of the account named in your letter, which bears a balance of $133. I think we shall meet with some other good friends, like Mr. Phillips, who will esteem it a privilege to reduce the sum still lower.'"

Walker was to go to Wendell Phillips for more financial help two years later.

Accounting for the money used to free Walker, Garrison added: "The sum of $133, which is specified by Captain Small, is the amount which he has paid out of his own pocket for the release of Captain W. (it was originally $300, we believe), which he [Walker] is not able to pay, and which ought to be cancelled by those who sympathize with the branded hand."

The newspaper report may have contributed to confusion. The introductory sentence may have led some readers to assume that Small had put up the full amount of release money. As a result, Dr. Bowditch wrote "Friend Garrison" a letter that appeared in *The Liberator* the following March 20, 1846:

A mistake is going the rounds of the anti-slavery papers, that Captain Small had been obliged to pay for the release of Captain Walker. Captain S. originally advanced, of the whole sum paid for the release of his friend, about one-third; the committee advancing the remainder. At present, however, I wish everyone who has given money for the relief of Captain W. to know that the money advanced by Captain Small has been wholly refunded by the Walker Committee. I feel that it is due to the Committee to state thus much – which has not been done, so far as I know, either by *The Liberator* or the [New Bedford] *Standard*.

Then, having announced that Zebina Small had been repaid and the Walker Committee had, in effect, completed its tasks, Dr. Bowditch went on to defend the Walker Committee's action, but not necessarily attorney Thomas Blount, in having given to the Florida lawyer in November 1844, the $750 intended to help pay for Walker's release and from which Blount alone benefited. In this March 1846 letter, Bowditch wrote:

With regard to choosing T. M. Blount to be our counsel at Pensacola, I am not going to decide, now, that all the results which he has chosen to influence have been decided; but I advise those who are so prompt at blaming the Walker committee to look at their Report. For my own part, I must say that, acting upon my usual principles of judging, from oral evidence, of the character of individuals, I should do again exactly as I did in regard to Mr. Blount. It is true, the events that have transpired have convinced me of the utter folly of attempting to obtain anything by courts of law, where slavery is concerned [in] clashes with Northern rights; but I was not so convinced at the time the subscription was asked for Captain Walker. Nothing has done as much to prove to me the utter absurdity of this Union. If so, not even the high-handed annexation of Texas. But, notwithstanding the result of Mr. Blount's embassy, it proves nothing in regard to our caution, or sincere attempts to choose the right counsel.

One word more and I have done. The sum of $750 paid to a lawyer for going (under written agreement) three thousand miles away from home, to spend, if necessary, several months in the engagement, did not, and does not now, seem to me to be extravagant, when I consider the common fees obtained at the bar. Mr. Blount had been eminent in the legislature of Florida. Our personal friends, acute and honest merchants, recommended him as able and honest, as having done business for them, and the sum seemed to me a mere [pittance] in comparison with, first, the freedom of Walker and, second, the carrying up to the Supreme Court of the various points of the law proposed by us, and which are stated in the Walker committee's Report. The fact that we failed on the second point is no proof of our squandering. In truth, the sum was a small one, when we consider that it has given all the evidence necessary to satisfy anyone of the absurdity of attempting to obtain justice for the North by Southern courts.

Walker seems to have been silent on Bowditch's letter. He had already made clear how misplaced he felt the committee's trust had been in Blount's honesty. Bowditch may have overstated the case by suggesting the money given Blount was expected to cover expenses of travel, his services in defense of Walker in Pensacola, perhaps bail money, and even his fee for carrying an appeal to the United States Supreme Court.

Writing in the Pensacola prison in December 1944, Walker had expressed his contempt for Blount. With *Trial and Imprisonment*, the reading public would have had no difficulty in deciding if Harvard's Bowditch was protesting too strongly.

This matter of the "ransom" to free Walker pretty much brought to an end the details needed to close the chapter on Walker's Florida jailing. The captain from Cape Cod had made his decision and he was about to throw himself, literally, into the battleground over slavery. Ahead lay seven years on the lecture circuit, covering all New England states and extending out into Pennsylvania and New York. In a way, all of Walker's Pensacola activities were preliminary to the long, trudging experiences about to take over his life.

Then lift that manly right hand, bold ploughman of the wave!
Its branded palm shall prophesy, "SALVATION TO THE SLAVE!"
John Greenleaf Whittier, *The Branded Hand*

Chapter 12   Good Times on the Lecture Circuit

J onathan Walker was a sympathetic figure on the public platforms of the abolitionist lecture circuit. In an age before sound amplification, the best speaker was the man – and increasingly in the 1840s, the woman – who could deliver a message in something more than a strong voice. Walker was probably not an inspiring speaker. He lacked the electric good looks, fierce delivery, and radical proposals of Stephen Symonds Foster. He could not charge an audience as Garrison did with his cold logic in morality.

The words Walker spoke were, on occasion, sufficient to anger pro-slavery and neutral audiences, but he was most often a comparatively mild figure on the platform. Garrison signaled this once in a report: "[The] speeches of Mr. Burleigh were characterized by great logical power and force of eloquence, and produced a very deep impression. Excellent remarks were also made by Jonathan Walker, Austin Bearse, and others." An Ohio editor commented: "He is not an enthusiast nor a fanatic, such as excite the passions of the people, and draw out their money under the influence of excitement, but [instead is] one of nature's noblemen, a plain, matter-of-fact man, with a heart full of humanity..."

In truth, it was the scarred hand that was attracting crowds to Walker's lectures. The palm represented a cruelty that people in Walker's audiences could

imagine themselves suffering. In an eerie way, the mutilated hand was to become better known than Walker.

He wrote in jest, but historian Josef Berger was accurate in stating, "Captain Walker advanced the anti-slavery cause by going on an illustrated lecture tour – the illustration being in the palm of his hand."

Buckmaster, in *Let My People Go*, put it this way: "Jonathan Walker was able to stand at an abolitionist meeting in Massachusetts and raise his branded hand against the slavocracy... Captain Walker, solid, blue-eyed, a son of their own, was asking them to give a thousand times less than he had."

The branded hand drawing was featured on signs that were prepared in order to help attract crowds at speaking engagements. A typical one proclaimed in letters more than an inch high: "A NARRATIVE OF THE TRIALS, IMPRISONMENT, AND OTHER PUNISHMENTS OF JONATHAN WALKER!" Beneath these words appeared three illustrations, including the right hand with the SS in the center. At the left was a sketch with the caption, "The Author standing in the Pillory, and pelted with rotten eggs, by George Willis; who in 1838 or 9 hung 3 men by their necks until they were dead" (a reference to when Willis served as U.S. marshal in Pensacola). Another on the right side had the caption, "The Author being branded in the right hand with the letters S.S. by the U.S. Marshal for the District of West Florida." And across the bottom of the sign was a message referring to Walker's report of his Pensacola adventure: "For Aiding Seven of his Countrymen to Escape from Bondage, inflicted by the U.S. Court in Florida. WITH FOUR ENGRAVINGS AND AN APPENDIX. FOR SALE HERE."

The hand was the attraction, promoted not only by the instant legend already grown around the "slave stealer" but also in poetry and song. Within weeks, Whittier's poem was being recited as far away as the Old Northwest. In Salem, Ohio, editors Benjamin S. Jones and J. Elizabeth Hitchcock proudly announced: "Copies of this tract can be had gratis, by applying at the office of [The Anti-Slavery] *Bugle*." The lines were being committed to memory by school children, and even set to music by an evangelistic abolitionist, George Clark. Also active on the lecture circuit, Clark sang "The Branded Hand" frequently with, as one newspaper reported, "thrilling effect."

Whittier's poem began:
Welcome home again, brave seaman! with thy thoughtful
    brow and gray,
And the old heroic spirit of our earlier, better day;
With that front of calm endurance, on whose steady nerve in
    vain
Pressed the iron of the prison, smote the fiery shafts of pain!

The most often quoted passage from Whittier's work included these
lines:

Jonathan Walker The Man with the Branded Hand

Then lift that manly right hand, bold ploughman of the wave!
Its branded palm shall prophesy, "SALVATION TO THE
   SLAVE!"
Hold up its fire-wrought language, that whoso reads may feel
His heart swell strong within him, his sinews change to steel.
Hold it up before our sunshine, up against our Northern air;
Ho! men of Massachusetts, for the love of God, look there!
Take it henceforth for your standard, like the Bruce's heart of yore,
In the dark strike closing round ye, let that hand be seen before!

The interpretation of the branded SS to represent "Salvation to the Slave" was published widely. For example, the *American Liberty Almanac* for 1846, printed in Hartford, Connecticut, carried this caption beneath "an exact representation of the brand":

Ponder it, fellow citizens, and as you [cringe], and blush, and weep at the disgrace of our country, the indignity done to a worthy neighbor, and the misery of the poor slaves, let the fire burn until your soul is enkindled to the high resolve that the letters on Jonathan Walker's hand shall be made to read, SALVATION TO THE SLAVE.

The *American Liberty Almanac* was published by the American and Foreign Anti-Slavery Society from 1844 through 1852 as an organ of the Liberty Party, the nation's first anti-slavery political party.

On September 4, 1845, the Yarmouth *Register* recognized Walker's decision to fight on for abolition. Its editorial said: "But that branded hand will give the slaveholders more trouble than did the mysterious hand to the king of Babylon."

Parker Pillsbury at least once introduced Walker with a light reference to his hand: "He is a man of letters, though 'having never learned.' Two letters, written and graven, if not in the fleshly tables of the heart, in the live flesh of his hand, by the baptized and sanctified branding-iron of American Democracy, are a speech of themselves, longer and more eloquent than ever shook as with thunderbolts the Roman Forum..."

Walker's hand was getting attention also as a result of his own grim wit. The New York *Tribune* seemed to be chortling when it exclaimed: "The brand on his right hand he styles the 'coat of arms of the United States!'" In fact, Walker went even further. He came to call it often, "The Seal, the Coat of Arms of the United States of America."

   *   *   *   *

Jonathan Walker, who for months had longed for the freedom to take a mere half-dozen unchained steps from wall to wall in his Pensacola jail cell, was now travelling miles outdoors almost every day, mostly by railroad and by horse, but sometimes walking. Early in this new career, Walker appeared with Frederick Douglass, perhaps the best-known former black slave of his life-time.

172

Good Times on the Lecture Circuit

They came together in August, 1845, in New Bedford, Walker speaking "in his simple manner... followed by Douglass, who turned on the oratory," Richardson reported.

Throughout the late summer and autumn of 1845 and into the winter that began 1846, Walker slogged into dozens of Bay State communities, carrying copies of his book for sale, and showing the branded hand. Walker's early appearances were arranged by agents of the Anti-Slavery Society.

Walker wrote of his early lecture tour: "The first four or five months, I traveled in company with Loring Moody... who has since been the general agent of the Massachusetts Anti-Slavery Society. I was then sustained by the liberality of a few friends, and small collections taken up occasionally to defray expenses, etc." Later, he was expected to rely on his own resources, as most agents did.

At first, Walker was greeted and treated like the celebrity he had become. Pillsbury reported for the newspaper, *Herald of Freedom*, on such an event in a town in central Massachusetts:

> I met Garrison and Jonathan Walker at Fitchburg, on the evening previous to the meeting at Westminster [where] Walker... was the central point of attraction... Slavery ought not to have stamped her own image and likeness and with her favorite instrument, too, the red-hot branding iron, upon Jonathan Walker. He told the story of the unheard of outrages inflicted upon him in a manner deeply to affect the heart. Had the same barbarities been inflicted in Mexico, for aiding American prisoners to escape, this whole nation would have embarked in a crusade of revenge that should have blotted the name of Mexico from among the nations... and all this by the Government, not of a slave State, but of the United States.

Despite the supportive publicity and often cheering crowds, life on the road was not always inspiring and commodious for the lecturing agents. Commonly, they sent word ahead through letters to regional newspapers of the dates and places they intended to visit. Friends, and sympathizers, were expected to arrange for the lecturer's room and board and to reserve a hall for the gathering. In 1842, a set of instructions for sympathizers was announced by John A. Collins, general agent for the American Anti-Slavery Society: "When an agent proposes to visit your town, let no pains be spared to get him a good house to speak in, and a large audience to listen to his address. Let me entreat you to excite the abolitionists to rally at these gatherings. When the weather is favorable, it would be well to have the conventions in a grove."

Walker must have hoped that Southeastern Massachusetts abolitionists had read Collins' suggestions. In April 1846, now living with his family in Plymouth, Walker sent his week's schedule for publication in Garrison's newspaper. He was to visit five communities over a forty-mile range south of Plymouth: South Carver, on Friday, April 16; Wareham, at Cape Cod's western entrance, that Saturday and Sunday; and in Sippican, Mattapoisett, and

Rochester, small towns along Buzzards Bay south of Wareham, over the next three days. His notice concluded: "And if the oppressed victims of the United States have any friends in these places who will make the necessary arrangements for meetings on this occasion, I will address the people, to the best of my ability, on the subject of slavery."

*   *   *   *

While Walker was lecturing that spring, he must have heard with interest the news coming from Mexico. Just ten years earlier he had gone there hoping to help found a colony for free black people and instead escaped with a wounded, permanently damaged left arm. When on May 11, 1846, Congress followed President Polk's request and declared a state of war existing with Mexico, General Zachary Taylor had established a military post at Fort Texas, on the banks of the Rio Grande River opposite the Mexican town of Matamoros, where Walker had lived in 1846. Now, on May 18, 1846, Americans entered Matamoros and chased the Mexicans sixty miles into the interior. Polk, and the federal government, were in for even greater disapproval, if that were possible, from abolitionists. In June, with Senate approval, Polk accepted Britain's compromise offer to divide Oregon territory, admitting only half as "free." Both Texas and Florida had been admitted as slave states, and only one free state, Iowa, had been added. That gave pro-slavery interests a majority in the Senate.

Walker, like many abolitionists, expected only the worst from the national government. He had long since made up his mind about politics and politicians: he didn't like them and he denounced what he repeatedly decried as their hypocrisy. Again, like the more radical abolitionists, Jonathan Walker seemed to relate every action in government to its impact on slavery.

Within a year of his return from Florida, Walker had written two more short books on slavery. W. R. Bliss of Boston assisted with the publication *of A Picture of Slavery for Youth*. Walker's introduction expressed a need to reach children while in their impressionable years. "Just as the twig is bent, the tree's inclined," he wrote. The examples he used were aimed directly at young people. He noted that black men, whatever their age, were called "boys." He told of auctions at which children and parents frequently were sold to separate bidders. But he could not watch, Walker wrote. It made his "heart ache to see them sold." He did not soften his rhetoric for the impressionable readers. He included newspaper advertisements for the sale of slaves and ads that offered rewards for runaway slaves. He commented: "[N]ot infrequently, the poor fugitives are shot badly, their flesh is torn in pieces by savage bloodhounds, and they are left in the wood to die."

Walker's second new publication came out with help again from the American Anti-Slavery Society in Boston. In *A Brief View of American Chattelized Humanity and Its Supports*, he set forth a stinging review of federal and state laws that oppressed people of color, both African-American slaves and Native Americans. In the preface of the 36-page pamphlet, he cited two Irish writers, Henry C. Wright and James Haughton, both of Dublin, as the authors of

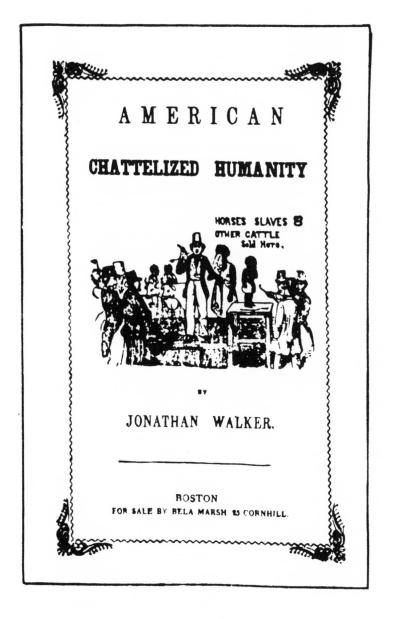

AMERICAN

CHATTELIZED HUMANITY

HORSES SLAVES &
OTHER CATTLE
Sold Here.

BY

JONATHAN WALKER.

BOSTON
FOR SALE BY BELA MARSH 25 CORNHILL.

his "copious extracts." The opinions, however, clearly belonged to Jonathan Walker of the United States, notably this one: "I renounce the present government of the United States, and the present American church, as anti-republican and anti-Christian..."

In *A Brief View*, he wrote with cynicism about the nation's beginning:

...[A]bout the same time the first emigrants were landing in the old Bay State, and introducing their civilization and religion to the natives with powder and bullets, the first cargo of slaves was being landed at Jamestown in Virginia. Since that time, both branches of the business have continued...

I know of no language adequate to express my feelings of abhorrence of a government like this... The history of this country for the last two years has demonstrated too plainly to doubt that the lovers of power and advocates of slavery are determined, at all hazards, to unite their energies, and at the expense of the people's money, rights, and liberties, to establish the institution of slavery upon a foundation that shall not be touched by the finger of freedom.... Every office of the government is filled at their pleasure and dictation, from the President to the light[house] keeper... Hang all the monuments of your country's pride in sackcloth and mourning till you dig up from the dust its character, which has disappeared from the gaze of the civilized world.

*   *   *   *

Jonathan Walker, like Stephen S. Foster and many abolitionists, detested what they saw as the sanctimonious hypocrisy of any organized religious group that spoke against slavery but did nothing actively to abolish it. They opposed "Pharisaism," which theologian Gustavo Gutierrez defined in his book, *The God of Life*, as "saying or professing one thing and doing another, separating theory from practice, doctrine from everyday behavior." The hypocritical church-goers for Foster, Walker, and others were those who prayed with their minister that slavery would be abolished but who would not allow black people to mingle with white people in church pews.

Abolitionists frequently cited their preference for the open enmity of a candid advocate of slavery over the passive church-goers who passed resolutions against slavery but really felt that what slaveholders did was none of their business.

The experience of the Roman Catholic Church was not much different, if any, from that of other sects. While earlier Popes condemned the enslavement of various peoples, it was not until 1839 that Pope Gregory XVI condemned the slave trade, which had continued then more than three decades beyond the adoption of national bans. The Pope, in his apostolic letter, *In Supremo Aspostolatus Fastigio*, explained that his pastoral concern led him to attempt to turn people away from "the unhuman traffic of Negroes." He wrote:

[We] do... admonish and adjure in the Lord all believers in Christ, of whatsoever condition, that no one hereafter may dare unjustly to molest

Good Times on the Lecture Circuit

Indians, Negroes, or other men of this sort; or to spoil them of their goods; or to reduce them to slavery; or to extend help or favor to others who perpetrate such things against them; or to exercise that inhuman trade by which Negroes, as if they were not men, but mere animals, howsoever reduced into slavery, are, without any distinction, contrary to the laws of justice and humanity, bought, sold, and doomed sometimes to the most severe and exhausting labors.

Writing in 1992 for Dear Padre Bulletins, the Reverend Maurice J. Nutt said:

[Pope Gregory] forbade any ecclesiastic or lay person to defend or teach anything that supported the slave trade. However, the general Catholic attitude in the United States was pro-slavery. Many Catholics owned slaves and were actively involved in the slave trade. They did not view slavery from a moral position; rather, they saw the abolishment of slavery as a threat to their economic stability. Bishops and a great many religious communities owned slaves. Some bishops even sought to defend the institution of slavery on theological and legal grounds. Given these circumstances, the American Catholic Church's position on slavery in defiance of Pope Gregory XVI's condemnation was to remain silent. It was felt that slavery was a national and political issue, and that it would be best that the church in America avoid making an official statement on slavery.

Walker was clear about how he could speak in favor of Christianity while denouncing any individual religious group. He said, in *A Brief View*, that he endorsed the explanation given by Frederick Douglass:

What I have said respecting and against religion, I mean strictly to apply to the slaveholding religion of this land, and with no possible reference to Christianity proper; for, between the Christianity of this land, and the Christianity of Christ, I recognize the widest possible difference – so wide, that to receive the one as good, pure, and holy, is of necessity to reject the other as bad, corrupt, and wicked.

While Walker was to continue with that attitude for years, he never had direct conflict with the church groups in his hometown. On December 3, 1846, Harwich's First Congregational Church, during the pastorate of Cyrus Stone, unanimously passed resolutions separating members from "those who hold and treat their fellow men as chattels or who advocate and approve of the system of human slavery."

Walker's not openly criticizing this church may have been owing to his gratitude for the help that so many of the members had provided him and his family during his imprisonment. Deacon Sidney Underwood was a good example. In addition, Walker would defer, if only for courtesy's sake, to his close friend, Loring Moody. In 1846, Moody was beginning a long period of activism in the cause of abolition. He was the first of Walker's traveling companions, and his first chief supporter; at the same time, he maintained membership in the Harwich Congregational Church. He had begun what developed into a long, strong relationship leading to his appointment as an active deacon.

* * * *

Some audiences were offended by Walker's rhetoric. The words would sting some of his listeners, even when Walker's understated, quiet personality was being reflected in his somewhat uninspiring platform manner – tough words delivered softly. One result would have been less success than other abolitionist speakers in motivating audiences to the financial support he needed not only for his family but also to continue his work. Walker decided that he could not compromise by toning down his speeches in order to offend fewer listeners and collect more money. He was a man of principle; he had to dispense truth as he saw it.

By winter 1846-47, he made his life even worse by abandoning free-will offerings and counting only on book sales for support. In addition to his own three books, he also carried anti-slavery literature prepared by other abolitionists. Such sales were a common supplement to abolitionists' income. For example, Elizabeth Hitchcock, the Salem, Ohio, editor, advertised in her *Bugle* that she had "just received, and has now for sale at her boarding house" a list of ten books, including Stephen Foster's *The Brotherhood of Thieves*, *Garrison's Poems*, and *The Disunionist* by Wendell Phillips.

Walker explained his decision to rely on books sales in a letter to the *National Anti-Slavery Standard*, printed May 3, 1847. The letter was a rare piece of writing for Jonathan Walker; probably scribbled in haste, it reads like notes strung together:

> I have dispensed with taking up contributions at meetings except to pay for the use of the house, etc., don't think it's a good plan – get but little, except from the Anti-Slavery folks, and they can give without a contribution; it produces more talk than money. People don't want to pay to have their errors exposed – they are not willing to buy the truth for truth's sake. All parties and sects want exceptions made – they are not so bad as others – anxious to shift the blame on their neighbors, the abolitionists, on the South, etc., etc. It is not good for the speaker to think of getting pay of the audience when lecturing to them – places him in a wrong position – an inducement to leave out some important truths – had better feel under no pecuniary obligations at such times.

In another letter, he wrote:
> The last year, I have distributed four- or five-thousand publications, and have no doubt but I have done much more for the cause by that means than by any other. It has also been the main pecuniary support of

myself and large family, though the profits were small. The urgent demands on my purse bring me considerably in arrears. But we have had up to this time sufficient bread and pure water in abundance from the never-failing spring, which is more than thousands of others have in this boasted land of equality, Democracy, and Christianity.

In fact, the Walkers also relied on gifts to survive. They were living in Plymouth, that winter, and Jonathan wrote "Friend Wm. L. Garrison" on February 1, 1847:

A few days ago I returned to my family at Plymouth from which I had been absent upwards of two months on a tedious anti-slavery tour, and was shown a neat and good bed-quilt, and two or three lesser articles, which had been received during my absence from an unknown source. More recently, I have learned that they had been presented us by the friends of the enslaved at Everettville, Princeton, as a token of sympathy, and in consideration of our need, sacrifice, and devotion to the cause of the more needy victims of American oppression. Be those practical friends assured of our heartfelt gratitude for their well-timed present. They could not have made a section of anything of the same amount that would have been more acceptable at this time and season. May the donors and their co-workers in the cause of humanity yet have the satisfaction of knowing that the three millions of American chattel slaves in the United States have, at least, the privilege of providing themselves with a quilt to shield them and their little ones from the inclement weather by their own labor and industry, instead of having their backs stripped and quilted, as at present, by the driver's lash under a relentless despotism.

Garrison tried to help Walker with his book sales. In one edition of his newspaper, he wrote:

Captain Walker has with him, for sale, excellent anti-slavery publications, designed to throw light on the dark system of slavery, and also his own narrative of his seizure, imprisonment, and trials by the courts of the United States, etc... This narrative he has published at a considerable expense, by the assistance of friends, to whom he is under pecuniary obligations, and he is desirous therefore to sell immediately as many copies at least as will cover the expense of publications. He is, moreover, in impoverished circumstances, and has a large family dependent on him for support. May he in every place be hospitably entertained, and receive generous assistance. Think of that "branded hand."

"Hospitable" and "generous" were words for an editor writing in Boston or New York; they were generally unknown to an agent of the American

Jonathan Walker The Man with the Branded Hand

Anti-Slavery Society working in the often barren field of abolitionism. On March 3, 1847, after his first full year on tour, Walker wrote from his home in Plymouth to Sydney Gay, editor of the *Standard*:

I have held meetings in places where the first anti-slavery man could not be found, and many towns where the third one was unknown. I have been over much ground where no faithful anti-slavery labor had been done, no good seed sown, and the consequence is, nothing of the right spirit has sprung up to bear good fruit. But party briars and sectarian thorns were in all places deep rooted, shooting forth their malignant points at everything that came in contact with them. But I have seen a few spots where the radicals have been throwing in their reformatory firebrands, which caused some crackling and stir among the trash, and finally cleared away a few breathing holes for humanity... I have been into places where no suitable house could be obtained for a meeting; at other places have had to wait on several committees, be questioned... and refused; and at other places procured some public or private hall, posted up my notices, lighted the house at my own expense, or paid for the use of it; then have had to go to a rum house for lodging.

Walker cited an example involving a planned lecture in the western part of Massachusetts, more than 150 miles from his Cape Cod home:

I gave notice in the *Hampshire Herald* that I would be at Greenfield at such a time (some ten days after), requesting the friends of the slave and of humanity to make the necessary arrangements for a meeting, etc. Knowing that a number of the *Herald*s were taken there, I took no other steps until I arrived, late in the day appointed for the meeting. I inquired if anything had been done, and found there had not. There was no other meeting in the place to interfere, and there were two empty halls, and four or five meeting houses; none had been applied for. It was then too late in the day to give notice for a meeting that evening. I made arrangements for a future time, passed on to other places to fulfill other appointments, and returned at the set time, talked to some sort of an audience an hour and a quarter, sold one dollar's worth of books, gave away one and a half dollar's worth more, paid for the use of the hall, and went to a James K. Polk grog tavern to get clear of sleeping in a snow bank. This was at a large, thriving village in Old Massachusetts, AYE, a hotbed of abolitionism.

It is not clear why non-drinker Walker, in his distress, should associate President Polk with a drinking establishment. Polk has been considered by some historians as the nation's hardest-working chief executive. Polk and his wife, Sarah Childress Polk, have been described as "pious Calvinist... strong-willed and earnest." And, more to point of "grog taverns," Mrs. Polk – presumably with

Good Times on the Lecture Circuit

her husband's full support – banned wine, dancing, and card-playing in the White House, and forbade the serving of refreshments at public receptions.

Walker would not have voted for Polk. He was pretty much a one-issue man. Since Polk opposed every attempt to interfere with slavery, he had earned Walker's disdain.

The editor of the Portland *Pleasure Boat* seemed to capture the essence of Walker's principled paucity in responding to a letter the newspaper published from John O. Wattles of Cincinnati. Wattles invited Walker "to come out here to the West. Thousands would flock to hear his story and see the BRANDED HAND." Wrote the editor: "I doubt whether circumstances will ever permit him to [visit Ohio]. He cannot endure hardships as formerly... I do not think the friends of humanity where he has traveled have all done their whole duty towards him..."

The editor exaggerated Walker's physical condition. But he was accurate about the poverty in which the Walker family lived. Walker wrote to "Esteemed Friend" Wendell Phillips on July 8, 1847, asking a loan of twenty-eight dollars:

> I am destitute of property except [for owning a cow] and a very little ordinary furniture, having been robbed twice within the last eleven years of my last mill. I have lived in this place but a short time, the most of which I have been absent from my family in the anti-slavery field. About the first of May, that great and true friend of humanity, Francis Jackson, came to this place and bought a piece of land a short distance from the [Plymouth] village and gave me leave to improve it. Since that time, I have labored hard and constant upon it with the hope of procuring a comfortable subsistence and shelter for my dependent family. Myself and family have lived for some time almost entirely on bread and water until within a few days we have been blessed with plenty of milk, and of which we are loathe to be deprived of.
>
> A few days ago, several friends from abroad met here in convention, and I was not in circumstances to invite them even to take a meal with me, neither could my wife and children attend the convention for the want of shame and clothes decent to wear... In the last two months, I have worked from 11 to 13 hours per day, rain and shine, seven days the week...
>
> It is not myself that I feel anxious about, for I can almost live on beach sand and salt water, and cloth myself with seaweed... I will pay you again soon as I can. I am in possession of an excellent cow which is much of our dependence at present, and if I cannot obtain the money immediately she will have to go to pay the bill. I do not know of any friend here who can easily afford this money now. The Anti-Slavery finances are few and of limited means. Yours for impatient freedom and right to the end.

Not everyone working the broad field of slavery was destitute. Stampp reported that "a good slave-catcher with 'Negro dogs' could earn $600 a year."

And in Pensacola, some slaves were being taken out of the fields and off the railroad track beds to work at the Arcadia Cotton Factory. On April 8, 1848, the Pensacola *Gazette* editor was continuing his way, dehumanizing African-Americans with the kind of praise usually given a yoke of oxen or a team of horses: "[W]ith the native skill and ingenuity of mere labor – the labor of the hands – the Negro is just as richly endowed as the white."

     *   *   *   *

Late in 1847, Jonathan Walker began to lecture regularly outside New England for the first time. Despite the fears of the Ohio editor that he was too weak to survive a trip to the West, Walker seemed drawn in that direction. Perhaps part of it was from the boredom of meeting with small-town farm audiences in western New England. Perhaps part of it was the need for a new challenge. And perhaps part of the attraction of going westward was his still unsatisfied desire to explore "the West." His childhood dreams still were not met.

Walker now was also traveling with escaped slaves who, in the free Northern states, were an attraction in themselves. One of the posters printed to advertise Walker's visits outside his home state was headed with inch-high capital letters and an attention-getting word.

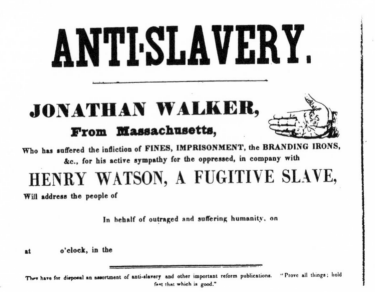

ANTI-SLAVERY.

JONATHAN WALKER,
From Massachusetts,

Who has suffered the infliction of FINES, IMPRISONMENT, the BRANDING IRONS, &c., for his active sympathy for the oppressed, in company with

HENRY WATSON, A FUGITIVE SLAVE,

Will address the people of

In behalf of outraged and suffering humanity, on

at   o'clock, in the

They have for disposal an assortment of anti-slavery and other important reform publications. "Prove all things; hold fast that which is good."

Good Times on the Lecture Circuit

Blank spaces were left to write in the name of the community, date, and time. In small type, the posters added, "They have for disposal an assortment of anti-slavery and other important reform publications. 'Prove all things; hold fast that which is good.'"

Through the first half of the winter of 1847-48, Walker traveled with John S. Jacobs, a free black man. Walker wrote "Esteemed Friend" Garrison from East Hamilton, New York, on January 24, 1848:

> We commenced our work [in November] of disseminating the melancholy facts of the power and influence of slavery and its kindred abominations (both verbally and printed) in the western part of Massachusetts, and have worked our way into the center of the "Empire State." We have spent about one month in the counties of Herkimer, Oneida, and Madison, but in a few days shall go into a more western part of the state. It is seldom an evening passes in which we do not have a meeting, and, with few exceptions, in different towns and villages each evening. We have traveled several hundred miles on foot, through colds and storms, slush and mud...

In a letter from Plymouth, on May 14, 1848, Walker added more details about that New York trip. Appearing in Herkimer and Oneida counties for two months, Walker and Jacobs often lectured to the converted. He wrote: "Many of the friends in this region dated their anti-slavery experience from the zealous labors of Abby Kelley Foster, who, some four years ago, had spent some time there, and met and refuted the squabbles, arguments, slanders, and misrepresentations of the priests and lawyers, who essayed to destroy the influence her truthful statements and scorching rebukes had made."

The rewards were not always pleasant: "On several occasions, a little rowdyism was manifested, but nothing of a serious character took place... On one occasion we were somewhat annoyed by the beating of a drum under the windows where we were talking. On another occasion, the bell was frequently rung overhead, a gun fired at the door, etc., and while speaking I was sprinkled with a shower of musket shot, but as they were not buried in powder, they fell harmless."

Walker, up to this point, seldom gave details about the bad moments in his life. He had far more time to devote to the good times. Concluding a list of "a few specimens of unmixed benevolence and large humanity," he singled out a person he met in Paris, New York, for praise.

> At the close of the meeting, a man by the name of John Stanton, of Casville, came forward and purchased three or four dollars worth of books, mainly for distribution. The next evening, we held a meeting at Waterville, six or seven miles distant. Here we found friend Stanton again on hand, who wanted three or four dollars worth more books, and presented me twenty-five dollars from two of his sisters, who had attended our meeting the evening before. He had walked upwards of

four miles through storm, snow, and slush, and returned again, after meeting, on his mission of kindness.

Walker also wrote warmly about one of abolitionism's strongest supporters: "We held a meeting at Peterboro, and spent a night with Gerrit Smith, who is another eccentric, good man. I say good, because he means to do good; eccentric because all land monopolists and speculators want all the land they can get, or all they can get for it, while Smith wants other people to have some, too; therefore, he has given titles to more than 2,000 individuals, and intends to increase the number to 3,000, to that poor, despised class called the African race."

One of Smith's best known gifts of land in upstate New York was to Frederick Douglass, who founded his newspaper, *North Star*, after receiving forty acres from Smith near Rochester in December 1847.

"Yes," Walker wrote, "the history of friend S. demonstrates that he has designedly, with good intention, stepped aside from the bloated aristocracy around him to administer relief to the needy, sable sons of grief, and provide for them a homestead in his state, instead of pointing them (as in days of yore) to their beloved country of Africa!"

The last comment appears to have been delivered as cynical reference to colonization, a movement still alive although supported by few whites or blacks.

Walker reported on another highlight of the New York trip: meeting with Samuel J. May, the first man Walker had heard lecture on the subject of slavery. He wrote: "I was prepared for a pleasant interview with him, which was fully realized on that occasion. When we meet with a true and active friend in the cause, it makes me feel joyful – for slavery has no resting place for the sole of its foot there."

These, then, were "the good old days" for Jonathan Walker.

The "bad new days" were not far off.

Perhaps no decade in the history of the United States
has been so filled with tense and crucial moments
as the ten years leading to the Civil War;
and closely connected with the majority of these crises
was the problem of slavery.
John Hope Franklin, *From Slavery to Freedom*

Chapter 13   The Bad New Days

If Jonathan Walker seemed sometimes to be casual about money, it was not his usual way. He had demonstrated often an ability to find and hide income. Nevertheless, he was not too proud to request, even plead, for financial help.

When he had money, he kept a record of its uses. In one of his letters from his long New York trip, Walker included an accounting of income and expenses – to the half-penny! As Walker recounted his trip, he and former slave John Jacobs had received a supply of anti-slavery books with a wholesale value of $215 as they left Boston in November 1847. They "had remitted at Utica," January 7, 1848, $92.50, giving them assets of $307.50. They collected $426.77 from the sale of books "and otherwise," and had remaining unsold books valued at $70.90. That gave them a net income of $190.08, from which they deducted $87.79 for "incidental expenses, such as conveyance, transporting books and other baggage, food and lodging, printing handbills, etc." That left them with $102.29, which they divided equally, each getting $51.14 plus a half-penny, "out of which we had to pay our expenses, home over 300 miles, which cost me a little more than ten dollars by the way of New York City, thus leaving to provide clothing, pay debts occurred by necessity, and support a large family, the enormous sum of about forty dollars, after four and a half months' hard service in the cause of suffering humanity. In addition to this, presents were made me, in cash and other articles, amounting to nearly fifty dollars, by benevolent individuals."

Jonathan Walker The Man with the Branded Hand

Walker's letter introduced a new argument against taking up collections at the meetings he conducted. He had decided a year earlier to discontinue the practice. In his 1848 East Hamilton letter, he emphasized why he would not seek donations:

> I am aware that some persons who read this will ask, "Could you not have done better by taking up collections at meetings?" To which I answer, emphatically, no! We might have done more for our pockets, but not for the cause in which we were engaged. It is my opinion that those who go forth preaching reformation from error to truth, taking up collections for their benefit, do as much to retard the cause as to promote it. At several meetings, where halls were to be paid for, etc., we consented to have a collection taken. But after one has been tearing off the mask of hypocrisy, exposing religious and political inconsistencies, and handling roughly the people's gods, to shove a contribution box in their faces, expecting to receive money for it, is quite preposterous. The fact is, friend Garrison, if you expect to get the people's money, you must make them appear better than what they are. Is that right?

That last remark might be taken as a simple yet insightful tip for any person in sales, whether it might be hard goods or ideas. It might also be seen as somewhat cynical. While Walker was generally inclined to see the good in people, he occasionally let his growing despondency, or melancholy, edge into his writings. His letter from East Hamilton seemed to hint of an increasing weariness. He wrote: "Though few seem willing to take a decided stand either for or against the system of slavery, there is much anxiety to know what is to be the result of the present agitation on this subject... The dreadful conflict between freedom and slavery is ere long (in my humble opinion) to be fought in this country; and though I dread the consequences, I am anxious for the event to take place, that it may the sooner be over, and the rising generation may take lessons from the consequences of `compromising.'"

Walker had now been on the road for nearly three years. The "dreadful conflict" was not to come, "the sooner to be over," during Jonathan Walker's lecture tours, although he continued for another three years. In fact, the "ere long" that Walker predicted for a civil war was to take thirteen more years of anxiety and agitation.

*   *   *   *

Even though Jonathan and Jane Walker were well into 19th Century middle-age after his return from Florida, they were still young enough – and brave enough – to have their ninth child. Their fourth son was born on February 13, 1848, about two and a half years after Jonathan had returned home from the Florida jail. Jonathan was almost forty-nine years old, and Jane, forty-four, ages not uncommon for grandparents.

The Bad New Days

As they had with their first-born, John Bunyan Walker, the parents named their last child for a famous religionist who had been imprisoned for carrying out his beliefs. George Fox, son of a Puritan weaver, was only twenty-three years old when he began the preaching that was to lead to his founding of the Society of Friends, commonly known as Quakers. While the Walkers apparently never were formal members of the Friends, they were faithful to the organization's principles.

With the arrival of George Fox Walker at the family home, now in Plymouth, the parents had five children at home. Besides the new baby, there were three other youngsters: William Wilberforce, then almost five years old, and the twins, Maria and Lloyd, who were about six and a half. One older daughter was around to help. Mary Gage Walker was fifteen, and surely at home. Sophia, who would be eighteen years old in another month, had been married at Plymouth only a few months earlier – on November 26, 1847 – to Zadock K. Chase, a native of Dennis on Cape Cod.

Mary was to leave in another year in order to work for a Plymouth man, Ivory Blackmer Lucas, whose wife was seriously ill. In 1852, soon after Lucretia Lucas died, and when Mary was only nineteen years old, she and Ivory Lucas were to begin a marriage that lasted a little more than a half-century.

George Walker was born almost twenty-five years after Jane and Jonathan's first son. John Bunyan Walker, who had been his father's companion at age twelve in the Mexican adventure, had married in late 1844 and begun his own career in Plymouth, first as a sailor, then a harbor pilot, and later as a ship's carpenter, following less spectacularly his father's vocations. Baby George had two other sisters. Altamera was twenty-one years old and Nancy had just turned twenty. Like John, they were out on their own.

The Walker children were born in four different communities. The twins had arrived while Jonathan and Jane were living in Florida. John and William were born in Harwich, and George in Plymouth. Altamera, Nancy, Sophia, and Mary were all born in New Bedford. The longest gap between children occurred between Mary and the twins, nine years.

*   *   *   *

Having a new son did not seem to distract Jonathan Walker from carrying on his anti-slavery work. Just two weeks after George's birth, Jonathan wrote a letter on "The Products of Slave Labor" to Garrison. The purpose was to point out that while he, like many abolitionists, tried to follow the motto Garrison promoted, "No Union with Slaveholders," to do so thoroughly would not be possible. He cited the difficulty of avoiding slave-produced materials:

> I have, for the last year and a half, spent more than three-fourths of my time lecturing on the subject of slavery in different sections of this country. Much of the food placed before me, I have reason to believe, is mixed with the products of slave labor. If I ask whether it is free or slave labor, I get no satisfactory answer. At night, the only bed I can sleep in is mostly composed of the produce of slave

187

labor. Most of the means by which I sustain myself and family are the little profits I derive from the sale of the anti-slavery publications, printed on slave-grown cotton. I have a family to clothe and feed, with my limited means, which compels me to procure the cheapest articles to meet their necessities as well as I can, and it is mixed with the products of unpaid labor. I subscribe for an anti-slavery or any other reformatory periodical. It comes to me through a postoffice managed by a slaveholder, printed on slave-grown cotton paper...

[I]f we try to evade the use of those slave-grown articles, and substitute imported articles in their place, we are paying a tax to support a slave-holding government, all steeped in innocent blood, and now carrying on a diabolical war against a feeble government, for the sake of establishing permanently the traffic in helpless men, women, and children on its soil, where it had been abolished by a half-civilized people. Yours for the annihilation of slavery and war by all right means.

Walker's practical and noble justification in no way eroded his unflagging opposition to slavery, or his intense desire for an immediate emancipation. This contrasted with the way some of his neighbors viewed slavery. Most of the men whose livelihood was made on the vessels that delivered slave-produced tobacco, cotton, and sugar did not defend slavery, but they were aware of the impact its abolition would have on their lives. Few looked forward to its end.

*   *   *   *

During this increasingly difficult time of his life, Jonathan Walker concluded another money-losing episode. There is reason to believe, however, that, rather than viewing this as a defeat, he managed to salvage an ironic smile for himself.

Repayment of the loan that he and Nathan Underwood had made to Jonathan's brother, David, which was due by January 18, 1846, apparently never materialized. The Barnstable County Registry of Deeds has on file a quitclaim deed: "I, Jonathan Walker of Plymouth...yeoman, in consideration of $64 to me paid by Nathan Underwood of Harwich... do hereby grant... and forever quit claim unto the same Nathan Underwood... the estate conveyed to me by David Walker by his mortgage deed dated 29 December 1842..."

In order to prevent any claims in the future, Jane Walker also signed off in the deed: "...I, Jane Walker, wife to the said Jonathan, hereby agree to quit all my right to dower in the premises..." Prepared in June 1848, the document was signed in November, 1848, and filed with the register on March 2, 1849. The spread of nine months between the decision to sell and the recording of the transaction was not uncommon in that era.

The deed does not, of course, explain why David defaulted, if indeed he did. It appears that one of two actions took place. David may have repaid

The Bad New Days

Underwood in full but Jonathan only about half the $117.59 he had borrowed, and then stopped paying. That would leave Jonathan with about $60 due. A charitable, and financially generous Underwood, might then have paid Jonathan the balance due him in order to give David a clear deed. More likely, however, is that David never repaid the partnership and, during a period of Jonathan's desperate need for money, Underwood bought out his partner at about half the total of Jonathan's investment.

This could be taken to illustrate another of Jonathan Walker's attempts at thanking those who had stood by him during his jailing. Assuming that David failed to repay his creditors, two of the three principals involved could claim some useful gain; the other was clearly a loser. The gainers were Nathan Underwood, who would have acquired the two-acre Harwich property for a total investment of $110.41, and, to a lesser degree, David, who had the benefit of the $164 as well as the use of the property for at least five years. The loser was Jonathan. He not only was out more than $50 of his investment principal, he never received a penny of the interest David had promised to pay six years earlier.

On the quitclaim deed, Jonathan had described himself as a "yeoman." The word is nowhere else associated with him. There are several meanings: citizen and common man are two of them. Walker, in fact, never thought of himself in any other way. Two other definitions are appropriate to the careful user of language that Walker was. From the British comes "a small landowner." A literate person, one perhaps playful with language, might have chosen this meaning in giving up claim to land that he had never really owned. Or, in claiming identity as "yeoman," Walker might have let another meaning cross his mind, that used in the expression "yeoman's service": "loyal service or assistance." Jonathan would have been pleased that, despite his own poverty, he had been able to provide loyal assistance to his brother.

Assistance for Jonathan, however, was not coming from the United States Congress. Walker was still trying to recover the thousand dollars he said Mexican custom officials in 1836 had taken from him and his son. On February 3, 1849, Walker wrote "Esteemed Friend" Horace Mann, the newly elected U. S. representative from Massachusetts. Mann, before and later one of the nation's most influential educators, had succeeded John Quincy Adams. The former president, then serving in his eighteenth year as a member of Congress, collapsed during a session of the House and died two days later, on February 23, 1848.

Wrote Walker: "...I should be glad if you would interest yourself a little in a case of mine, which was submitted to John Read [sic]... a little more than twelve years ago. . . At the expiration of his term at Congress, I wrote him to know what disposition had been made of my memorial and was informed by him that he lodged my document in the office of the Secretary of State. From that time to the present, I have heard nothing more from my petition to

Congress. I shall be extremely glad if you can inform me if anything has, or, can be done in the case."

Walker concluded with perhaps the most self-pitying plea he ever issued:

> I have a large family dependent on me for their support, while I am destitute of property and have to meet constantly pressing wants and demands by what little I can earn in my crippled state by day's labors. The U.S. Court in Florida in 1844-45, after loading me with irons in a miserable jail for many months, and inflicting other barbarous punishments for showing mercy to American-born men, wrung from me my last cent to pay unjust and infamous charges of their own creating. Thus, having been plundered and robbed of my last mill by a Mexican *banditi* and our government and by American slave-catchers and government, insulted, abused, scarred, and every principle of justice outraged, with a family of nine children and one at the breast... you may imagine something of my present condition. A line from you giving information in this matter will be greatfully [sic] received..."

In fact, Walker was never to receive anything.

This must have been one of the low points of Jonathan Walker's life. Weary from his three years on the abolition lecture circuit, worried more than usual about finances, and finding new proof that the government he had once trusted was not going to help him – all of this had helped sink his spirits.

And yet, this yeoman in the war against slavery had years more of battle before him.

*   *   *   *

The issues of slavery were becoming like a roaring fire, heating to overboiling the national stewpot of concerns, and affecting politics, the economy, religion, social affairs, personal relationships, and even immigration. By January 1850, leaders in the South had seen the admission of a new series of free states, creating for Southerners a minority status. Henry Clay presented a package of bills already introduced in Congress, hoping to persuade Southern colleagues to accept. It was Clay, John F. Kennedy wrote in *Profiles in Courage*, who "initiated, hammered, and charmed through the reluctant Congresses [in 1820, 1833, and 1850] the three great compromises that preserved the Union until 1861..."

From Congressional negotiating came compromises on both sides. Southerners agreed to permit abolishment of the slave trade – but not slavery – in the District of Columbia, and the admission of California to the Union as a free state. For their part, Northeners yielded to the Fugitive Slave Law. This Act required every American – even the uncommitted and uncaring – to capture and return runaway slaves. No longer could a fugitive expect to find sanctuary and legal freedom in the states that had made slavery illegal.

The Bad New Days

Two other measures were seen as serving both free state and slave state interests: local decisions were to determine the slavery status of the territory ceded by Mexico to become New Mexico, Arizona, and Utah; and Texas, already in the Union as a slave state, was to be awarded $10-million to settle claims of adjoining states.

Clay challenged: "Let him who elevates himself above humanity, above its weaknesses, its infirmities, its wants, its necessities, say if he pleases, 'I never will compromise;' but let no one who is not above the frailties of our common nature disdain compromise."

Supporting the measures was Daniel Webster. His "Seventh of March" speech in the Senate represented, in the view of many Northerners, no less than surrender. Whittier, whose poem had celebrated Jonathan Walker, now humiliated Webster with a poem called "Ichabod!," in which Webster was adjured:

> Walk backward, with averted gaze,
> And hide the shame!

Webster was to explain: "If the chances had been one in a thousand that Civil War would be the result, I should still have felt that thousandth chance should be guarded against by any reasonable sacrifice."

Wrote Kennedy: "It was because Daniel Webster conscientiously favored compromise in 1850 that he earned a condemnation unsurpassed in the annals of political history."

In the North, and especially in New England and Massachusetts, abolitionists pondered Webster's stand. Like Lincoln, Webster was opposed to slavery but placed above that burning issue the safety of the still adolescent union of sovereign states.

Jonathan Walker's reaction to Webster's speech was immediate. Walker wrote *The Liberator* that he had "no vials of wrath to pour on the poor man's devoted head, for his lamentable exhibition..." He suggested that he had expected such weakness, as he regarded it, from "prostituted" political leaders such as Webster, as well as Calhoun and Clay.

Harwich's Loring Moody, speaking at the New England Anti-Slavery Convention a few months later, picked up on Walker's theme, and went much further. Webster, suggested Moody, had lost his mind.

* * * *

The Massachusetts Anti-Slavery Society decided to return to Harwich in 1850, having skipped a visit in 1849, the year after the riot. As part of the New England Anti-Slavery Society's 1850 schedule of "The One Hundred Conventions," August 30-31 and September 1 were set aside for the same Harwich grove at which a mob had brought the 1848 convention to a halt. This time, Jonathan Walker would attend, and speak, at a hometown gathering.

Garrison filled more than one of his newspaper's wide columns on September 9 in reporting on "the largest local gathering we have ever witnessed

Jonathan Walker The Man with the Branded Hand

in the State (the largest, certainly, with very few exceptions)." Adopted were several familiar resolutions denouncing the silence of religious groups.

Another excoriated "the hypocrisy of such men as Lewis Cass, Daniel Webster, and Henry Clay..." One resolution alluded to the kind of crime for which Jonathan Walker had been punished: "Resolved, that 'free trade and sailors' rights' can neither be exercised nor protected on our American coast while... our shipmasters trading at the South [are] being placed under fearful liabilities in case they succor any slave on board of their vessels, and [are] subjected to imminent peril if they venture to speak out their free sentiments against the enslavement of any portion of the American people."

*　　*　　*　　*

While Loring Moody was still traveling as an agent for the Massachusetts Anti-Slavery Society, Jonathan Walker took his mission into Vermont. In November 1850 he said his good-byes to Jane and the children still living at home in Plymouth. All four youngsters were still under the age of ten. George Fox Walker was still a baby, not yet three years old. Jonathan was soon to reach his fifty-second birthday. He had been home from Florida for more than five years, and had spent most of that time lecturing. He was weary when he sat down on February 3, 1851, and wrote a long letter (about 1,200 words) that Garrison printed in *The Liberator* under the heading, "Travels in Vermont." Walker reported:

> I have traveled several hundred miles, and addressed many audiences on the subject of slavery, some small and others large, as circumstances permitted. The first few weeks [in November 1850], I was under the necessity of traveling on foot, till a fall of snow and the kindness of a friend at Randolph provided me with the means of traveling with a horse and sleigh... [I would] say a word about the withering and blighting effects of slavery there, as elsewhere in the United States; for I have not yet been able to learn of any place, in all this broad land, where slavery has not shed its baneful and demoralizing influence on the inhabitants thereof. Great is the work to be done... [T]heir political and religious teachers have been guided by such a narrow, selfish, and cringing policy, tending to moral bankruptcy, that their flocks have been made, under their influence, greatly insensible to equal justice and impartial humanity... I am of opinion that if half of the real anti-slavery work had been done in Vermont that has been done in Massachusetts, that state would, before this, have been prepared to endorse the declaration, "No Union with Slave- holders," politically or religiously.

Walker went on to tell the editor that the "word Garrisonian, with many, is associated with the rankest atheism." He urged Garrison "and another friend or two [to] spend a few weeks in that state, holding conventions at different places." It wouldn't be easy, Walker promised. "With but few exceptions, I have received any other aid than an occasional meal or a night's

The Bad New Days

lodging; yet they are... careful not to crowd one's pocket or purse in the way of donations, or in purchasing anti-slavery and other reform books. Anti-slavery proper don't pay, in dollars and cents; this fact has long been abundantly experienced by those who have labored earnestly and faithfully in the cause, and consequently the laborers are few."

But there were also rewards, he acknowledged: "...the satisfaction of being engaged in a good work – approved by their own consciences, by the imbruted slave, and by all good men who comprehend their principles."

Walker returned home, dejected that "the same lamentable fact stared us in the face there as everywhere, that those who are the best able to help the cause along, with their abundance, possess the least disposition, generally, to overthrow the grinding system of oppression and outrage. If such be the influence of wealth, may I never be brought under its hardening and deleterious influence, but remain as at present, struggling with the cold atmospheric and moral elements to meet present pressing family wants," he wrote Garrison.

*   *   *   *

While Walker was trudging homeward, his famous hand was being used by John Brown to shame free black men into joining the revolution still taking shape in his eroding mind. On January 15, 1851, Brown formed the League of Gileadites as an organization for the protection of fugitive slaves. "Words of Advice, written by Brown," began with "Union is strength." He demanded of his black readers, "Have any of you seen the Branded Hand?" Brown seemed to be asking, "If this white man can accept so much suffering in pursuit of freedom for black slaves, how much are you willing to accept?"

Frederick Douglass, after meeting Brown in Springfield, Massachusetts, in 1847, had written of Brown: "Though a white gentleman, is in sympathy with a black man, and as deeply interested in our cause as though his own soul had been pierced with the iron of slavery." "Brown...was trying to put into action a fighting doctrine that other militants only talked about," Stephen B. Oates concluded in his biography, *To Purge This Land with Blood.*

*   *   *   *

During their years in Plymouth – where Jonathan's ancestors had arrived from England among the Pilgrims – the Walkers occupied a small house near the harbor. There, Walker worked occasionally. In a *Liberator* letter published June 6, 1851, Walker alluded to the poverty in which he and his family lived – sometimes with escaped slaves. He and Jane, apparently, were active in helping fugitives resettle as free people in New England, and perhaps also were serving as conductors on the Underground Railroad. Walker described their living conditions in responding to a reader's letter:

Had friend [B. S.] Whiting been intimately acquainted with me and my circumstances for a few years past, he would have been slow to attribute to me anything of a niggardly or begrudging disposition; or only, for a few weeks past, to have witnessed our condition, and worked with me in mud-docks, under the bottoms of

193

vessels, in all possible positions, from day to day, in order to meet the demands of hunger, cold, and oppression; yes, or even today, shut in by the storm, seated in a rough and humble cabin (the best habitation I can have), writing this scrawl, surrounded by a dependent family of wife and small children, an invalid relative, and a half-dozen others, not gentlemen of cloth and standing, not safeguards of the American Union, but fugitive slaves, with their little ones, terrified, from their whips and chains – victims of American barbarity, unable, after being here three weeks, to find any other habitation to shelter them from the violent storms which have visited our coast recently, in the town sacred as the landing place of our liberty-loving Pilgrim fathers from foreign oppression, solely because they are guilty of the unpardonable sin of being a fraction darker than most of our neighbors. Is there no escape – is there no avoiding – is there to be no end to this dastardly, cruel, and infernal prejudice, in the vicinity of the Puritan Rock?

It is with much difficulty that I scratch these lines, with a hand crippled and scarred with a Mexican bullet and an American branding iron, and a half-dozen large, fresh cracks caused by hard work in the dock, to procure an honest temporary subsistence.

I now close abruptly, in haste, as the time has arrived to meet a few friends, under the name of a Vigilance Committee, to devise means, if we can, to aid and protect outraged and down-trodden humanity, directly now with us...

N.B. Between three and four weeks ago, two fugitives came here with their families, last from Lancaster County, Pennsylvania, to avoid being kidnapped. They are apparently smart, well-behaved, and likely men; but, up to this hour, they have not been able to find any house to live in, though there are houses to let here to persons of low character, and these men have offered to pay rent in advance...

Having the money to pay rent in the "free" founding community of Plymouth "avails nothing" for the blacks, Walker wrote, "so long as they belong to the abused class; and the Vigilance Committee has not been able to provide for them – so we are here, all huddled up in our little cabin. Others have come here and gone away for the same reason."

Using words similar to those he had written several years earlier in describing a disappointing lecture stop in Greenfield, Massachusetts, Walker concluded: "Are we not great anti-slavery folks in Old Plymouth?"

Walker seemed ashamed that even here, in white America's hometown, black people wore the shackles of discrimination.

*   *   *   *

Now, in 1851, old warrior Walker was suffering the burden of fatigue, in spirit as well as in body. Walker's Vermont report to Garrison had repeated a

The Bad New Days

conclusion that he had several times recently suggested: "I shall, in all probability, have no more reports to make of my anti-slavery tours abroad..."

Was Jonathan Walker finally ready to give up his efforts in the abolitionist cause entirely? Or was this rather a hint of a change to be made? What did he mean by saying he could no longer assist "in this branch of the work"?

Perhaps he had used some of the long trips on foot between Vermont communities to plot his future. Perhaps he had concluded that he had more to offer in the cause that had occupied him actively for more than fifteen years. As if to suggest that idea, he wrote in his letter to Garrison that "the enormous and corrupting institutions of our country [provide] no just cause why the friends of human redemption should in the least relax their efforts to hasten the good time coming! Though

> 'We may not live to see the day,
> 'Yet earth shall glisten in the ray
> 'Of the good time coming...'

when man shall behold in every man his equal brother."

Walker was steeped in disappointment. He seemed to have concluded that New Englanders were turning their backs on the national crisis over slavery, just as he seemed to be turning away from his native New England. He wrote Garrison: "Whatever enterprise or movement is to be advanced or sustained by New Englanders calls up the great American question, 'Will it pay?' If it pays in the estimation of the inquirers, their sympathies are immediately enlisted; otherwise, procrastination is a more acceptable idea."

The "good old days" were behind Walker, and the "bad new days" upon him. Displaying more than ever a snapping cynicism, Walker had reached another crossroad in his long and colorful career.

Which path would he choose?

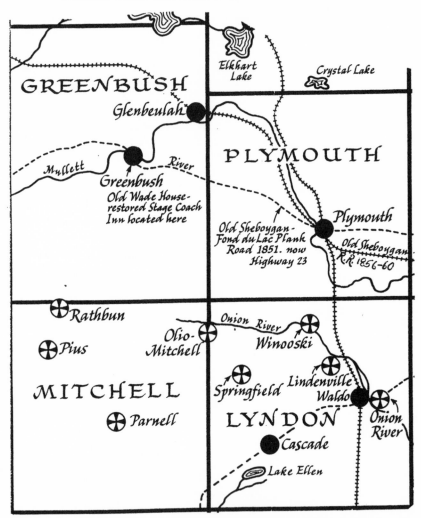

Winooski, Wisconsin, was named, along with other places in that region, after New England communities and streams by a former Vermonter. The Walkers lived in the Mitchell-Lyndon area, arriving in 1852, only four years after statehood had been granted Wisconsin. Jonathan and Jane Walker are believed to have helped fugitives from slavery by hiding them in their home and, when threatened with discovery, in a hideaway tunnel or ditch nearby. The younger Walker children went to the Old Northwest with their parents, and settled there. Before the Walkers relocated to Michigan, in 1864, their twin son Lloyd Garrison Walker had enlisted in the Union Army in Michigan. He returned to Wisconsin later as a physician and served his community into his own elder years.

America is West and the wind blowing.
America is a great word and the snow,
A way, a white bird, the rain falling,
A shining thing in the mind...
Archibald MacLeish, *American Letter*

CHAPTER 14   The Dream Fulfilled

When he was fifty-three years old, Jonathan Walker decided to move his family to Wisconsin. At last, he was headed West.

During his youth, and in his careers as a sailor and then as a lecturing agent for abolition – during most of those five exciting, wearying, impoverished, determined decades – Walker had expressed an interest in helping to settle the westward moving nation's frontier.

He was apparently so well known for his wistful wish that he had successfully used it in 1844 in Pensacola to camouflage his departure with the black men. Citing three sources, Joe M. Richardson wrote: "When local whites noticed his preparations, he said he was going to Mobile to sell his boat and then return to Massachusetts by way of a western route."

He left no record of why he chose to act at last in 1852. But it is easy enough for us to guess.

His health may have been a factor. He had never regained full strength in the arm that was wounded in Mexico. He had complained openly a year earlier about the wounded left arm, and about the branded right hand. In the end, his wandering lecture tours for nearly seven years surely had worn his tall, rugged body more than such a period of sailing or farming would have done. But it's not likely that his health was a major determinant. He would live another quarter-century and, in fact, leave behind memories of a man of unusual strength well into his eighth decade of life.

Jonathan Walker The Man with the Branded Hand

Walker's strength had permitted him to endure physical punishment longer than most men would have accepted it. But he was weary. He had reached a point of exhaustion, physically and emotionally. Driven by the self-set challenge of reaching the neutral masses, he was in turn beaten down by the disdain he perceived in the nation's leaders. He never lost faith that the people themselves would abolish slavery; his discouragement came from the slight and feeble efforts shown in government's halls and in religion's praying places.

Writing in his book, *The Year of Decision: 1846*, historian Bernard DeVoto described this era:

> They were an inchoate people between two stages of the endless American process of becoming a nation, with their heads down and their eyes resolutely closed to the desperate realities which a few years would force them to confront in the deadliest of awakenings. They were a people without unity and with only a spasmodic mutual awareness, at this moment being pulled farther asunder by the centrifugal expansion of the frontier and the equal explosiveness of the developing industry... A people going blithely into a war of conquest whose certain ending few tried to foresee. A people divided by racial differences, sectional cleavages, cultural antipathies, an enormous disparity of assumption, expectation, hope, and philosophy...

Walker had none of DeVoto's century-later perspective, but nevertheless he possessed an understanding of these circumstances of American life in mid-Nineteenth Century. One can imagine Walker coming to believe that he was an abolitionist Don Quixote, jousting with a windmill of rejection.

His family's finances, or the lack of them, may have been the most defining reason for his decision to leave the lecture circuit. He had provided Jane and the children some support from time to time, but he had not brought home the amount of money he would have earned had he continued his career as a sailor or boatwright, or even in farming on Cape Cod. Walker would have been mindful of his recent experiences in the "mud-docks" at Plymouth, requiring contortions few men in their fifties could execute without pain.

Jonathan and Jane might also have given thought to their family status. Their offspring were, in a way, two generations of children. The first five had been born between 1823 and 1833. By the time Jonathan had plodded home from his long Vermont tour, these five had reached adulthood. With Mary Gage Walker's marriage in Plymouth on January 11, 1852, the eldest had all settled into their own homes. That left at home the four youngest, ranging in age from baby George, then not quite four years old, and William, who was eight, to the twins, Lloyd and Maria, then only ten years old. It would be more than a dozen years before the youngest was old enough to leave home. Jonathan and Jane then would be into their mid-sixties. They would have thought about that, and how they wanted to spend those years with their children.

The Dream Fulfilled

Perhaps the decision to leave Massachusetts came as Jane once again urged Jonathan to consider finding work that would not take him away for long periods from their home – wherever that was to be! She would not have asked him to retire from the causes of abolition. She knew that would be unlikely. His conviction was too strong for him to just quit and walk away. His weariness from the years of long lecture tours, however, could have led him to seek out a more passive role. He hinted at that in his final letter to Garrison before relocating: "...[C]ircumstances forbid my further labors *in this branch of the work* [emphasis added], though I shall always hold myself in readiness to aid this and every cause, to the extent of my ability, which has for its object and aim the amelioration of the condition of any part of the human family."

As they may have done twice before, in relocating to Pensacola and to Plymouth, the middle-aged couple may have renewed their avowed compromise: he would stop traveling if she would let him choose the place where they would live.

They chose to live never again in Massachusetts. Leaving their home state, however, did not mean abandoning adventure. Just the opposite. The West was being settled, and Jonathan Walker would approach this new effort with the baited patience of a veteran sailor scanning the horizon, comfortably aware that somewhere beyond lay the excitement that he had so far found throughout his fifty-three years.

The "Old Northwest" would have seemed attractive to an abolitionist. The Northwest Ordinance of 1787 had banned slavery in any of the six states to be made from that territory. Just as the Mason-Dixon line separated the eastern free and slave states, the Ohio River had become the line of separation to the west.

When the Walkers were looking to their future, the Old Northwest was made up of five states and Minnesota Territory. Between 1803 and 1837, Ohio, Indiana, Illinois, and Michigan had achieved statehood, each when its population reached the ordinance's requirement of 60,000. In 1852, Minnesota was still six years from statehood. That left Wisconsin, admitted to the Union in 1848, as the youngest state in the Old Northwest and the newest frontier. Jonathan Walker's decision was made. His choice was the newest frontier.

*   *   *   *

The Walker family's trip west probably was made through the Great Lakes, the most common route for new settlers. Gustave W. Buchen, in *Historic Sheboygan County*, wrote about the trip connecting Buffalo, New York, and Sheboygan, Wisconsin. Walker would have known about the steamship service, having lectured into central New York State and beyond, and having a sailor's interest in the Erie Canal. When completed in 1825, the canal ran nearly four hundred miles from Albany to Buffalo. The trip from Buffalo to Wisconsin took sail vessels and steamers up to a month, and sometimes longer, depending upon the weather.

Jonathan Walker The Man with the Branded Hand

Not all travelers chose the Great Lakes. Settlers from the eastern states often chose the land route below the lakes. One observer counted as many as two hundred fifty covered wagons moving west in a single day along the south shore of Lake Erie. The wagon's speed – only fifteen to twenty-five miles a day – must have seemed intolerable to a family anxious to resettle.

Walker left no record of his choice of travel, but a sailor and his family would most likely have gone over water. In seven months in 1853, immigration agents for Wisconsin logged 13,400 immigrants at Sheboygan and Port Washington. The following year, the number of passengers disembarking at Sheboygan was 20,914. Most of these settlers were young people. "A man fifty years of age was considered an old man," Buchen said. Jonathan was older.

Much of Wisconsin's 56,000 square miles were in undeveloped land when the Walkers arrived. A territory cut out of Michigan territory since July 4, 1836, Wisconsin had become the Union's thirtieth state on May 29, 1848, only four years before the Walkers' arrival. The state's admission brought, once again, equal balance between free and slave states, between North and South representation in the United States Senate. The settlement of Sheboygan County, where the Walkers were to land, had been sputtering for four decades. In 1836, the village name was chosen and a postmaster appointed to serve the seventeen dwellings. The Panic of 1837, which had caught the Walkers in Florida, resulted in Sheboygan's becoming "a destitute village," Ray Van Handel, Jr., wrote in his postal history of Sheboygan County. "In 1840, a second wave of settlement began, and on October 25, 1844, the [new] postoffice at Sheboygan was established."

Wisconsin's population had grown rapidly, from 31,000 in the federal census of 1840 to 305,000 in 1850. Miners from Kentucky, Missouri, and other areas, attracted to lead deposits in the southwestern part of Wisconsin, founded the state's first permanent white settlements in the '20s. The Black Hawk War of 1832, followed by a series of treaties, led by 1848 to U.S. acquisition of all Indian territories. The opening of this land to the public brought a wave of Yankee farmers and land agents from New England and New York.

News of this attractive opportunity would have reached Massachusetts. Equally important to Walker would have been the adoption, in 1848, of the state constitution – it outlawed slavery but withheld voting rights for African Americans. He was not now, no more than ever, willing to settle for half a loaf of freedom for slaves. He was to write: "[W]ere it not for the infamous clause in the Constitution of the State disfranchising the man of color, Wisconsin might present as manly an attitude as any other state in the Union. But the great deference paid to the slave-breeding, slave-trading, and slaveholding lords of the land will cost years of hard toil and human sacrifice to remove."

In that he was more accurate than he would have wished to be. More than a decade remained in the struggle. If he didn't know it before arriving in Wisconsin, Walker was to learn soon enough that not everyone in the state embraced what he came to call "progressiveness." Elmer Koppelmann, in his

The Dream Fulfilled

book, *Branded Hand: The Struggles of an Abolitionist*, cited an editorial published by the Sheboygan Lake *Journal*, on October 25, 1851: "Ought not Negroes be excluded from residence in the North? This is the question deserving serious consideration. We have reflected upon it, and the more we reflect upon it, the better we are satisfied that the peace and safety of Northern communities demand that the impress of runaway slaves into the Northern states should be entirely prohibited."

*   *   *   *

Where to live once they stepped off the ship in Sheboygan probably was not planned by the Walkers. Arriving, however, they would have made up their minds quickly. "During the 1850s, when the stream of newcomers was at its height," Buchen wrote, "Sheboygan presented much the appearance of a western mining camp in the days of the discovery of gold." Jonathan and Jane Walker, whose homes had been in the relatively rural quietness of Cape Cod, Plymouth, and Pensacola, would not have welcomed living in such frenetic activity on the western shores of mighty Lake Michigan.

The few major roads fanning out from lakeside Sheboygan were owned in the 1850s by the Wisconsin Stage Company and used by its coach lines. The most important was the route to Fond du Lac. Among the eighteen four-horse teams on this route was a coach that left after the arrival of the evening steamboat and reached Fond du Lac next morning. The Walker family very likely were on one of those trips in 1852 when Fond du Lac was just being incorporated. That the Walkers picked a place on the southern tip of Lake Winnebago would not have surprised friends and relatives back East. They had always lived on the water. In Fond du Lac – the French settlers' name translates as "End of the Lake" – they were on Wisconsin's largest lake – thirty miles long, up to ten miles wide. Although less than a day's travel from the excitement of Sheboygan, Fond du Lac was a region not unlike the Walkers' Cape Cod.

Jonathan wrote Garrison after settling down on his own farm: "The climate here is about the same as that of the southern part of Massachusetts, Rhode Island, and Connecticut, but with fewer violent gales and severe storms. It is as healthy in this section as any part of the Eastern states; but few localities are subject to the ague and fever, and those not much."

Fishing in Lake Michigan, as well as in Winnebago and other lakes and streams, would have appealed to Walker. But his first vocational interest now was farming. He had grown up on the farm of his father, who in turn had inherited farming interests and skills, as well as land, from his parents. Seth and Mercy Walker were probably living with Jonathan's brother David when Jane and Jonathan left Massachusetts in 1852. For Jonathan, the future was in the land. Wisconsin farmers were planting corn, potatoes, hay, and fruit.

In 1852, Harriet Beecher Stowe's novel, *Uncle Tom's Cabin, or Life Among the Lowly*, was published. The Walkers may have been the only family in America to have hanging in their home pictures of Harriet Beecher Stowe and Frederick Douglass.

The Walker family stayed in Fond du Lac about two years, and then made the first of two major moves in Wisconsin, both predicated on establishing an organized community, the type that 20th Century Americans would come to call a "commune." During the 1840s and '50s, these communities enjoyed a brief popularity among literary, liberal, reform-minded leaders in New England and elsewhere. Collins, the general agent for the Anti-Slavery Society, for example, was an advocate of "communitarianism." One of its cardinal tenets was that the community shared the property, none was to be privately owned. Collins founded the Skaneateles Community in upstate New York, which lasted three years after its founding in 1843.

Transcendentalists A. Bronson Alcott and Charles Lane had begun a utopian estate, called Fruitlands, in the town of Harvard, Massachusetts, in 1843. Members included Louisa May Alcott and her daughters. Alcott, author of *Little Women* and *Little Men*, later wrote that residents ate only fruits and grains, took cold baths, and wore linen almost exclusively, because "cotton, silk, and wool were forbidden as the product of slave-labor, worm-slaughter, and sheep-robbery." Fruitland failed within a year.

In Massachusetts, a community was formed in 1842 by the Northampton Association of Education and Industry, where Garrison had stayed in 1843 during a period of poor health; the Hopedale Community, founded in Milford in 1842; and the utopian Brook Farm in West Roxbury, whose residents included Ralph Waldo Emerson, Margaret Fuller, Nathaniel Hawthorne, and Charles Dana among other writers during its 1841-1846 existence. Most lasted only a few years.

After Fond du Lac, the Walkers decided to act on their hopes for an organized community. In 1854, they went southeast a few miles to the Town of Mitchell, a tiny village at the headwaters of the Onion River, and Walker began efforts to reactivate Spring Farm. This was a community begun in 1846 under the leadership of Benjamin Trowbridge by families from New York State. New York newspaper editor Horace Greeley visited the farm in 1847. Spring Farm residents adopted a motto that would have appealed to Jonathan Walker: "Union, Equal Rights, and Social Guarantees." When fully established, the colony was to have 400 families or 1,800 residents, but by the time the Walkers arrived in 1854, most of the eleven families at Spring Farm had departed, discouraged by crop failures and the territorial legislature. In 1847, denying a special charter for Spring Farm's incorporation, the legislature expressed fear the community would contribute to making Wisconsin "a breeding place for reformers." Spring Farm's buildings, some of them only half-constructed, were standing. That encouraged Walker and others to attempt a reopening.

Even with the new energy that the Walkers brought, Spring Farm was not to be. By March 1, 1855, Walker had given up on Mitchell, but not on the idea of a cooperative community. He explained why he had quit the venture in a letter to "dear friend Charles Hazelton" of Littleton, New Hampshire:

The Dream Fulfilled

Several weeks ago, I wrote you a line in relation to the contemplated progress in a movement at Mitchell... Since that time, I have come in possession [of] some facts in the case which utterly forbid all hope of its success, and have despaired of any healthy, radical, reformatory movement at that place, under the present state of affairs. It has cost me much time and some money in consequence of being deceived in relation to the title of the land and those that claim them. I mentioned in my last [letter] that half the names subscribed to the circular should not have been there. I also might have said that more than three-fourths were unqualified and unprepared to cooperate in any such an enterprise as the circular [for Spring Farm] indicated. The circular was written by myself and the sentiments were mine, but after it passed *from me* the quantities of lands and all the signatures were appended by others...

Walker seemed to be suggesting that the information added to that which he had prepared was inaccurate, or perhaps it either exaggerated or simply expanded on Walker's conservative claims.

More likely, Spring Farm was doomed simply by the idealism of its invention. Buchen explained: "In distributing the reward to labor, the usual method was to be reversed [at Spring Farm], in that necessary labor would be best paid, useful labor would come next, and pleasant labor would be worst paid. The poorest person in the organization was assured of comforts and pleasures greater than the existing order of society could give to princes and millionaires, and beyond anything he had ever dreamed of."

Buchen quoted a "first-hand account of this unique social experiment" from an unnamed member as concluding: "Though we failed in this attempt, yet it has left an indelible impression on the minds of one-half the members at least, that a harmonious association in some form is the way, and the only way, that the human mind can be fully and properly developed; and the general belief is that community of property is the most practical form."

Jonathan Walker could not have been the author of such a statement. Not one to sulk, he was anxious to continue the search for the right place. He had been in Wisconsin nearly three years now and still had not found a place in which to settle. He and Jane made their second major move, to the village of Winooski in the town of Lyndon. The Walkers were among the pioneers in settling this area, only a few miles west of Sheboygan Falls and Lake Michigan. The Mitchell-Lyndon-Lina region had seven little villages along the twenty-eight-mile stretch of the Onion River. Several had names familiar to the Walkers. Nearby, for example, were Plymouth and Hingham, names much earlier given to Massachusetts towns. The name, Winooski, according to Raymond Van Handel, was chosen in 1854 by postmaster James Stone, "who came from Vermont, where there is a Winooski and an Onion River..."

In coming to Wisconsin, Walker had not left behind a lifetime of aggressive independence and entrepreneurial action. Once he abandoned his hopes for Mitchell, he almost immediately began publicizing a new proposal – to create a community for reformists in Winooski. And, again, typical of his luck in finding a dawning unexpectedly early in the darkness of his night, assistance came from rejection. In his 1855 letter to Hazelton, he noted that the Spring Farm supporters had publisahed the information that Walker disliked. That turned out to be good news, he wrote, because it "has induced a number of progressive friends to make further inquiries in relation to the enterprise, and the probability is that a number will be this way in the spring and summer."

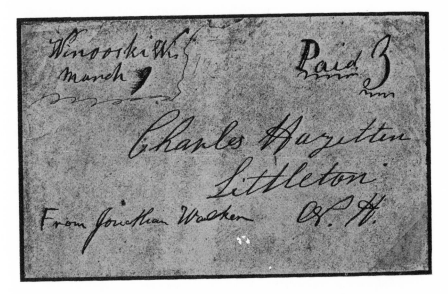

Cover for Walker's letter to Hazelton, bearing Jonathan's signature.

So buoyed, Walker encouraged Hazelton to consider his new proposal:

I have therefore bought sixty acres of good land within a quarter mile of a small, pleasant village and am now on it myself, and am disposed to share it with such practical reformatory friends as may be disposed to come here *on the cash principle*, which will be this season not exceeding ten dollars per acre on the average value." If that sounds inexpensive, note that in 1855 one Sheboygan County company was paying a laborer seventy cents a day; and tollgate keepers earned from fifty to two hundred dollars a year, although they also may have received housing as well. ..

At our village we have a store, a flour [mill] and a saw mill. The two mills are owned by William M. Ellis, a liberal-minded anti-slavery friend, and [he] is ready to enlarge his water pressure when needed and in otherwise assist in industrial pursuits. I have charge of the sawmill and can furnish lumber to friends at about eight dollars per 1,000 feet...

I do not wish to persuade but am anxious for you to come here and *see* how you like it. It will not cost much, and [there is] no occasion to be idle here. Write me on the reception of this.

Running up the left margin of the paper was a scribbled post-script: "You can make a good beginning here with $200."

There is no record of how Hazelton reacted. However, nine months later, on December 18, 1855, Walker was still proselytizing. He convinced Garrison to publish a letter to "Dear Friend S.M.B." This lengthy, detailed report covered the cost of farmland ("from three to six dollars per acre"), wheat ("one dollar to one dollar and thirty cents per bushel"), and cows ("thirty to forty dollars"). He added: "In regard to society, we have nothing to boast of; yet, in some respects, it will bear a comparison with that of the older states. There are rough edges and sharp corners that need to be trimmed off; but that must be the work of time, with labor and patience."

In 1856, Walker wrote of new arrivals from the eastern states and Germany, and he called again for "a social community of Equality." Despite his prolonged efforts, there is no record to indicate that Hazelton, or "S.M.B.," or anyone else, had been persuaded to join Walker. That he had tried was not unusual for him. If nothing, he had always been dedicated to any principle or action that he believed to be right.

*   *   *   *

Jane and Jonathan Walker were to make their Wisconsin home for a decade in Winooski. Homesickness was never mentioned in Walker's writings, although a report he prepared for the curious back East suggested that he had felt the pull of "home." He wrote:

...To leave behind all our old associates and associations, which years of familiarity have given a strong hold upon our habits and feelings, and attempt to create others, among strangers in a strange land, [is] what many dispositions find it difficult to accomplish. The difficulty, however, may be much modified by several families of kindred habits, feelings, and associations moving at or near the same time to the same locality. This prevents, to some extent, the isolated and melancholy feelings that make life tedious and gloomy.

Again using the word newly popular with him – progressive – he concluded: "This is not a bad section of the West for progressive minds to emigrate to, in order to associate together and cooperate to aid on the needed reforms of our age."

Jonathan Walker The Man with the Branded Hand

Winooski in winter, some years after 1900, showing the present Drewry home at left center. The Walkers' home was up a hill in left background.

Walker concentrated his early efforts on developing his farm in the planting and growing season. But he would have kept up with his interests in anti-slavery events. He was living not far from Ripon, Wisconsin, when on February 28, 1854, a group of about fifty met in a schoolhouse there to help found a new political organization in favor of abolishing slavery. They were planting the seeds for what became the Republican Party. There is no record that Walker attended that meeting. Nor did he record his reaction to other major slavery-related activities during this period, yet surely he would have cheered in 1854 when Sam Houston stood alone among Southern senators to vote against Stephen Douglas' Kansas-Nebraska Bill. The act repealed the Missouri Compromise of 1820 and permitted all new states from Iowa to the Rockies to decide the question of slavery on the state level. In reversing his own vote as a Tennessee Congressman in 1820, Houston was to declare later that his 1854 stand was "the most unpopular vote I ever gave... [but] the wisest and most patriotic." Here he was – the heroic Mexican War general, the man who had been declared the first president of the Independent Republic of Texas, and the United States senator from a state with 150,000 slaves – being denounced by his

The Dream Fulfilled

state Legislature and his own political party. Houston spoke like a Texan George Washington: "I know neither North nor South; I know only the Union."

It's likely that such noble actions stirred the abolitionist fires within Jonathan Walker. With fewer demands from farming during the winter, he would have been able to help the cause for which he was best known. His anti-slavery activities were not so celebrated. He wrote Garrison on July 6, 1854, from his home in Winooski, about the visit of his old colleague, the former Harwich visiting lecturer, Charles C. Burleigh. As if longing for his once active role, Walker called Burleigh's visit "a God-send..." Walker spent "about two days" with Burleigh while he gave five lectures.

The former sea captain's report indicated how virgin was the new territory for abolitionist activity: "But very few of those who heard him had ever before heard the subject presented other than in connection with politics. The doctrine of 'No Union with Slaveholders' was new, but with many found a hearty response... The people of this new country, as everywhere else, have been nose-led by designing priests and demagogues; but, not content with their present position, many of them, who dare to think for themselves, are disposed to take a more progressive stand."

Wisconsin was not without the dishonest. Walker wrote that "some villain" broke into Burleigh's trunk and stole two hundred dollars that he had earned selling anti-slavery literature. In words that so often in the past could have been applied to himself, Walker added: "Physically, he is fast wearing out in the cause of humanity, and should not be allowed the vexation of pecuniary embarrassment."

$$*\qquad*\qquad*\qquad*$$

Throughout this period, Abraham Lincoln was wrestling with his emotions, his conscience, and his own public stand on slavery. On October 16, 1854, he shared his anguish in a public statement that displayed the eloquence and legal logic that still was maturing within this great figure of destiny. He was writing about the Wilmot Proviso of 1846, which would have prohibited slavery in any territory acquired by treaty with Mexico. Here is how Lincoln wrote of it, carefully stepping through the philosophical brambles and political thorns of slavery:

> [The proviso] created a great flutter; but it stuck like wax, was voted into the bill, and the bill passed with it through the House. The Senate, however, adjourned without final action on it, and so both the appropriation and the proviso were lost for the time... This declared indifference, but, as I must think... real, covert zeal, for the spread of slavery, I cannot but hate. I hate it because it deprives our republican example of its just influence in the world, enables the enemies of free institutions with plausibility to taunt us as hypocrites, causes the real friends of freedom to doubt our sincerity, and especially because it forces so many good men among ourselves into an open war with the very fundamental principles of civil liberty, criticizing the Declaration

of Independence, and insisting that there is no right principle of action but self-interest...

I surely will not blame [Southern people] for not doing what I should not know how to do myself. If all earthly power were given me, I should not know what to do as to the existing institution. My first impulse would be to free all the slaves, and send them to Liberia, to their own native land. But a moment's reflection would convince me that whatever of high hope (as I think there is) there may be in this in the long run, its sudden execution is impossible. If they were all landed there in a day, they would all perish in the next ten days; and there are not surplus shipping and surplus money enough to carry them there in many times ten days. What then? Free them all, and keep them among us as underlings? Is it quite certain that this betters their condition? I think I would not hold one in slavery at any rate, yet the point is not clear enough for me to denounce people upon. What next? Free them, and make them politically and socially our equals? My own feelings will not admit of this, and if mine would, we well know that those of the great mass of whites will not. Whether this feeling accords with justice and sound judgment is not the sole question, if indeed it is any part of it. A universal feeling, whether well or ill founded, cannot be safely disregarded. We cannot then make them equals. It does seem to me that systems of gradual emancipation might be adopted, but for their tardiness in this I will not undertake to judge our brethren of the South...

* * * *

Jonathan Walker apparently did more than pay tribute to Burleigh, Stowe, Douglass, and others active in abolitionism by hanging pictures and writing letters. In the 1854 letter to Garrison about Burleigh's visit, he again hinted at some other activity. He said, "I devoted some time last winter to the anti-slavery cause, and intend to devote more time the coming winter, if possible."

Koppelmann suggested that Walker was a conductor on the Underground Railroad. Those who aided runaway slaves faced six months in jail and a thousand dollars fine in addition to civil liability to the owner, a thousand dollars for each fugitive. That did little to slow or halt the traffic. Between 1810 and 1850, more than 100,000 slaves valued at thirty-million dollars had escaped. The Michigan Lines of the Underground Railroad alone carried between 40,000 and 50,000 passengers into Canada, according to one estimate.

In Wisconsin, three communities – Madison, Beloit, and Milton – became known as stops along the Underground Railroad. Koppelmann suggested the possibility that Walker began his Wisconsin efforts to help runaway slaves while in Mitchell, and continued the action after building his simple two-story home in Winooski.

The Dream Fulfilled

By 1855, Koppelmann said, the Walker family had built their house in Lyndon, a village just east of Winooski. Ruth and Dave Drewry, who bought the Walker farm a century later, interviewed a man who claimed he had been told as a child that Walker was involved with the Underground Railroad. Alvin Kirst recalled a trench perhaps two hundred feet long and deep enough for a man to stand in it, running near the apple orchard on the former Walker property. Boards covered the top of the trench, and dirt covered the boards.

Koppelmann wrote: "It is my speculation that Walker regularly received fugitives at his home. I believe that he provided them with food and shelter until he was able to lead them to the next station, located, perhaps, at Ripon, Appleton, an Indian reservation, or some other point North, on their trek to freedom."

As he had earlier, Walker in 1856 wrote *The Liberator* to attack those abolitionists who supported armed overthrow of the slaveholders. There were more peaceful means for "settling difficulties with our erring brothers," he wrote. Achieving freedom through violence was using evil to fight evil, he believed. He was, it seems, actively demonstrating one way, serving as a conductor on the Underground Railroad.

Walker never faltered in believing that freedom ultimately would be declared for all people of color. He was to write, two years after arriving in Wisconsin: "[A]lready, slavery's death-knell begins to toll, and a few more slave cases like those of Shadrach, Jerry, Glover, Sims, and Burns will do a mighty work for the toiling millions now in Slavedom." He was referring to men whose escapes and captures had come under the notorious Fugitive Slave Act of 1850. Walker advocated a simple regard for the Fugitive Slave Law: disobey it. The Act, he believed, charged all *free* Americans "to become substitutes for Southern trained bloodhounds, to bark on the track of the panting fugitive from degradation and chains."

*   *   *   *

In January 1857, Governor Coles Bashford delivered a message to the people of Wisconsin: "The day seems not far distant when, in agricultural and mineral wealth, in commercial advantages, in educational facilities, and all that tends to make us truly great and prosperous as a state, we shall be among the first in the Union."

Jonathan and Jane Walker followed the same rainbow. They expanded their sixty-acre holding in Lyndon. On September 11, 1858, the local register recorded a deed for the sale to Jonathan of twenty acres from Frederick and Helen Joerns for $221. William Ellis's sawmill, which employed Walker, was on the bank of the Onion River; the Joerns owned a large tract north and northeast of Waldo Mill Pond, and it was part of this plot that they sold to Walker. No matter where he called home, as a sailor or farmer, Walker always managed to settle near a body of water.

If Jonathan Walker had known about an adventure reflecting his own escape with slaves of fourteen years earlier, he would have cheered when learning of the Pensacola *Gazette* account on February 2, 1858, of a dozen slaves stealing a boat in Key West and sailing to freedom in the Bahamas.

There was not much else now to swell the heart of a devout abolitionist. It must have seemed sometimes to Walker that the decade of the 1850s had brought repeated political defeat on the heels of another legal loss. The Kansas-Nebraska Act, the latest Congressional attempt to find equal balance in free and slave states, turned the middle of the continent into armed conflict. John Brown went from the futility of the 1856 Kansas battleground to the madness of 1859 at Harpers Ferry, Virginia. There, in the quiet and darkness of a Sunday evening, the fifty-nine-year-old Torrington, Connecticut, native set about his driven task of freeing all the slaves -- not those in Virginia alone, but in all of America. Brown's mad efforts were not without irony. In his attack on the United States Armory arsenal on October 16, 1859, the first man killed was a black porter at the depot. In the thirty-six hours of Brown's bloody symbolism, death had taken both his sons and two slaves. Brown was hanged for treason in Charlestown, Virginia, on December 2, 1859, the eighteenth to die from the Harpers Ferry invasion.

Jonathan Walker, like most abolitionists, opposed the use of violence. Despite such shocking attempts in the decade of the '50s to foreclose on slavery – perhaps because of them – abolitionists had had just cause for their unrelieved outrage. Stampp wrote in his study of slavery: "In 1860, the peculiar institution was almost precisely what it had been thirty years before. If anything, the chains of bondage were strengthened, not weakened..."

  *   *   *   *

By 1860, Jonathan Walker's parents had died. True to family tradition, both had made it into their ninetieth year or beyond: Seth Walker died on July 26, 1858, age eighty-nine, and Mercy Bassett Walker on July 18, 1860, age ninety-one.

In 1860, the United States took a census in all thirty-four states. Nineteen of them, plus eight territories, prohibited slavery. Of the thirty-one million people recorded, about twenty-seven million of them were white. Of the nearly four and a half million people of color, less than a half million were categorized as "free colored." The remaining population – 3,950,000 men, women, and children – were slaves. There had never been so many in the United States. One of every eight Americans was a black slave.

Massachusetts' population was placed at about 1.2 million, only 9,400 of whom were "free colored." Florida's 140,000 population included more than 62,000 people of color, virtually all of them slaves. Jane and Jonathan Walker were among 775,000 people counted in Wisconsin, where there were no slaves and only 1,481 "free colored." They were still living in Lyndon with all of their "second generation" of four children. Maria and Lloyd, the twins, were now eighteen years old; William was seventeen, and George, twelve. Also listed at the Walker home was twelve- year-old Lewis Berry, apparently the son of Lewis Berry and his wife, Nancy Child Walker, who was the first of two daughters the

210

The Dream Fulfilled

Walkers named for Lydia Maria Francis Child. The boy would have been visiting from Massachusetts, where the Berrys lived.

For the maturing Walker children, rural Wisconsin had been the only home they remembered. Not until 1881 was Winooski to reach its peak population – eighty-eight inhabitants. Some of the Walkers were to live there as adults, as they married and raised their own families. The five older siblings made New England their home.

In 1860, Jonathan Walker was sixty-one years old and Jane was fifty-seven. They were still living in Lyndon. Walker's occupation, he told the 1860 census-taker, was in carpentry. But he kept busy at other odd jobs, as he had all his life. It's probable that the Walkers were still helping runaway slaves as the nation plunged closer to a civil war.

The Walkers' Wisconsin real estate was valued at $600, the census recorded, and their personal property at $150. It wasn't much, even by the standards of the 1860s, but it was more property than Jonathan and Jane Walker had ever owned.

In fact, Walker may have begun exploring land across Lake Michigan as early as 1859. From later developments, it appears that the adventurous Jonathan regularly sailed the ocean-like lake, and may even have spent time on the opposite shore preparing land for farming. He may have had his son Lloyd homesteading in Michigan. A father who had taken his eldest son to Mexico when he was only twelve years old would not have had second thoughts about assigning seventeen-year-old Lloyd to live across the lake, perhaps alone for a few months at a time. After all, Jonathan had left home to begin the life of a sailor at seventeen.

As it was to turn out, Jonathan Walker had not yet shed the restlessness that had driven him for almost a half-century. More adventures lay ahead for the old captain, not only in Michigan but in a Union Army camp in Virginia.

The Walker home at Winooski, Wisconsin.

Jonathan Walker The Man with the Branded Hand

Leslie's Illustrated Newspaper (1861)

During the Civil War, Fortress Monroe, on Virginia's peninsula east of Richmond, became the first major site for the Union Army to provide safety for African-Americans fleeing bondage in the South. This drawing was labeled, "The Black People Seeking Refuge at Fort Monroe in 1861." The former slaves came to be regarded as "contrabands," based on General Benjamin Butler's reasoning that if southern slaveholders regarded them as chattel property they could be seized and claimed along with real estate and other real property. By 1863, the federal government was conducting schools for the children and otherwise helping the tens of thousands of men, women, and families prepare for their new freedom. Jonathan Walker went to Fortress Monroe in 1864, hoping to help provide education in the fields in which he claimed knowledge: fruit farming, mechanics, carpentry, and writing. The Army eventually decided to permit civilians to volunteer their services, but not until after Jonathan Walker, now sixty-five years old, had become ill and was forced to return to his new home in Michigan.

Our political problem now is, "Can we as a nation
continue together permanently – forever –
as half slave, and half free?"
The problem is too mighty for me.
May God in his mercy superintend the solution.

Abraham Lincoln (August 15, 1855)

CHAPTER 15   One Final Effort

J onathan Walker seemed attracted to a small settlement being put down in the
late 1850s among the forestlands on the Michigan shore almost directly across
Lake Michigan from Sheboygan, Wisconsin. Perhaps the romanticist in the old,
world-traveled sailor was drawn by its name – Crimea, Michigan. As a young
sailor, Walker may have stopped at one of the Black Sea ports in the Ukrainian
resort peninsula with that exotic name.

Perhaps, however, the site appealed to his entrepreneurial interests.
When Crimea first caught Walker's eye, the town was not much more than a
name for an area almost given over to trees and wild animals. His eye was good,
however. Within a quarter-century, the land on the edge of Lake Michigan was
to become a resort area.

But now, Walker was to relate, it was:

...three or four small unfinished houses and several shanties, with small
cleared patches for growing garden stuff which generally proved a
failure, as it was mostly harvested by deer, woodchucks, and roaming
shoats. The raccoons, minks, and skunks paid nightly visits to the
chicken roosts, relieving the owners of collecting eggs or dressing
poultry. Civilization had provided a P.O. named "'Crimea," which was
mainly kept in the pocket of the postmaster.

A Michigan historian claimed that in 1862 Walker established a small
fruit farm on land "where he had spent earlier summers." This slender rise of

213

land, which juts into Mona Lake (also called Black Lake) near the channel leading into Lake Michigan, was to be called "Walker's Point."

These sources indicate that Walker had explored the lake shore eighty miles east of Wisconsin, perhaps as early as 1858. Other evidence suggests that he cleared land and farmed there for a few summers. Patient and methodical, he would have used his carpentry skills to begin erecting a house, and it seems certain that his son, Lloyd Garrison Walker, lived there prior to 1862, for he enlisted in the Union Army at Grand Haven, Michigan, on December 19, 1862. Jonathan, however, probably did not move there to live with Jane and the three children who were still at home until 1864. The old sailor, now halfway into his seventh decade, was still able to juggle property, homes, and family on opposite shores.

*   *   *   *

By 1860, the North and the South were almost literally at sword's points. The War Between the States was the inevitable result of a union politically paralyzed by slavery.

As wanton – and wasted – as John Brown's 1859 raid on the Virginia arsenal may have seemed, it served as one of several triggers to blast off the war. Only one hundred days passed between the election of Abraham Lincoln, running in the 1860 United States presidential campaign on the Republican Party's anti-slavery platform, and the election of Jefferson Davis as president by the seven Confederate States of America, which had been established on February 8, 1861. Five states had seceded by January 21, 1861, when Davis and four others from the Deep South resigned from the United States Senate.

Davis took office, a month before Lincoln did. A week after Lincoln's inaugural, on March 11, 1861, the Confederate states in convention adopted a permanent constitution much like the United States Constitution, including a section prohibiting the African slave trade. A main difference was in allowing interstate commerce in slaves. Of the break-away states' population of nine million in 1861, more than a third – 3.8 million – were slaves. The Union states' 22 million population included a half-million slaves.

On April 15, 1861, only five weeks into his first term, Lincoln declared a state of insurrection and called out Union troops. By the third month of his tenure, Lincoln was president of a Union that had lost eleven states: Alabama, Arkansas, Florida, Georgia, Louisiana, Mississippi, North Carolina, South Carolina, Tennessee, Texas, and Virginia.

The hard-line abolitionists, of whom New Hampshire's Stephen Foster usually seemed the most militant, were not certain about Lincoln during the early, rapid developments of the war. Foster was still broadcasting his jaunty jingoism: "Revolution, not dissolution."

As the war began, abolitionists found themselves maligned by public figures who otherwise were opposed to slavery but who insisted the war must be fought to preserve the Union. Urging President Lincoln to resist abolitionists' pressure to free the slaves, publisher Samuel Bowles in his Massachusetts

One Final Effort

newspaper, the Springfield *Daily Republican,* wrote: "The abolition of slavery is not the object of his administration. He has no right to make that the purpose of war. His present duty is to prosecute the war and to overpower and punish the rebels who seek the destruction of the government."

In Boston, some abolitionists formed the Emancipation League, which supported freedom for slaves as a military necessity for the Union. Foster, no less shocking than in his religious rampages, called Lincoln a better slave-catcher than Jefferson Davis. He referred to Union forces having captured 6,000 slaves in South Carolina alone by November, 1861. Lincoln offered to ship freed slaves to Haiti, or Liberia. Foster said he would join the rebel confederation if Davis would emancipate slaves living in Confederate states. Lincoln signed the Congressional act freeing District of Columbia slaves, and paying compensation to the slaveholders thus denied the slaves' services.

Lincoln issued his first call for Union Army volunteers in 1861. Volunteers were called up for ninety days, all the time necessary, some thought, to crush the rebellion. Walker's native town of Harwich sent 341 Union volunteers. At least three of Jonathan and Jane Walker's family served in the Union Army. Lloyd Garrison Walker, one of the twins, was twenty-one when he enlisted at Grand Haven with Company B, First Regiment, Michigan Sharpshooters. He took part in fourteen major battles, and was wounded twice in the Army of the Potomac. Apparently endowed with some of his father's dry wit, he later told family members: "Father tried to free the slaves, but they had to wait until I went to war before anything was done."

The other two family members serving in the Civil War were sons-in-law of the Walkers. Nearly forty years old at the outset of the fighting, Ivory Lucas, Mary Walker's husband, enlisted in the 4th Wisconsin Cavalry. A blacksmith, he and Mary were living in Plymouth, Wisconsin, until he began his five-year military service. Ervin Underhill, the husband of Maria Child Walker, was a member of the 10th New York Artillery.

Jonathan Walker would have paid special attention to war news from Mobile Bay, where he had lived in the winter of 1843-44. In 1862, Admiral David Glasgow Farragut directed his Union Navy fleet into Mobile Bay, which Confederate troops had heavily mined. Farragut sent the fleet onward, declaring, "Damn the torpedoes."

Pensacola historian Leora M. Sutton wrote of this era: "More and more cases involving slaves show more compassion for the blacks in the South between 1850 and 1862. More whites were charged with aiding slaves to run away. More arrests were made for selling slaves liquor or to permit them to work for themselves. More slaves were freed by their masters."

Some slaveholders never changed. When George Willis, one of the three accusers of Jonathan Walker in 1844, died in 1861, his will identified forty-four slaves. Had Walker known of the Probate Court case involving the will, he would have appreciated the irony of the justice that came to the last wishes of the man who had pelted Walker with eggs as he stood in a pillory.

Willis' will had not been fully probated when the Union Army arrived in Pensacola. Most of the population fled. As a result, the late George Willis not only failed to pass along this chattel property, which his will valued at $40,350, but his estate was reduced by the bills charged for maintaining the slaves from December 1861 through February 9, 1862.

*   *   *   *

The politics of war intensified. The greatest pressure on Lincoln was to issue an order ending slavery. Such a declaration would, he feared, "not only undermine our cause, but smack of bad faith." He explained, "We didn't go into the war to put down slavery, but to put the flag back..."

Frederick Douglass later supported Lincoln's judgment: "Had he put the abolition of slavery before the salvation of the Union, he would have inevitably driven from him a powerful class of the American people and rendered resistance to rebellion impossible."

Lincoln was to change his attitude as part of changing his strategy of governing. In juggling the reasons for maintaining the Union and the need to resolve the crisis of slavery, the president moved step by gradual step towards full emancipation. At the first acts of secession, Lincoln supported a proposed constitutional amendment providing federal protection to slavery in the South. That failed. He ordered Union troops to return to the slaveholders any runaway slaves who crossed the Union lines. On March 6, 1862, he proposed a thirty-year transition towards the abolition of slavery, a plan that included a voluntary colonization program in which the federal government would support the resettling of liberated blacks outside the United States. He ended slavery in the District of Columbia. Congress set aside funds for volunteers relocating to Haiti and Liberia, black colonies that the government now recognized. By July, Congress had appropriated a half-million dollars for resettlement of confiscated blacks in "some tropical country." In September, Lincoln warned that if the rebels had not withdrawn within a hundred days, he would authorize the Union military forces to free all the slaves in the break-away states. That led to the proclamation signed by Lincoln in the White House on January 1, 1863, ending slavery in America. He took this action, the proclamation said, "as commander-in-chief of the army and navy of the United States, and as a fit and necessary war measure for repressing said rebellion..."

The proclamation added: "And I further declare and make known that such persons of suitable condition will be received into the armed service of the United States..."

That cleared up the question of employing black troops. Several states had proposed forming such regiments, each time to be rebuffed by Federal authorities. Of the 209,000 black men who were eventually to serve in Union forces, 93,000 were recruited from the South. Nearly a third of the African Americans were to die in service – 68,178, one in every three. Unlike white soldiers, the black men were not allowed to surrender.

One Final Effort

A leader in organizing Union troops, including the nation's first all-black unit, was John Albion Andrew. He was elected to five one-year terms as governor of Massachusetts during the Civil War. An ardent abolitionist, lawyer, and former state legislator, Andrew had supported Abraham Lincoln at the 1860 Republican Party convention. While he rejected the extreme positions of Garrison and Wendell Phillips, he is said to have had a leading part in raising funds for John Brown's defense. Pro-slavery mobs taunted Andrew with the chant:

> Tell John Andrew
> Tell John Andrew
> Tell John Andrew
> John Brown's dead.

Governor Andrew was to extend a helping hand to Jonathan Walker.

*   *   *   *

After moving to the Northwest, Walker returned at least three times to the eastern states. He first went in the fall of 1862, hoping to find a publisher for his autobiography. He may have tried to interest the anti-slavery press, which in the 1840s had printed three of his small books. Perhaps by this time, twenty years after Walker's rise to national recognition, his story was seen as too well known, or of little interest. Whoever decided, and why, Walker failed to find a publisher.

Jane was probably along on the trip, as perhaps were one or two of the children still living at home. It appears that the visit lasted into the winter. A letter Jonathan wrote years later used the pronoun "we," and described the return trip in the spring of 1863. Having been gone from Massachusetts a decade, seeking a reunion with family and old friends would not have been remarkable. Some of the older Walker children were married and living in the Plymouth and New Bedford areas. Jane and Jonathan would have wanted to see their grandchildren. And on Cape Cod they had brothers and sisters, and long-time friends, all of them elderly now. Jonathan was then sixty-three years old, and his brother David, who was to die in 1866, was seventy-two.

To return to Wisconsin, the Walkers left by railroad train. It is possible that Jonathan used this trip to introduce Jane to the property he had been developing in Michigan. Perhaps by now, having exercised the patience of a long-married man, he decided the time had arrived to convince Jane that they should move from Wisconsin to Michigan. Jonathan described the trip in a letter in the possession of Walker descendants in Shiocton, Wisconsin. The paper, not dated or signed, carries a notation, "This was written by Jonathan Walker." The account is in the style of Walker, dancing with playful wit around the urgent detail of pioneer life. Walker's long habit of recording his activities and attitudes would not have failed him when it came to telling about "tramping" the eastern shore of Lake Michigan. Walker wrote:

Jonathan Walker The Man with the Branded Hand

On our way from Philadelphia to Wisconsin in 1863, we left the [railroad] cars at Grand Haven and took a tramp along shore to Black Lake. There was then no other route to the place and on that one we had to climb steep sand banks or wade around the tops of fallen trees in deep water. Lake Michigan was then higher than it has been since. At Black Creek I found a sawmill partly built and a boarding house ditto.

He went on to describe the geographic pinpoint called Crimea, a few miles northwest of Lake Harbor. In the years to follow, camps and resort hotels were to be built in the area, some fronting on Lake Michigan. But the area that Walker wrote about was, as he suggested, barely inhabited in the 1860s. Located in Michigan's Muskegon County, Black Lake was a finger-shaped pond with uneven shoreline extending eastward from Lake Michigan. During the region's development, a bridge was built, nearly halfway from the western channel entering Lake Michigan, to carry traffic north and south over the lake. The name Black Lake remained with the pond on the eastern side of the bridge. For the pond on the western side of the bridge, at the mouth of Lake Michigan, a more resort-sounding name was chosen: Lake Harbor. The same name was given to the neighborhood that the Walker family was to help found soon after.

If Jonathan had arranged to have the westbound rail trip end in Grand Haven so he could show Jane the wild attractions of the land he and Lloyd had been farming, it was a successful bit of selling. They moved to Michigan in early 1864, taking with them a "team." This was one of the few times he mentioned having farm animals.

Walker told about the trip in his usual spare style, although the writing chortles with the zest of one who has overcome the difficult, if not the impossible, and exaggerates its formidability by making light of it. In the Hogoboom account he wrote:

The following spring we crossed Lake Michigan from Milwaukee to Grand Haven with a team on board a steamer, put the team in a boxcar, and out again at Ferrysburg, and started on the old mail route for Muskegon, but before we had reached Crimea the road disappeared among the hemlocks in dense darkness where we could neither go forward or return. The advent of the next glad morning revealed our whereabouts and the next day we "squatted."

Up to this point, Walker was recording factually his own experiences. His narrative continued in a more literary fashion, taking poetic license to cover years rather than the mere hours of his own stay with Jane:

The woodchopper came, too, with his shining axe, threw off his coat, rolled up his shirtsleeves, and the tall trees tumbled. A little later, the man with his oxen and log chain 'pitched in' and the next exhibition was a cloud, formed in the heavens by the smoke of what had been the forest; behold, it had taken wings and flown away, gone but not annihilated; only changed in form. Then followed the plow share, and the soil was turned topsy turvy.

The site Walker showed Jane was on the south side of Lake Harbor, a thumb-shaped hill thrust into the water about midway between the channel to Lake Michigan and the site of a north-south "float bridge," itself at mid-lake. The Walkers were again to be home on the quiet water of a tidal pond, perhaps only a mile-long walk from the ocean-like Great Lake to the west.

The Muskegon River, a few miles north, was a principal waterway carrying lumber to Lake Michigan. Having worked with lumber most of his life, most recently at Ellis' sawmill in Wisconsin, it was only natural that Jonathan Walker should help out with lumbering in Michigan. Early settlers around the Great Lakes cleared the forest so the land could be used for crops.

Farmers kept some wood for buildings and fuel, but most of the trees were simply felled and burned.

During these years, Michigan's rivers and lakes also were being used for passage on the Underground Railroad. It is possible that Walker was helping carry runaway slaves over Lake Michigan, connecting with the well-established Michigan network that included Muskegon, Grand Rapids, and Lansing. Fugitives could enter Michigan from underground stations in Illinois, Indiana, Minnesota, and Wisconsin.

A case could be made for the possibility that Walker served in some capacity. By the time he and Jane relocated, slaves had been freed. Earlier, however, Walker may have ferried runaways to Michigan from his Wisconsin home. In his style, he would have roamed from the Grand Haven or Muskegon Underground Railroad "terminal" and explored the Crimean forest and nearby lakeside area.

Settlers named the new community "Norton Township." Whenever it was that Walker actually took up residence in Michigan, he was remembered as one of Norton's early settlers. Benjamin Brist and John Kittle, both German immigrants, had been the first settlers, planting orchards on their virgin farmland in 1853. Other orchardists were to follow: Frederick Coston, William Hile, and Milo Rowe. H. N. Rowe, Milo's son, captained a tugboat on Lake Michigan. Another tug skipper was Hubert G. Bowles. Walker and the tugboat men would have had sailing stories to exchange. Active during the lumbering years around Muskegon, Bowles later claimed a close relationship with Jonathan. Perhaps Walker confided to Bowles that, having moved his family and household from Wisconsin forever, and settled permanently in Michigan; that, having undergone all this activity, he was already leaving. Something inside Jonathan Walker had determined that he had to return to the East for a new mission.

*   *   *   *

In April of 1864, apparently only days after moving to the Lake Harbor home he had built, Walker would make his last major attempt to assist African-

Americans. He headed east for his second trip away from the Old Northwest. Jane would not have objected. What good would it have done?

Walker explained in a letter to Garrison how he began what turned out to be a trip of at least five months to Massachusetts, New York, Maryland, and Virginia: "I left Grand Haven, Michigan, April 26, 1864, and after fifty-two hours' ride reached Boston. After visiting a few friends, I called on Governor Andrew, who readily gave me a letter of introduction and commendation to General [Benjamin] Butler, then at Fortress Monroe."

While Andrew and Walker may not have known each other personally – Walker was nearly twenty years older – each would have known and respected the other's reputation. In 1860, when only forty-two years old, Andrew had been unexpectedly nominated for governor and was swept into office. His reelection in November of 1864 was assured.

Walker wrote of his plan to go South: "My main object in going there was to devote myself to the aid of the newly-emancipated slaves in that part of the country in their industrial pursuits, having had previous experience in that work."

The Union army had gathered at Fortress Monroe in Virginia thousands of former slaves, many of whom had been caught in the vise between the warring forces from North and South. Besides those who took advantage of battles to escape North, there were present the slaves who had been forced into labor for the Confederate Army. Congressional Republicans had sponsored a bill that allowed the seizure of any slave employed in the Confederate war effort. In war, the argument went, the government had every right to confiscate enemy property – including slaves.

As the war years went on, and Union victory seemed certain, the Lincoln administration developed a program that put former slaves to work in military and civilian pursuits and prepared them to live in freedom. By 1863, many of the former slaves were working directly for the Union army; others were on government farms. A soldier in the Massachusetts 52nd Regiment wrote to newspapers in Northampton, Massachusetts, sympathetic to the plight of the finally freed slave: "Untouched, except in brutality, ground down through successive generations to a position little higher than that of the beasts, it is not strange that we find him unfitted for self-care..."

Walker believed his farming and mechanical background might be useful at such camps in supervision or instruction, but, he discovered, putting his skills to use would not be easy:

When I reached New York, I learned that General Butler had already left Fortress Monroe with an expedition up the James River, and had issued an order that no civilians should be allowed transit within the lines of his command. I waited some time, thinking the order might be withdrawn or modified; but got somewhat restless after waiting nearly three weeks, and started on, accompanied by two female teachers from the American Missionary Commission.

One Final Effort

Just ahead lay prime examples of bureaucratic red tape. It was already June, Walker had traveled from Michigan to Massachusetts to New York, and he was not much closer to executing his volunteer service than when he had decided to make this final gesture of help. "At Baltimore," he continued:

> I succeeded, by dint of exertions and the force of my letter from Governor Andrew to General Butler, in getting transportation to Fortress Monroe, where I presented my letters to Colonel J. B. Kinsman, in charge of the freedmen in Eastern Virginia, who sent his secretary with me to Norfolk, where I was introduced to a subordinate superintendent, who gave me a letter to another subordinate, requesting him to furnish me with a situation on a government farm in that district. By him, in turn, I was furnished with a military pass, and a note to an overseer upon three government farms from twelve to sixteen miles east of Norfolk, but he had all the aid he needed from detailed soldiers on the place. I passed on, therefore, to a number of the government farms, both east and south of Norfolk, for some distance, without finding a suitable opening. I slept several nights under the roof of ex-Governor Wise's house, a part of which was then occupied by three schools. Had I been there three years sooner, he would have doubtless been anxious to furnish me with a necktie, as he was [word or more missing] John Brown at Harper's Ferry.

The Liberator omitted words in Walker's account. As the lines appear, they leave the impression that Henry Wise would himself have hanged an abolitionist like Walker. Walker may have been suggesting that Wise "would have doubtless been anxious to furnish me with a necktie as he was *among those who favored hanging* John Brown at Harper's Ferry."

Walker could have been misinformed, of course. In *From Slavery to Freedom*, John Hope Franklin quoted Governor Wise: "They are themselves mistaken who take him [John Brown] to be a madman... He is a man of clear head, of courage, of fortitude and simple ingenuousness."

"But then," Walker's letter continued, Governor Wise "... wasn't there, and the songs of freedom were shouted out between the white teeth of the little blacks daily."

In this recounting of his stay at the former governor's place, Walker revealed important traits of himself as a writer and as a warrior on abolition's frontline. As a writer, especially in his later years, he used his wry humor to point up the potential dangers of anti-slavery activities. One can imagine, from his suggestion that Governor Wise would gladly have hanged him, that the non-violent Walker nevertheless seemed proud to be associated as a reformer with John Brown. And if we can overlook the stereotype of "the white teeth of the little blacks" as a writer's attempt at imagery, we hear Walker expressing rhetorical joy that at last a new generation is shouting "songs of freedom." A century later, Dr. Martin Luther King, Jr., was to dream of shouting from the mountaintop, "Free at last!"

    *   *   *   *

Spring faded, summer arrived, and, several months after leaving Michigan, Walker languished in Virginia. He wrote:

> After waiting, by request, in suspense and at expense, for three weeks, I received an official order to go directly to a certain farm, and act with the overseer on the place. On arriving there, I saw the overseer putting his musket in shooting order. I naturally inquired if there was game about there, and was told there were some d----d niggers that he would like to shoot. I soon saw there had been some trouble on the place, and that the man whom I was there to 'act with' was a rough customer, of the copperhead type, and that disorder was the order of the day -- because the man who had been put there to govern the place was not able to govern himself, much less others. After giving close attention to the disturbed elements for a few days, matters settled down rather quietly, and when I left the colored people expressed many regrets.

Walker described the plantations as "pauper farms." He was to spend a month or longer at one of them. He wrote:

> The one at which I stayed for a time would not probably half pay the expenses. Yet it is better that these homeless people be spread out over the farms than left in idleness without doing anything towards their support; for but few of the resident, oath-bound citizens have the means and disposition to furnish them with remunerative employment, and many of them cannot sustain themselves at the present time of high prices, etc. Many of the able-bodied men and many of the women are employed by the government as soldiers or in some other capacity, leaving but few for farm laborers other than the aged, the children, and women encumbered with the infirm and small children, many of whom are orphans.

Again, in a typical Walker account, he went on to fill a column of Garrison's newspaper with his experiences, all meticulously categorized under such headings as "Health," "Wages," "Schools," and "Religion." He continued:

> The whole number of names on the books of the farm [where he stayed] was 187, drawing 132 full rations. Children under fourteen drew half rations. About thirty of this number were employed as field hands, five-sixths of whom were women and children, and a large percentage under eighteen years of age. The soil was hard to work, tools badly worn and awkward. Hoes, weighing from one and a half to two pounds each, with a two-inch hole for the eye, and five and a half-foot handle, were used by girls of fourteen years. No wonder the crop

One Final Effort

of 400 acres was far behind the season, nor could all the gross and abusive language of the overseer, with any amount of threats, make it otherwise...

Small food rations and poor health also contributed to the farm's falling behind schedule. "Many of those on the place had been down with the smallpox, fifteen had died, and quite a number of others were then sick of various diseases," Walker wrote. "The place was notorious for its sickly location, surrounded as it is by swamps, frog ponds, and forests... Nearly all the whites (fourteen) who had been stationed on the place since its confiscation were obliged to leave on account of sickness."

About the food and diet, he wrote: "For the month of July, the rations served were, each, eighteen pounds corn meal, nine pounds flour, seventeen pounds beef and pork (two-thirds of which was beef, very bony, and all extremely lean), one pound of beans, two of salt, one and three-quarters of sugar, three-quarters of soap, and one pint of vinegar..." Himself a vegetarian, Walker must have winced when he added: "... no vegetables."

The workers paid for this food. "The charges were deducted from their pay. For farm hands, the wages were from five to ten dollars a month, with rations deducted leaving but a trifle due at pay day, if such a time should come. The men had not been paid since last March and the women not for the last year..." Walker wrote.

These newly recognized free Americans were abiding by the wishes that Lincoln had included in the Emancipation Proclamation: "And I hereby enjoin upon the people so declared to be free, to abstain from all violence, unless in necessary self-defense, and I recommend to them that, in all cases when allowed, they labor faithfully for reasonable wages."

Walker wrote:

Men wearing the United States uniform, who can openly and exultantly boast of their brutality towards those they have in charge, females not excepted, are not the best guardians for the simple and defenseless whom grinding oppression has had for long years beneath its iron heel... A simple change from a Southern to a Northern overseer is no proof that the condition of the underling is better. Northern masters and overseers are often the most exacting and avaricious. Notwithstanding the free use of the lash is not allowed, yet there are various other modes of punishment and torture at hand.

Walker left Virginia in late July because he was ill. Referring to Virginia's "swamps, frog ponds, and forests," he wrote: "With such associations and surroundings, and with poor provisions, badly prepared, etc., my health gave way, the ague and fever came on, and finding myself rapidly running down, and seeing no sufficient reasons for remaining there longer under existing circumstances, I left, with just strength and life enough to reach New York..."

Jonathan Walker The Man with the Branded Hand

Discouragement probably led to Walker's decision to quit Virginia and to abandon his hope of assisting the downtrodden to whom he had dedicated much of his life. Walker wanted to help, and felt that his services were unneeded. He was aged enough, at sixty-five, to feel the helplessness that the elderly of all generations have faced in trying to adjust to the strong assertions of younger authorities.

Once more, he was off in retreat, but finally he knew that, despite his failure to serve in Virginia, his thirty-year efforts on behalf of African-Americans were not in vain.

Ain't long now, 'fore nobody gonna say come,
and nobody gonna say go. Naw, Lawd, gonna be
parlor-time, gonna be rockin-cheer time,
set in de parlor, rock and fan.
Robert Penn Warren, *Band of Angels*

Chapter 16   The Final Years

Jonathan Walker arrived in New York from Virginia on July 29, 1864, flat broke and barely able to function, only to learn that he had lost some of his belongings. Despite that, he wrote, he "there found the most kind and hospitable reception at the hands of our old and true friend, Wm. P. Powell, at No. 2 Dover Street, who, with his family, had been made to suffer severely by the fiendish barbarity of a New York mob, for his identify with the colored race."

Writing late in August, he added: "Since my return to New York, I have been stopping with a relative at Astoria, Long Island, having been principally confined to the house, and much of the time to the bed; but I am now slowly improving, and am in hopes in a few weeks to be able to go to work again, as that is our main dependence for support. A part of my baggage was stolen on my passage, and when I got here, the last dollar had vanished."

     *   *   *   *

The Civil War was ending. The nation was preparing for peace. Walker, who had devoted his adulthood to working for equality, sent his assessment – a plea for caution, patience, and non-violent action – to *The Liberator*: "We should not expect too much from the present generation. It is not one Proclamation that lifts the life-long chattel to the angelic plane! There must be *growth*. Much cultivation has to be done. The blacks of this land are now in a transition state. They are just entering the red sea, 'whose surges are of gore.' The wilderness is some distance on."

Jonathan Walker The Man with the Branded Hand

The assassination of Abraham Lincoln took place only six days after the war's end, four years to the day from his order on April 15, 1861, calling out Union troops. Lincoln was not to rest in peace. For thirty-six years, threats of kidnapping resulted in his body's being hidden while the public paid tribute at an empty sarcophagus. Not until 1901 was the body to be buried permanently at Lincoln's Tomb in Springfield, Illinois.

Gone was the fighting and the killing of tens of thousands of Americans – Northerners and Southerners, whites and blacks. Disappearing also was the violence of emotion and unrestrained hatred over the issue of slavery. That is not to say that racial relationships were suddenly harmonious; there was no perceptible change in personal relations. To the land instead had come a wariness and hope, anxieties and anger, bitterness and happiness. It was almost as if the people on both sides of the massive issues that fueled the Civil War were now frightened with what they had done. The enormity of the misdeed outweighed temporarily the relief that came with its conclusion. And yet, for most militant abolitionists, their struggle had ended; the victory, they thought, was theirs. That victory was, in fact, as difficult to hold as the sunshine they thought emancipation had brought to the slaves.

Walker had given thought to this concern. He wrote Garrison:

The great and immediate want among these people is remunerative employment, good and trusty advisers who will secure their confidence, and protection in the exercise of their legitimate rights. They need protection from the avariciousness, usurpations, and vices of Northern men as well as of Southern men; but give them a fair chance and, with few exceptions, they will prove themselves self-sustained. Their little corn and potato crops, their gardens, poultry and pigs, and everything they can turn to account, demonstrate that they will take care of themselves as well as any other class with the same conditions. The freedmen's Aid Associations and some others have done much to aid and encourage them in their agricultural and industrial pursuits. Their gratitude is never withheld, where kindness and favors are honestly bestowed.

Kinsman and Walker, both using the Virginia farm schools system as evidence, saw great hope in the generation of black children. Kinsman reported:

Thirty-nine schools have been established, over which there are ninety-nine teachers, with an attendance averaging 5,930 [or approximately sixty per teacher]. This experiment has been truly successful. The energy, industry, and perseverance of these people in learning to read and write, and their capacity to learn, is far greater than has been claimed for them by their most enthusiastic friends.

Walker supported that opinion:

The Final Years

The children acquire the knowledge of reading, spelling, writing, etc., as readily as any other class would under the same circumstances. I visited a number of the schools, both in and out of the city [of Norfolk], and was informed by the teachers generally that their pupils were more orderly and attentive to their lessons than white children were of the same age whom they had previously taught. Many of the adults attend school as they have opportunity, either in the daytime or evenings; and it was pleasant to see those who were not regular teachers giving freely their time and attention in assisting them. Had I now the constitution and the years that have passed and left me a wreck, I would be glad to dwell among them and cheer them on to manhood, if nothing more.

The political forces were being changed also. The freed slaves were now "whole" in the eyes of Congress, rather than the three-fifths assigned politically, and that meant the addition of at least twelve Southern representatives in Congress.

The Thirteenth Amendment, ratified late in 1865, began the moves towards establishing a legal foundation for achieving equality. The series of laws and constitutional amendments introduced between 1865 and 1876 included the Thirteenth, Fourteenth, and Fifteenth Amendments, which formally abolished slavery and enfranchised the Negro; the Freedmen's Bureau bills of 1865 and 1866, setting up an organization to care for African Americans; the Civil Rights laws of 1866 and 1875, which guaranteed social privileges to all men in public places; and the Force and Ku Klux Klan acts of 1870 and 1871, providing machinery to enforce the recent amendments and to break up organized white resistance to Republican decrees.

Once again, the disappointments from realities more often overshadowed the visions of equality. Laws were not enough.

    *   *   *   *

Life was changing for almost everyone in postwar America. Lloyd Garrison Walker, a wounded veteran of the Michigan Sharp Shooters, was discharged on July 28, 1865, in Jackson, Michigan. In a reverse of their pre-war residences, he returned to live in Wisconsin while his parents remained in Michigan. After a few years in lumbering – following a trade that three generations of Walkers before him had pursued – Lloyd Walker studied medicine for three years and, at the age of twenty-eight, began a practice near Pound, Wisconsin, that continued until his retirement in 1916 at the age of seventy-four.

The man for whom the Walkers had named their twin son, William Lloyd Garrison, completed his thirty-fifth volume of *The Liberator* on December 29, 1865. His work, he declared, was done. He had achieved what in 1831 he had set out to do; he had helped lead the young nation from the shame of slavery. In his final edition, he published U.S. Secretary of State William H. Seward's proclamation of December 18 declaring that, with the twenty-seventh state's ratification, the Thirteenth Amendment was the law of the land. Garrison not only published it; he set the type. "With our own hands we have put in type this unspeakably cheering and important official announcement," he wrote. "Not a slave is left to clank his fetters, of the millions that were lately held in seemingly hopeless bondage... It is, consequently, the complete triumph as well as utter termination of the anti-slavery struggle, as such."

Garrison's final front page featured a reminiscence under the byline of "Mrs. L. Maria Child," the author and journalist for whom Jane and Jonathan Walker had named two of their daughters. She began, "It seems but yesterday that the South called Massachusetts to account for allowing the publication of a newspaper that expressed sympathy for the slaves... Now, the black man is introduced to me in every form of art and literature."

The Liberator's final edition carried also letters from several of Garrison's admirers and co-workers in abolitionism. With the retirement of *The Liberator,* Jonathan Walker, like dozens of others, lost the tablet on which they had etched the record of their humanitarian acts as well as the emotional highs and lows of the struggle.

The contributions to emancipation made by Garrison, however, had been recognized almost from the beginning, although not always in praise of the editor. Boston Mayor Harrison Gray Otis had apologized to the governors of Georgia and Virginia. The Massachusetts city, he wrote, "had ferreted out the paper and its editor; that his office was an obscure hole, his only visible auxiliary a Negro boy, and his supporters a few very insignificant persons of all colors."

The Mayor lived to admit his grave error of judgment; the city erected a monument fifty years later to the editor.

One reason so little is known of Jonathan Walker's life after 1865, following the demise of *The Liberator*, is that Walker seems to have stopped writing for publication. Except for a family letter or two, nothing that came from his pen is known to exist today.

Writing in that final year of slavery, Walker had put it this way:

...I have lived long enough to see the old venerated institution crumbling. Its adhesiveness is passing off. The acid is in motion throughout the whole fabric. Its rumblings may sound horrible to the modern conservative, but in due time it will be a mass of rubbish. Meantime, the Temple of Freedom will go up; and if it shall become visible to the inhabitants of this country, and inquired after in the "old" [country], it will be enough for this century.

When his health improved enough to travel, Jonathan Walker returned to Jane and their home in Michigan in late 1864. There was not much left for the old warrior to contribute to the battle for equality. Like Garrison, he could say he had done his job; the strife for freedom's sake was over. Like the character

The Final Years

"Walker's Point," it was called, when Jonathan and Jane lived in the little farmhouse (upper right) by the lakes feeding into Lake Michigan to the west. Walker sailed these waters and managed his small fruit farm from 1864 until his death in 1878.

Dollie, in *Band of Angels*, by Robert Penn Warren, Walker could exult: "Ain't long now 'fore nobody gonna say come, and nobody gonna say go. Naw, Lawd, gonna be parlor- time, gonna be rockin-cheer time, set in de parlor, rock, and fan. Fedder-fan. Dis Lawd's chile."

*   *   *   *

Compared to his earlier life, Jonathan Walker was finally settling down as he neared his sixty-sixth birthday. For him, "settling down" meant improving his little fruit farm to being one of the best around, and striving, always, for more productive crops and farming methods.

Fruit had become the principal commercial crop almost immediately upon the region's settlement a decade earlier. In July 1870, newspapers carried this advertisement: "Jacunda Strawberry Plants For Sale by Jonathan Walker near the mouth of the Black Lake, Muskegon County, at fifty cents per hundred, fifteen dollars per thousand... anytime after the 20th of August."

By this time, Walker had slowed and even mellowed. There was now a gentle satisfaction in his writings, as few as they had become. Gone was the sting of his anger with slaveholders, and with the government that he considered only half-heartedly opposed to slavery. The year that Walker wrote about his 1864 move to Michigan was probably around 1870. He and Jane now had the opportunity to enjoy each other's company. Yet, some small strife remained in the home. M. Berry Wood wrote in "The History of Lake Harbor" in 1933: "He was a vegetarian, and not only never touched meat, tea, or coffee, but also imposed these rigid restrictions upon his wife. She, poor soul, used to make periodic but surreptitious trips to her sympathetic neighbors, in order to satisfy her normal appetite."

Jane also made longer, less secretive, trips. When the 1870 census was taken, she was visiting in Wisconsin, across Lake Michigan, with the Walkers' daughter, Mary Gage Walker Lucas, and her husband, Ivory B. Lucas. With Jane was the Walkers' youngest son, George Fox Walker, then twenty-two years old. Consequently, Jane and George were listed by the census takers as residing with the Lucas household in Plymouth, Sheboygan County, Wisconsin.

The 1870 census also listed Charles Hubbard and Fred Duele as living at the Walker home. Jonathan was now seventy-one years old; having a couple of farm hands would not have been unusual. There was much work to be done. From the home he had built at Lake Harbor he wrote, proudly, one imagines:

> And now we see all about us the broad acres of fruit trees, grape and strawberry vines, raspberries, etc. Of the strawberries this season, over 3,000 bushels were shipped from here in a steamer for the Chicago market. We have also our corn, wheat, and oat fields with an ample supply of all kinds of vegetable production that can be grown in this climate. And instead of the wild animals, which had no respect for the "rights of man," we have the domestic animals to provide us with bread and butter. And "Lo," the poor red man that roamed over our section with rifle, spear, and traps, has fled to other parts in pursuit of business. These changes have been gradual. A large steam sawmill in full operation, three district schools well attended, and two railroads passing through our township speed us on our way to progress.

*   *   *   *

Walker was remembered by some of his neighbors as a person with odd habits. Wood's Lake Harbor history said:

> Those who knew him describe him as a very large, tall man, curiously double-jointed, tremendously strong, and exceedingly peculiar... When [he] wished to go to town, he would put his pony and wagon on an old scow, ferry them across the lake to the Bend, and then drive Lakeside. He always ferried his cow across to pasture. It is reported that he took his morning plunge in the lake all the year around, even when he had to break the ice in order to do it.

Bowles, the tugboat captain, remembered "the sight of Walker galloping across the countryside about Lake Harbor on his white horse."

The Final Years

Walker was regarded, even in his final years, not simply as a large and odd man, but as a man of significant presence. His Michigan neighbors knew of his role in abolitionist history and respected him for it. His branded hand remained an identification that was unique among white men, and it seemed never to fade.

Even as he slowed, Walker was not one to set out his berry plants and idly keep them weeded. Well into his seventies, he was attacking agriculture's problems. "Powell & Hovey, Agents, Muskegon, Mich.," advertised in the Muskegon *Chronicle* in April of 1877 under this heading:

JONATHAN WALKER
Invented Weeding Tooth Hoe.

Under common practices in newspapers of the times, the advertisement ran as a news item, distinguished from the news only by the agents' signature at the end. After introducing Walker as being "somewhat famous in anti-slavery history as the 'man with the branded hand,' [s]omething like forty years ago," the article candidly added, "This, however, has nothing to do with the Improved Weeding Tooth Hoe which Mr. Walker has *invented*, as will be seen from the following testimonials..."

There followed statements attributed to seven farmers.

*   *   *   *

Through their children and grandchildren, the elderly Jane and Jonathan had much joy to share during their Wisconsin and Michigan years. The family was spreading throughout the Northeast and the Midwest. All nine children outlived the parents.

That two of the Walkers' sons, Lloyd and William Wilberforce, turned to medicine was perhaps less a coincidence than a result of encouragement from their father. Especially during his years in the South, Jonathan had developed a reputation as a self-taught physician. He had practiced successfully on himself during the flight from Pensacola and in the first two months in jail. He noted unhappily in his account, *Trial and Imprisonment*, that he had been deprived at Key West of his "small trunk of botanic medicines." Also among his "patients" had been the slave William Cook, whom he had nursed back to health in 1840 in his own home, using cayenne, lobelia, and steam to overcome the symptoms of dropsy.

The golden years for Jonathan and Jane Walker ended with her death in 1871, at the age of sixty-eight. The county clerk's office in Muskegon has no record of the death of a woman by that name. The office received a notice on May 27, 1872, for the death on October 12, 1871, of a "Mrs. Mary Walker," whose birthplace was given as Massachusetts. Her age was listed as sixty-six, and her late home as Norton Township, Michigan. Cause of death, the certificate said, was "nervous debility." It would be pleasant, and probably more accurate, to regard this error-strewn document as the product of a casual report system, or even a careless 1872 clerk. A similar disregard for precise detail showed up seven years later when Jonathan himself died. No one familiar with the couple's

JANE WALKER posed for this portrait while living in Wisconsin. She was in her fifties and was believed active with Jonathan in helping fugitives from slavery as they made their way to Canada on the Underground Railroad.

mutual devotions could conclude that the 1871-72 errors were a result of Jonathan Walker's casual acknowledgement of the death of his life's partner. He had many reasons to love and honor Jane, and the only records surviving indicate that he did so without reservation.

Not unlike most married women of her time, Jane Walker had been the nucleus of her large family. Despite her husband's heroism and even fame, he was frequently only a visitor to the home she maintained for their nine children. In many ways, Jane Walker led a life like that of Mary Brown, whose radical husband was hanged for attempting to arouse Southern slaves to insurrection. John Brown, like Walker a faithful correspondent, left a written record of his failures as a home-based husband and father. Early in 1847, while living in Springfield, Massachusetts, Brown wrote to "the partner of my own choice, and the sharer of my poverty, trials, discredit, and more afflictions, as well as what of comfort and seeming prosperity has fallen to my lot." Brown confessed: "I really feel, notwithstanding I sometimes chide you severely, that you are *really* my better half." One can easily imagine Jonathan Walker making the same admission to Jane. If he put his sentiments in writing to her, they have not been preserved.

Such 19th Century women accepted the role expected of them. While the men were away at sea, or at war, or like John Brown attempting to establish a profitable business, the women were at home for months on end, alone with the children and carrying all the responsibilities of home and family. Their historical identification has been generally restricted to being "Mrs." or "his wife." Historians often neglect to record women's own first names. Even a couple's children are often listed only as "his."

Picturing Walker as a lonely stalker of freedom for blacks in the jungles of prejudice and apathy would be wrong. As unique as some of his experiences were, Jane's shadow followed him. Jane Walker supported her husband's devotion, not only to their family but also to the anti-slavery cause. If she did not, how else can we explain her maintaining the marriage partnership for nearly a half-century? Would a practical early 19th Century wife and mother have permitted in the home from which she seldom moved pictures of Harriet Beecher Stowe and Frederick Douglass if she did not welcome them?

If Jane Walker corresponded with her absent husband, we can assume she offered encouragement and love, and probably words of caution. No record of those words remains, which is our loss in trying to understand the important role she carried out.

That Jane should not be remembered only as a wife and mother was probably intended by her husband. On the death certificate filed with the Muskegon County authorities, her occupation is listed as "farmer."

Jonathan left few hints of his love for Jane, but there can be no doubt that they loved each other, and that each had deep respect for the other's achievements. Aside from his personal esteem for Jane, Jonathan would have respected her rights as a woman to the benefits of equality. Indeed, he earned a reputation as an advocate for women's right. Late in life, while living in Michigan, he wrote about the invitations-only opening gala at the Lake Harbor House and praised the "substantials and luxuries unsurpassed by city hotels." But, he chided, a "screw appeared to be loose somewhere in the committee's arrangement. It seemed to us rather too masculine. As we glanced over the whole company, we failed to discover the inability of the female department to do ample justice to the occasion. The tables and the hall contained abundant evidence of their judgment and skill."

And then, as if forgiving the male decision-makers for simply behaving as men had for centuries before, he concluded: "For this time, we shall censure nobody, for they [women] have been so long classed politically with criminals and idiots that we [men] fail to recognize their just position in our social doings. Make way, gentlemen, ladies are coming to the front."

Walker was later honored as a feminist by A. J. Grover, a newspaperman from Chicago:

> Jonathan Walker was a strong woman's rights man. He believed in and worked for the emancipation of women as well as the Negro man; and, strange to say, we have those among us who oppose the political freedom of women, and predict as they did of the liberty of the Negro that all the dire consequences that can be named will follow the emancipation of women. It is really true that the freedom only of one half of the people of this country has yet been achieved... God hasten the day when this republic shall take the last step which shall make us a

nation truly free – the political emancipation of women. The fact that Jonathan Walker forty years ago was an advocate of liberty to women makes him to us a real prophet as well as a martyr.

Suffrage for all women was yet another forty years away. Women, white and black, would not be given voting rights under the Constitution until 1920 with ratification of the Nineteenth Amendment.

The often invisible impression on history of such women as Jane Walker was conveyed by O. W. Firkins in his 1915 biography of Emerson. Writing of Lidian Emerson, the poet's wife of forty-six years, he said: "The tread of this lady through the unfrequented paths of Emerson's domestic life is so noiseless that only a rare footfall here and there reaches the ear of the questioning biographer."

After Jane Walker's death, Jonathan had her body buried in a small cemetery in Norton Township. The grave is marked by "a simple sandstone slab," the Muskegon *Chronicle* reported on July 3, 1937. The inscription, while not unyoking her from her husband of nearly a half-century, gives this resourceful, strong woman her own permanent identity without invoking her spouse's fame:

JANE
Wife of
J. WALKER
Died
Sept. 28, 1871
Aged 68 years

Jane and Jonathan had acquired two large plots on the cemetery's far east side. Numbers 127 and 128 each contained three grave sites Their intention may have been to provide sufficient space for any of the children who might wish to be buried there also. Two of the spots in number 128 were to be for the couple, and so it was that, soon after her death, Jane was buried in 128.

Both lots are now the source of a mystery. No explanation exists for the burial there of four people, all with the same names as Jane's parents: Gage and Ellis. About the same time as Jane died, a man named James Ellis was buried in 128. According to Norton cemetery records, Ellis was born in 1822, the year the Walkers were married, and died in 1871 at age forty-nine. The three buried in number 127 are listed as Elizabeth and William Gage and a child. The man is described as a member of Post 7, Grand Army of the Republic, and a veteran of Company M, 6th Michigan Regiment. A notation on the cemetery records adds: "This lot owned by J. Walker (Jonathan, the Man with the Branded Hand.)" There are no birth or death dates for William and Elizabeth Gage. Beside the word "child" appears a question mark, which today represents the mystery that shrouds this burial site.

One conclusion is possible: that Jane would have wanted family members to be with her, as they had been throughout her life. As it developed,

234

The Final Years

she was to remain in death as she had for much of the time of her adult life – without her husband.

*   *   *   *

Jonathan Walker's health continued strong as he moved well into his eighth decade. The Muskegon *Chronicle* recalled his later years at Lake Harbor: "Here he continued to reside, and although affable and intelligent, was a quiet and unobtrusive old gentleman, beloved and respected by all those who enjoyed the good fortune to form his acquaintance."

In the autumn of 1872, now a seventy-three-year-old widower, he went east for the third and last time. He was attempting for a second time to find a publisher for his journals. When he returned to Michigan in 1873, he brought back, along with the rejected ream of paper, a new wife. She was Levina R. Gay. Born in Dedham, Massachusetts, about 1815, she was at least fifteen years younger than Jonathan.

Thirty years after Walker's branding, and a decade after the Emancipation Proclamation, he was still being eulogized. In June 1874, a group of formerly active abolitionists had a reunion in Chicago. Ira Porter, apparently the former neighbor and orchardist from Norton Township in Michigan, wrote Walker about the attention given him. The event was highlighted by the singing by George Clarke (also spelled Clark) "with thrilling effect" of Whittier's poem, "The Branded Hand." Porter enclosed "gifts from personal friends" plus $65.10 that had been "dropped into the box with the personal magnetism of the giver adhering to each piece of coin or paper..."

Porter wrote Walker:

I trust that the palm of that hand that unflinchingly popped and hissed beneath the red-hot brand that our government pressed upon it more than thirty years ago will find something soothing in this spontaneous expression of sympathy so fully merited, and so peculiarly fitted to be a blessing to him that receives and to him that gives. Could you have witnessed the deep feeling and the breathless stillness that pervaded the convention while the song of the "Branded Hand" was being sung, you would not doubt but the blessing of the contributor is stamped upon every one of the items contributed.

Porter signed the note, "With great sympathy." He sent a copy of the letter to the Chicago *Evening Journal* with a note: "Ebenezer Dorr, the Yankee marshal who procured the branding iron, heated it, and in open court at Pensacola pressed it upon that palm, was but the agent of every voter of the nation."

Porter, calling on some of the indignation that fired the earlier crusades, concluded his letter to the editor: "It is but truth that no incident of the abolition movement better deserves to be remembered long and well by those abolitionists who asserted that the then United States Constitution was an agreement with

Courtesy of Massachusetts Historical Society

Jonathan Walker posed for photographer J. D. Westervelt in Muskegon, Michigan, probably in the mid-1870s. His residence is identified in notes on the back of the old print as "Black Lake, Muskegon County."

death and a covenant with hell, than the cruel punishment inflicted under the sanction of law by branding with a red hot iron the hand of Jonathan Walker."

In 1874, Walker was still active on his farm. To the end, he maintained an interest in his New England birthplace and the communities where the Walker children were born. The New Bedford newspaper reported proudly in February 1877:

> Among the new subscribers to the *Republican Standard* is Captain Jonathan Walker, of Lake Harbor, Michigan, who was immortalized by Whittier in verse as the man with the branded hand. Mr. Walker is 78 years old 22nd inst., and his daughter sends him a year's subscription as

The Final Years

a birthday present. Captain Walker is a native of Cape Cod, and is still hale and hearty, though time has somewhat stooped his shoulders, and is nearly six feet tall.

Perhaps Walker was able to read in that newspaper in 1877 of the appointment of Frederick Douglass as United States marshal for the District of Columbia. Now in frail health, cared for as a patient by his second, younger wife, Jonathan Walker would have been cheered to learn of this recognition given an old comrade in arms, one whose career in abolitionism had started on Nantucket island, only twenty miles from where Walker was born. Even as his strength faded, Walker could smile. The man whose portrait hung in his home, beside the likeness of the author of *Uncle Tom's Cabin*, was now the first black person appointed to a federal position requiring Senate approval. The nomination of the fifty-nine-year-old Douglass, by President Rutherford B. Hayes, came almost a century after the Declaration of Independence had asserted that "all men are created equal."

Just as William Lloyd Garrison had quit publishing his abolitionist newspaper within days of the Thirteenth Amendment's becoming law, putting an end to slavery under the Constitution and to his determination – it could be said his need – to campaign for slavery's end, perhaps this news about Douglass brought a final sense of justice, of vindication, of fulfillment, and even of contentment, to the old anti-slavery warrior from Massachusetts.

    *   *   *   *

As difficult as Jonathan Walker's life had always been, the last months were perhaps the worst. While he had found in Levina Gay Walker a fond and caring wife, he had lost his first love. His children apparently had little or no contact with the old man. And he was as financially strapped as he had ever been in a lifetime of poverty. No longer able to farm, and his hopes gone for income from his autobiography, he and Levina were virtually destitute.

In 1877, former Michigan Governor Henry H. Holt came up with a plan to raise funds for the Walkers. He wrote an article about Jonathan, citing the glory of his egalitarian struggle and the agony of his poverty. The story was distributed to newspapers around the country, soliciting donations and offering for sale at a dollar each photographs of Captain Walker and his branded hand. Among the contributors was John Greenleaf Whittier, who wrote to Holt: "I beg leave to send to thy care a small sum [five dollars] for my old friend Capt. Jona. Walker. I hope others will aid him more abundantly out of their abundance. He should not be forgotten in the woods of Michigan, who suffered for Freedom. Thy frd, John G. Whittier."

Helped by the money, and perhaps buoyed by the good wishes and prayers of friends and admirers, Jonathan Walker lived over the winter, passed his seventh-ninth birthday in February, and came into the season of blossoms and new growth.

Jonathan Walker The Man with the Branded Hand

Among friends who came to visit Walker in the final weeks was the Reverend Frank Edward Kittredge, who served Muskegon's Universalist Church. The two had long, deep discussions about the eternal questions of divinity and morality.

Herbert G. Bowles, the man who told of Walker's riding a white horse around Lake Harbor, was among those who kept a vigil at Jonathan's bedside. He told of spending the night of April 28-29, 1878, with Walker, and of then being unable to continue his vigil.

Death came on Tuesday, April 30, two months into the eightieth year after his birth in his mother's bedroom on Cape Cod.

Jonathan Walker did not die suddenly; he faded from life. Lois Wightman, of Plymouth, Wisconsin, a Walker descendant and family historian, has a newspaper report suggesting his gentle departure: "He made the choice of a very estimable companion for his declining years, one who possesses an amiable disposition, and who had faithfully watched over and soothed him in his many months of enfeebled sickness and sorrow with untiring patience and affection, until the pulse had ceased."

Strangely, none of the contemporary accounts named his second wife.

The sickness that ended his life, according to the death certificate, was "consumption." But, like the information filed after Jane's death, this report is also questionable. According to the county clerk's records, the death was not recorded for thirteen months, until May 22, 1879. It gave Jonathan's age as "seventy-nine years, one month, eight days," cutting a full month off his lifespan. The certificate listed his parents as "unknown" and gave Jonathan's occupation as "sea captain." In some ways that was not inaccurate; the old man had not captained a working boat for nearly thirty-five years, but he would have been pleased to have been considered in death, as he probably had always thought of himself in life, a sea captain.

"Jonathan Walker, who died at Lake Harbor, Muskegon County, Michigan, on the 30th day of April, 1878, at the advanced age of 79 years and two months, has a life record interspersed with more thrilling incidents and Philanthropy than most persons in our Country during his time," The Muskegon *Journal* reported.

Walker's obituary – published in the *Journal* on May 7, 1878, and copied in area newspapers in the weeks that followed – continued with what came to be a standard, heroic recitation of his escapes from death on the Atlantic Ocean and in India, Cuba, Mexico, and Florida. As with other accounts since, slight exaggeration resulted from imaginative flourishes; for example, Walker was not simply caught as a slave stealer near Cape Florida, according to the *Journal*, he was "piratically captured on the high seas under the American flag..." In the *Journal's* account, he did not simply die: "...the great physical frame and powerful constitution of Jonathan Walker had yielded unto death."

The Final Years

Michigan neighbors knew of his background, although apparently there had never been a local effort during his lifetime to recognize him for his work. The *Journal* obituary seemed to be trying to make up for that as it continued:

The deceased was a man of genial and pleasing nature, but of strong will and purpose in all his undertakings. He aimed to be just and honorable in all his dealings with his fellow men. His strong anti-slavery principles and hatred of human Slavery prompted him early in life, purely out of fixed principles, to engage without the promise or hope of *pecuniary gain* to be one among the few prominent outspoken anti-slavery men, whose aim of life was the emancipation of American Slavery. Jonathan Walker was as equally prominent in that direction as was Sumner, Gerrit Smith, Joshua R. Giddings, old John Brown, Lucretia Mott, and others, but on account of his limited means and occlusion of life, his name and fame have been almost forgotten by the liberty-loving people of this Country, for which he has suffered so greatly. The cause of freedom should ever be held sacred. And the occasion of the branding of that bold right hand at Pensacola, Florida, thirty-three years ago, to appease and gratify a class whose traffic was that of human flesh, should be handed down to posterity in commemoration of his long and useful life upon the side of human freedom, equal in exalted honor with any who were earnestly engaged at that time aiding in the emancipation of human slavery in this Country.

Walker's death followed within weeks that of Edward Knight Collins. The two probably had never met, although they had grown up within thirty miles of each other on Cape Cod. Walker was born in 1799 in Harwich, Collins in 1803 in Truro. Their careers were to bring each of them international recognition. Walker had given much of his active life to anti-slavery efforts, yet he became known to history as "the man with the branded hand" for an adventure that covered only a few weeks. He never seemed comfortable with this fame, and never attempted to capitalize on it for himself. Collins, on the other hand, was a showman with a flair for publicity. For his more than thirty-five years as a successful merchant and passenger line owner, he had earned celebrity as a patriot, rallying pride for America's efforts to wrest Atlantic Ocean cruise leadership from Great Britain.

In death, the recognition given the two men also was in contrast. Despite Collins' success at building the world's largest ships for the Collins Line, a series of maritime disasters in 1854-1856 had led him to retire to Brooklyn in 1858, at about the same time that Walker was settling into his new life in Wisconsin.

When Collins died on January 22, 1878, his death was scarcely noted. "A few old gentlemen... attended the funeral," wrote maritime historian Ralph Whitney. Collins' body was laid to rest without a headstone at Woodlawn

Cemetery, "on the edge of the huge city he helped build into the world's greatest port."

At first it appeared that a quiet farewell also was to mark the passing of Walker. Perhaps unnecessarily bitter, the *News and Reporter*, a twice-weekly newspaper published in Muskegon, told its readers a week after Walker's death: "The sneering assertion that republics are ungrateful holds true in his case. Jonathan Walker, who died near Muskegon Wednesday, devoted a lifetime to freedom, and died miserably poor, and an effort [by former Governor Holt] made some months ago to place him above want was a wretched failure."

Like the *Journal's* account, the *News and Reporter's* obituary linked him with a few of the well-know figures from American history: "One by one, the figures once so prominent in the old days when slavery agitations shook this land are dropping from view. Old John Brown, Charles Sumner, Gerrit Smith, S. P. Chase, Joshua R. Giddings, and a host of other leaders have gone."

For the former Harwich sea captain, however, death was to bring a recognition long absent.

> There was something about his whole air
> self-respecting and dignified, yet united
> with a confiding and humble simplicity.
>
> **From *Uncle Tom's Cabin*, by Harriet Beecher Stowe**

CHAPTER 17   In Death: Recognition and Reward

The final tribute for Jonathan Walker, the one that would bring the lasting recognition and reward absent during his lifetime, would be delayed. In fact, the old abolitionist's body was to be buried three times before being placed in its final resting place beneath a tall memorial in a small park in Michigan.

The first funeral service was held on May 2, 1878, beginning at noon at the Walker home. The "widow and the youngest son of Mr. Walker [were] the only relatives present," according to the May 4 edition of the *News and Reporter*. George Fox Walker was, at age thirty, apparently living either with his father and stepmother, Levina, or independently but near enough to attend the funeral service. The *News and Reporter* also named a Muskegon couple on hand with the Norton neighbors, and added: "Had it not been for the very stormy weather, a much larger number would have attended the services at the house."

The Muskegon *Chronicle* reported:

A goodly number of his neighbors then formed a procession and came to Muskegon, having services again at 2 p.m. at the Universalist Church. Rev. F. E. Kittredge officiated. The Reverend Gentleman occupied an hour and upwards in reading extracts and relating many incidents from his eventful life, which was very attentively listened to by a large audience. The pallbearers upon this occasion were William Jones, A. Parker, J. B. Murphy, S. Ingham, S. B. Peck, and Mr. Fassett, many of them with whitened locks and showing advanced years.

Jonathan Walker The Man with the Branded Hand

Mr. Kittredge read excerpts from Walker's autobiographical accounts, as well as John Greenleaf Whittier's poem, *The Branded Hand*.

The *News and Reporter* added that Mr. Kittredge was assisted by the Reverend Thomas Wheeler of Muskegon, and "the choir, led by ex-Mayor Ireland, furnished excellent singing."

From the church, the body was taken to the Norton Township Cemetery and placed in the final grave site in Lot 128, beside the 1871 graves of Jonathan's wife of forty-nine years and that of William Ellis. There, only three miles from their small farm home on a hill overlooking the lake, Jonathan's body may have rested in peace, but not in permanence. As he had in life, the former sailor was to travel, even in death.

*   *   *   *

News of the Michigan death would not have been placed in general circulation hundreds of miles away for days, and even weeks. The news needs of people on Cape Cod were still served only by weekly newspapers. The Harwich *Independent* was silent on the subject until summer. That weekly never did run an obituary.

Michigan's former governor, Henry Holt, wrote a note to Whittier informing him of Walker's death. On May 4, Whittier responded:

> I had hoped our friend Jonathan Walker might live many years longer, but perhaps it is well for him. One after another, the old actors in the anti-slavery movement are passing on. The few of us left must soon follow. I do not know precisely what Captain Walker's religious views were, but in noble self-sacrifice for others he practiced christianity, and I trust his welcome in the new life has been "Inasmuch as ye have done it unto one of the least of these my brethren, ye have done it unto me."

Whittier concluded in the Quaker vernacular: "As one of the old-time abolitionists, I am grateful to thee for thy interest in our friend in his last days."

The *Chronicle* reported in June that while Walker's "quiet, unostentatious mode of life [had not] kept him prominently before the people [he] had not been forgotten... by his old friend, Reverend Photius Fisk... Soon after Mr. Walker's death, on learning that his relatives were unable to erect a suitable monument to his memory, he generously offered to do this at his own personal expenses."

About the middle of June, as Holt was to recall, Michigan "first heard of Reverend Photius Fisk's generous donation." The retired Navy chaplain also was credited with contributing to memorials for other abolitionists. Parker Pillsbury cited Fisk for a "generous contribution" towards the monument erected earlier in Boston's Mount Auburn Cemetery over the grave of the Reverend Charles Torrey. The Congregational minister had died in the Maryland jail cell to which he had been sent for committing the same illegal act as Walker had. Torrey had helped a black slave woman and her two children seek freedom.

In Death: Recognition and Reward

Cape Codders first learned of the memorial on July 2, when the Harwich *Independent* reported that "Whittier's 'man with the branded hand' is to have a monument [even] if he did die poor."

On July 9, the *Independent* carried a letter over the pseudonym "Argus" which gave a florid kind of obituary:

I was glad to notice in your last issue the fact that Jonathan Walker is to have placed over his grave a monument, and trust the time is not far distant when a centograph will be erected in his memory in this, his native town. East Harwich Cemetery would be the most suitable spot for it to be placed as it is not far distant from his birthplace. An epitaph something like the following would be appropriate:

Cape Cod was the land of his birth, old ocean his cradle.

His country though styled a land of liberty he soon found contained millions of slaves.

He attempted their liberation and became himself bound and imprisoned. His persecutors finally set him free bearing (as they thought) the marks of infamy, but he at once became famous.

The Branded Hand was the royal seal placed on his passport to honor and celebrity.

Tablet honoring Walker at Brooks Academy Museum in Harwich, MA

Jonathan Walker The Man with the Branded Hand

He lived to see the work of emancipation conceived by him, consummated by the immortal Lincoln, and after reaching a good old age, through penury and want in a land of plenty, death, the grand liberator, came and transported him to a realm where the slave and his master, the poor and the rich, and the king and his subjects are on an equal footing.

The *Independent* published no response. (Not until 1994 was a commemorative plaque placed in Harwich for Jonathan Walker.) In 1878, the Barnstable *Patriot* came as close as possible without apology to recanting some of the earlier criticism, even disdain, expressed for the jailed Walker. Reprinted in the July 30, 1878, Harwich *Independent*, the *Patriot* editorial recalled

...when Captain Walker was characterized as a fanatic, as an enemy of the peace and order of the country, as foolhardy and rash, and we think we might find, if we looked back to see, some pretty strong utterances to that effect in the columns of *The Patriot*. The opinion of his folly and rashness was only too common...

But time works strange results, and now it comes to pass that he of all men of his generation, born and going out of Cape Cod, is to be honored and remembered. Of all those who set out on the work of life with him in this [Barnstable] county, no other one is to be distinguished as he is to be... While it is proper to do honor to Jonathan Walker by erecting a memorial stone above his mortal remains, Cape Cod may well honor him by being proud of his character and sensitive of his honor...

*   *   *   *

Fisk, a retired U.S. Navy chaplain living in Boston, was born on the Greek island of Malta as Photius Kavasales. He had been taken under care, as a twelve-year-old orphan, by a missionary, the Reverend Pliny Fisk of Shelburne, Massachusetts. Mr. Fisk arranged for the youth to be brought to the United States. Educated in Massachusetts, Connecticut, and New York, Photius was ordained and served a pastorate briefly in Halifax, Vermont. But, Parker Pillsbury noted at Walker's memorial service, he "had become quite too much an abolitionist to be patiently tolerated in an American pulpit. So, aided by such men as John Quincy Adams and Joshua R. Giddings in Congress, and Gerrit Smith and other equally well-known men outside the government, he received [in 1842] the appointment of chaplain in the United States Navy." He served thirty-six years. A decade later, through a bill sponsored by Congressman Adams, Photius Kavasales was allowed to change his last name to Fisk.

Fisk's announcement in the spring of 1878 of his gift to honor Walker led to a Muskegon committee "for the purpose of receiving the proposed monument and for arranging for its unveiling with appropriate ceremonies on the occasion," the *Chronicle* reported. Appointed to the committee were the Reverend Mr. Kittredge, who had announced that Walker on his death bed had

In Death: Recognition and Reward

chosen him to conduct the service and deliver the eulogy; William Jones, who had been a pallbearer at the Norton Township burial; M. L. Stephenson, a local judge; Joshua Davis, and Daniel Upton.

The committee, with the approval of Levina Walker, decided that the body should be moved. Such an impressive monument as Chaplain Fisk planned should not rest in the plain environs of "a country cemetery," as the Evergreen Cemetery records call the old Norton Township burial grounds. Jones offered one of the plots he owned on the cemetery's west side. There was, apparently, room only for the remains of one Walker.

For Walker's monument, Fisk chose granite from Hallowell, Maine. Ironically, that was the birthplace of the man who branded Walker, Marshal Ebenezer Dorr. Hallowell's quarries were to provide the stone and artistic efforts for hundreds of such memorials and many national monuments, including those in Plymouth, Massachusetts; Yorktown, Virginia; and Gettysburg, Pennsylvania. Weeks were available for the Muskegon committee to prepare for "receiving the proposed monument." The engraving alone would take an artisan many days. Three sides were to bear messages. As it became clear that this second service would not take place before summer, the planners found an appropriate date: August 1, the sixtieth anniversary Emancipation Day of the West Indies. Great Britain in 1818 had freed all slaves in the islands, an act that so fired new energy for emancipation in the United States that abolitionists, Walker among them, had been celebrating the date for more than a half-century.

On Cape Cod, the July 16 Harwich *Independent* reprinted a report from the New Bedford *Standard* on plans for Walker's commemorative service: "It is intended to make these exercises interesting historical exercises, the occasion for calling together the old friends of freedom generally throughout the country. Wendell Phillips, Fred Douglass, Parker Pillsbury, Austin Blair, and other eminent members of the 'Old Guard' have been invited to be present and to participate."

The newspapers gave a minute description of the obelisk, a four-sided stone pillar to be mounted on a three-section base, itself nearly four feet high. The foundation was to consist of a "base, one foot high; plinth, one foot high; die, one foot nine inches high... size of foundation, two feet ten inches surface." The base was to rest half below the ground. The second part of the base, the plinth, was to be fully exposed above ground, and the third part, the die, was a dado, or the part of the pedestal between the base and the shaft. The shaft was to be six feet high and to rise in a taper to a pyramidal top. The total height would be nine feet nine inches; the total weight, two and a half tons.

As preparations went forth in Michigan, it became apparent that Michiganers, not unlike those in Massachusetts, had not fully realized the prominence among reformists and many others that their humble farmer-neighbor had achieved. Not untypical of the new recognition was a poetic cry for a permanent recognition for Walker, published in the *Western Rural* and reprinted in other regional newspapers. Somewhat resonating Whittier's famous cry of 1845, Lucius C. West proclaimed in two of his ten stanzas:

> From eyes of sable sons are flowing
> A mourner's tears. A nation's heart
> Throbs in unison, that one more
> Of Freedom's vanguards should depart.
>
> Lovers of Liberty! Sculptors! Raise
> A granite form for e'er to stand
> To future men, a sermon preaching,
> Bearing aloft a "Branded Hand."

Poets everywhere seemed moved. "W. S. B. of Nashville, Tennessee," wrote five verses "on the goodness of the Rev. Photius Fisk, the South, Friendship, Unity, etc." The poem concludes with a salute to all the abolitionists whom Fisk had help honor with memorials:

> And when by fate the Master called them home, each he reared a
> monumental tomb;
> Resolved their memory should not fade away
> Till marble shafts and granite stones decay.

*   *   *   *

A paradox was taking place. Plans for Walker's second ceremony were being made, not for the few friends and neighbors who attended the first program in Norton Township but for thousands from all over the nation. The principal speakers, it was decided, were to be ordained men, some active in pastorates, some dedicated in their younger years only to abolitionism. This was being done – ironically, some might think – for a religious man who never practiced his faith as an adult in a church.

The Reverend Mr. Kittredge, the ordained Unitarian who had spent the final days conversing with Walker, said of him: "[H]e could not technically be called a Christian. He did not even call himself one. But if Jesus was right when he said, 'By their fruits shall ye know me,' he was as loyal a Christian as any saint or martyr the church has ever canonized. He was not, indeed, a theological Christian, but far better, he was a practical one."

Kittredge went on about Walker: "He entertained an exalted opinion, an almost affectionate regard for the personal character of Jesus. He looked upon him as the world's greatest reformer... [H]e placed Jesus on so high a pedestal that he was willing to call him 'the pattern man of the world.'"

"Reformers" such as Walker may have been more open to religious experimenting than the more settled and satisfied traditionalists. Stephen S. Foster, who had called church leaders "the brotherhood of thieves," wrote to his wife, Abby Kelley, in the 1850s of attending a Cape Cod seance. Perhaps because Walker was reportedly "leaning towards" Spiritualism, some followers attempted to reach him after his death. A scrapbook of clippings maintained by

In Death: Recognition and Reward

Helen Johnston, a family historian, has an 1879 report of contact being made in the spiritual world by a "Circle of Spiritualism" known as "Voice of Angels." It quotes Walker as communicating to a Circle member.

There are some historians who believe that abolitionists were practicing a kind of personal ministry. "We still need to explain the extraordinary fortitude of the abolitionists," wrote John McClymer in *An American Portrait.* Some abolitionists, he wrote, "adopted the movement against slavery as a vocation, a form of ministry..."

In the end, dedication to what McClymer had called "moral purity and good will" may have been the best definition one could give to Walker's beliefs and practices.

*   *   *   *

The sun came up gently and warm on August 1, 1878, giving notice of the temperatures in the nineties to come that afternoon. Days before, Walker's casket, and the contents, had been removed from their place in the Norton Township cemetery, beside the grave of Jane Walker, and reburied in William Jones' gift lot. No mention was made of bringing Jane's remains. Later, a new note was added to the Norton cemetery records: "Story is that Jonathan was buried here, but was moved when the grave was found to be a tourist attraction. He is buried in Evergreen Cemetery in Muskegon."

The *Chronicle* reported:

> At an early hour in the morning, the streets of the city put on a holiday appearance and people began to pour in from the surrounding country. The Goodrich Steamer from Chicago arrived about 9:00 and brought about five hundred people from Chicago and Grand Haven, and at near 11:00 an excursion train of six cars arrived [from Allegan], crowded with people. Among the hundreds of people assembling for the march to the cemetery were three musical bands.
>
> A little before noon, the procession formed in front of the Opera House on Western Avenue. It was nearly one mile in length and yet a large proportion of the people in attendance were not in the line, a great many having gone to the cemetery in advance.
>
> The line of march was led by A. B. Miner, marshal; and F. L. Reynolds and O. B. Jones, assistant marshals.

Among the famous and well-known people on hand were former Governor Holt, who presided at the cemetery program; Pillsbury, the abolitionist lecturer who had frequently visited Walker's native Cape Cod, who was to give the eulogy; and General Benjamin O. Pritchard, whose military actions included the capture of Confederate President Jefferson Davis. He and General W. B. Williams were introduced for recognition.

The next day's *Chronicle,* under the headline, "A Hero Honored," attributed the size of the gathering to a cause that the late hero might have doubted, to a

247

Jonathan Walker The Man with the Branded Hand

... great doctrine of human equality... so deeply imbedded in the hearts of the Northern people and the maintenance of the principles involved in this doctrine... Hence, when it was announced that the memory of Jonathan Walker, the old hero who had periled himself for the good of his down-trodden fellow men... was to be honored, the pulse of the people quickened and they said we will do him honor, and they did by turning out on yesterday to the number of about 6,000 people, and spending the day in commemoration of the events which have rendered the life of Jonathan Walker famous... Perhaps no event that has ever transpired in Muskegon has attracted so many people of intelligence and culture together...

*   *   *   *

The Walker grave site, on the west side of the ten-acre Evergreen Cemetery, must have been barely recognizable to William Jones, who had donated it. "Yesterday," the *Chronicle* reported,

...the Ladies Cemetery Association had taken a good deal of trouble to decorate the portion of the cemetery in the vicinity of the monument in a very tasteful manner. On the monument was a wreath of evergreens; and on the west side was a beautiful anchor made of myrtle; just to the west of the monument and at the head of the grave was a sheaf of ripened wheat symbolizing the fact that Captain Walker had completed his labors and had been gathered home at a ripe old age. On each corner of the lot was a beautiful pyramid of flowers, and over the grave were festoons and baskets of flowers, while at the head of the grave was an elegantly wrought evergreen cross and crown. The monument was veiled with the stars and stripes, and remained so till the unveiling ceremony took place...

A neat stand had been erected on the west side of the cemetery and facing the Walker Monument, for the accommodation of the speakers and reporters.

All around the platform, spectators avoided the sun's heat under umbrellas and the shade of the few nearby trees.

The service opened with a choir selection and prayer by Mr. Kittredge, appointed chaplain for the program. Greeting the assembly, Holt said: "[A]lthough we anticipated a goodly attendance on the occasion, we had little reason to hope to see the immense throng which greets our eyes today... The immediate friends of Captain Walker are particularly grateful to the large number of his old-time associates and fellow laborers in the anti-slavery cause whom it is their good fortune to meet today..."

Mr. Kittredge, in his eulogy, left a picture of

...a saintly man, who regarded the kindnesses that he performed somewhat like deposits from which he could later make needed withdrawals. He loved to tell during his sickness how much faith he

In Death: Recognition and Reward

had put in the 'bank of humanity' and had never been cheated or deceived... He never hated a man because he was poor, or because he was ignorant, or because he was black. And he told me not long ago that he never entertained hard feelings, even towards the slaveholders or those who used him harshly...

But the life work of our friend is ended. He has achieved an early immortality and entered into rest. He felt impressed always with the idea of man's innate possibilities and of the undeveloped powers and resources wrapped up in his being, that he thought there must be a career awaiting him beyond the shore of this life, where full scope would be given to all his faculties... The lessons of his life to us are those grand but simple ones, of loyalty to conviction and faithfulness to duty...

Holt, noting that "ill health and other causes have prevented" some of the invited notables from attending, introduced A. J. Grover, who read letters from Douglass and Whittier.

Writing from his home in Danvers, Massachusetts, on June 21, 1878, Whittier alluded to a request that he compose a new poem for the occasion. He wrote: "Immediately on receiving the latter announcing Captain W's death, I sent it to Garrison with the suggestion that we should take measures for a monument. He came out to see me and informed me that Reverend Photius Fisk... had volunteered to give the monument himself... I don't think I could write anything without repeating my former poem on the same subject." Whittier signed the note, "Thine truly."

The *Chronicle* reported: "Everybody seemed anxious to hear what the venerable Fred Douglass would have to say on this occasion, and many had doubtless come expecting to see him and hear him speak. Therefore, the interest was intense when it was announced that Mr. Grover would now read Douglass' letter."

Dated July 15, 1878, and written at the "United States Marshal's Office, Washington City, D. C.," the letter was addressed to Photius Fisk. It said:

Yes, I knew Jonathan Walker, and knew him well, knew him to love him, and to honor him as a true man, a friend of humanity, a brave but noiseless lover of liberty, not only for himself but for all men; one who possessed the qualities of a hero and martyr, and was ready to take any risk to his own safety and personal ease to save his fellow men from slavery. It is meet and right that one who was such as he should have his grave marked as you propose. His name deserves remembrance, and should be mentioned with those of John Brown, Charles T. Torrey, William L. Chaplin, Elijah P. Lovejoy, Thompson, Work and Barr, Calvin Fairbanks, Abraham Lincoln, and other noble men who suffered at the hands of the slave power. Jonathan Walker is not less entitled to grateful memory than the most honored of them all.

Jonathan Walker The Man with the Branded Hand

He was one who felt satisfied with the applause of his own soul. What he attempted was not intended to attract public notice. He was on the free, dashing billows of the Atlantic when the voices of nature spoke to his soul with the greatest emphasis of love and truth; and responsive to those voices, as well as to those of his own heart, he welcomed the panting fugitives from slavery to the safety of his deck, though in doing so he exposed himself to stocks, prisons, branding irons, and it might have been to death.

I well remember the sensation produced by the exhibition of his branded hand. It was one of the few atrocities of slavery that aroused the justice and humanity of the North to a death struggle with slavery. Looking into his simple, honest face, it was easy to see that on such a countenance as his no trace of infamy could be made by stocks, stripes, or branding iron. SS meant at the South, Slave Stealer, but was read by the North and all civilized men everywhere as Slave Savior. His example of self sacrifice nerved us all to more heroic endeavor in behalf of the slave...

Grover later offered his own comments: "The memory of the man we honor today will grow greener and brighter in the hearts of good men wherever the history of this country shall be known."

C. J. Chaddock read Whittier's poem, "The Branded Hand," and a band played as the stars and stripes covering the monument were removed. There stood the ten-foot granite shaft. Facing the platform guests, on the stone's east face, was an engraving of Walker's branded hand. Above it were the words:

Jonathan Walker

Born in Harwich, Mass.,

March 22, 1799

Died in Lake Harbor, Muskegon

Co., Mich, Apr. 30, 1878

To the guests' left, on the north face of the monument, were the most often quoted eight lines from Whittier's poem:

Then lift that manly right hand,

Bold ploughman of the wave,

Its branded palm shall prophecy

Salvation to the slave.

Hold up its fire-wrought language,

That who so reads may feel

His heart swell strong within him,

His sinews changed to steel.

In his main address, Pillsbury said:

In Death: Recognition and Reward

[T]hough he failed in his purpose, as men count failure, his work was no less a part of the great conflict for freedom and independence. The work of Washington and LaFayette was not perfect. It had all to be done over again... But Washington, Jefferson, and Patrick Henry were slaveholders before, during, and after the Revolutionary War, and founded a Republic and a Union of slaveholders... The foundations of our temple of Liberty and Independence were laid in the crushed-out manhood, mindhood, soulhood, of half a million human beings, 500,000 chattel slaves...

Washington builded a Republic of men only, and only of white men, at that. White male citizens were all he knew. Garrison demanded the equal, untrammeled freedom of every human being – every human man, woman, child, irrespective of race, complexion, or sex; in spite of man-made codes, constitutions, creeds, or catechisms, he demanded that equal freedom "in the name of humanity and according to the laws of the living God." And of such as Garrison was Jonathan Walker...

An ancient philosopher said, "It were far better that posterity should ask why I have not a monument than why I have." Probably all of us would say the same. My task today is done, and well done, if I have shown to my audience and to posterity with what good right the humble pillar we today unveil should guard the dust and hallow the name of Jonathan Walker...

Forty years ago, the name "abolitionist" was below every name. Today, who, especially in the Northern and Western states, is not proud to be known as an abolitionist, or the son of an abolitionist? The blood of Lovejoy and Torrey, the fiery baptism of Jonathan Walker, the prostrate body of Sumner, felled to the floor of the Senate chamber by the murderous bludgeon of slavery, and, last of all, the gallows of the immortal John Brown, now sacred as Calvary's Cross – all these have hallowed the name of abolitionist forevermore!

The *Journal* obituary reported on the burial, and on the response of Levina Walker: "The widow expresses her gratitude to the many friends and neighbors, both of Lake Harbor and Muskegon, for the numberless acts of kindness extended to them during the sickness, death, and burial of her husband, when true disinterested friendship were exhibited by William Jones, who offered a portion of his family plat in the cemetery, which was most gratefully accepted by Mrs. Walker, and where the body of Jonathan Walker now reposes in peace." Not quite. One more trip lay ahead for the old sea captain.

  *   *   *   * .

American newspapers continued that summer to carry the news of importance in their communities. Amid the inspiring reports of the Muskegon ceremony relayed across the country were the routine announcements of the

Jonathan Walker The Man with the Branded Hand

farmers' harvests and the news from the nation's capital. On August 27, 1878, only two weeks after its report on Muskegon's salute to one of America's best-known anti-slavery workers, the *Courier* in Hickman, Kentucky, reported under the headline, "A Negro Sold at the Block":

The novel spectacle of selling a Negro to the highest bidder was witnessed in the streets of Hickman on Saturday last... [A]s the Negro man stood on the block, and the voice of the auctioneer rose and fell, crying the bids, it revived reminiscences of old and bygone days. The colored people crowded around in anxious expectancy. The Negro sold was one Jone Cooper, who had been previously tried and convicted as a vagrant, and the verdict of the jury was that he should be sold into servitude for six months as the law provides...

*   *   *   *

Not everyone remembered Jonathan Walker with charity. On October 25, 1878, six months after Walker's death, the Pensacola *Gazette*, now grown to a twice a week publication, carried a bitter commentary from William Dorr, whose brother, Ebenezer, had branded Walker in 1844 while serving as the district's United States marshal. Dorr's brother was, perhaps, responding to the scathing description of Eben Dorr given by Pillsbury during his dedicatory address three months earlier. Pillsbury called Marshal Dorr a "willing pimp and panderer to the slaveholders. His bills and accounts were curiosities..."

William Dorr wrote:

...[F]or more than a third of a century [Walker] has been paraded as a martyr. He made his living by exhibiting himself as a martyr and selling his book, which contained more solid lies than one of the voyages of Sinbad the Sailor. He was one of the original bloody shirt-bearers of radicalism to incite sectional animosity. He long antedated John Brown – who was hung as a murderer, while he was branded a man-stealer.

Nor were all of Walker's descendants dedicated to his memory as an abolitionist. Lois Wightman, of Plymouth, Wisconsin, wrote in her family records on the one hundredth anniversary of her great-grandfather's death:

Another side was written to me by Miss Alta Chase of West Harwich, Massachusetts, July 10, 1978. She was the granddaughter of Altamera Maria, who was the daughter of Sophia and Zadock Chase. Her father was Robert Walker Chase. Her grandmother remarked to Miss Chase when she was a young girl that it would have been more to his credit if Jonathan Walker had stayed home to take care of his family than to go off to free the slaves.

*   *   *   *

Nearly a year after the Muskegon *Chronicle*'s lengthy front page coverage of the Walker ceremony, the newspaper published a booklet under the name of Chronicle Steam Printing House "A Short Sketch of the Life and

In Death: Recognition and Reward

Services of Jonathan Walker, The Man with the Branded Hand." Included were Whittier's poem, the text of the address by Pillsbury, and "a funeral oration" by the Reverend Mr. Kittredge. Publisher W. M. Harford explained, "This little pamphlet is the result of an expressed desire on the part of friends of Mr. Walker, to have at least a short sketch of his life and services put in such a form that it can be preserved... If all the events of interest in the life of Jonathan Walker were put in book form, it would make a much more pretentious volume, but it has not been considered advisable to attempt this at present."

Not until 1899 was a longer account attempted. Minister Kittredge, now living in Albion, New York, capitalized on the dedication of the monument erected to Frederick Douglass in Rochester. Kittredge called this new booklet, *The Man with the Branded Hand.* The subtitle was, "An Authentic Sketch of the Life and Services of Jonathan Walker." In fact, it was a slightly enlarged reproduction of the 1879 "Short Sketch." The forty-six pages included the Emancipation Proclamation, a short biography and photograph of Fisk, and portraits of Walker, Douglass, Garrison, Pillsbury, Whittier, Wendell Phillips, Walker's monument, and, in the final pages, what a *Zion's Herald* reviewer termed on July 12, 1899, "an interesting history of the Frederick Douglass Monument" dedicated only a month before the publication was distributed. The *Herald* writer claimed his "thrilling interest" in "interesting and important history... with which the public hitherto has been unacquainted..." The book included a "picture of [Walker's branded hand] taken from an original daguerreotype now in the possession of Dr. Vincent Y. Bowditch, of Boston," the son of the Harvard physician who had ordered the image made. This was a rare printing made from photographer Southworth's plate correctly showing Walker's branded right hand. Other prints, reflecting the mirror image of the daguerreotype process, made it appear that Walker's left hand had been branded.

Kittredge's tribute to Walker was distributed widely. Among America's leaders in civil rights who responded was Booker T. Washington, the former slave who became a leading educator and followed Frederick Douglass as a prominent voice for African-Americans. Washington wrote: "I read 'The Man with the Branded Hand' with a good deal of pleasure and interest. I am always glad of these references to the heroic band of those who did so much toward the freedom of this race."

*   *   *   *

On August 16, 1921 – nearly a half-century after Jonathan Walker's death, burial, and reburial – his grave again was relocated. The Muskegon *Chronicle* headline read: "'Slave Stealer's' Monument Given Prominent Place." The body, the newspaper reported, "has been removed from an obscure grave in Evergreen Cemetery here to a plot of prominence near the cemetery entrance." The stone stands just inside the main entrance, over the grave in a triangular grass-covered open area. The reason for the relocation, according to local residents, was to make the tourist attraction easier to find. Incidental to that or not, the move also resulted in bringing even more posthumous prestige to Walker.

Some thought may have been given in 1921 to reuniting Jonathan and Jane in Evergreen Cemetery. Another search was launched in 1928. But the location of Jane Walker's grave had become lost. In the decades after the deaths of the Cape Cod couple, Jonathan Walker and his grave site had continued to gain prominence, and Jane's had become so neglected even her children could not remember where it was. In 1929, the twins, Lloyd and Maria, planned a visit from their Wisconsin homes to their father's memorial. Noting his mother's grave had been "lost," Lloyd wrote: "It is our hope that her body may be placed beside that of our father."

One reason Jane's burial site might have been difficult to find was the lack of a death certificate in her name. Not until 1937 did the location of Jane's grave return to public knowledge. As Muskegon prepared to celebrate the centennial of its first settlers, the *Chronicle* published stories about some of the county's historic residents. One of the reports, about "the man with the branded hand," mentioned his burial, and reburials, and noted the unsuccessful efforts of the 1920s to find the site of Jane's grave. That brought forth Mrs. Hubert G. Bowles, wife of the former tugboat captain who, a half-century before, had carried on a death-bed vigil for Jonathan Walker. Mrs. Bowles had located the thirty-inch high gravestone over Jane's grave at the little cemetery. The grave remains there, in the shade of a tree that probably did not exist when she died. The once quiet, rural community, renamed in the 1970s the City of Norton Shores, now absorbs the sounds coming from the nearby Muskegon County International Airport. The burying grounds' name has been changed to Norton Cemetery.

Like Jane Walker's grave, Walker's second wife drifted out of sight. Five years after his death, Levina Walker of Norton was married, on March 18, 1883, to James P. Crotty, a native of Ireland who had enlisted for Civil War service from Boston. She was sixty-eight years old; he was sixty-three. That, too, must have been a short-lived active marriage for Levina. In 1885, Crotty was living in a soldiers home in Grand Rapids.

     *   *   *   *

As for the old abolitionist, his name and, less frequently, the Southworth photograph of his hand, have continued to appear in print. Jonathan Walker left some record of his life's work, most of it in his published books and the letters to newspapers and relatives. But he must have had more – for example, the journal he kept while in the Pensacola jail. Twice in his twilight years, Walker went off in search of a publisher. There is no evidence that he had completed his autobiography. But he was such an addict for detail and an unforgetting collector of information, it is probable that he had many handwritten reminiscences.

Despite this absence of original records, Walker's story comes alive every generation or so. The 1902 essay prize at Harwich High School was

In Death: Recognition and Reward

awarded Mabel Weekes for "The Man with the Branded Hand," an account taken almost exclusively from Walker's own report. The twelve-page essay was "printed, not published," according to the guarded copy at the Brooks Free Library in Harwich.

In October 1941, Whittier's poem was given a dramatic reading over Detroit radio station WWJ by Canada Lee, a noted black actor of the time.

Muskegon has never forgotten Walker. The abolitionist was honored on "Jonathan Walker Day," July 27, 1937, during the Muskegon Centennial, and again in 1987 at the sesquicentennial. As part of the city's centennial observance, the Muskegon *Chronicle* republished the booklet it had prepared in 1879, "A Short Sketch of the Life and Services of Jonathan Walker, The Man with the Branded Hand." The publication was "inspired by E. A. Stowe, veteran editor of The Michigan *Tradesman*," who had covered the 1878 ceremony for a Grand Rapids newspaper.

The Urban League of Greater Muskegon conducts a ceremony at Walker's grave in Evergreen Cemetery every Memorial Day. And he is saluted every second year by the Urban League through the Jonathan Walker Brotherhood Award, considered one of the city's most prestigious honors. It has been given biannually since 1956. Among the recipients have been whites and blacks, and men and women, including a Roman Catholic priest, a real estate agent, a dentist, a juvenile court services director, a Protestant minister, educational administrators, and an eighty-eight-year-old "grassroots citizen." Each was cited as "the person in the community who has done the most to further the cause of brotherhood" during the previous year.

Walker's own publications occasionally pop up. *Trial and Imprisonment* was reprinted in 1969 by Arno Press of New York and in 1970 by Negro Universities Press of New York. The University Press of Florida reprinted the autobiography as part of its Bicentennial Floridiana facsimile series of 1974. Elmer R. Koppelmann of Sheboygan Falls, Wisconsin, reprinted most of *A Brief View of American Chattelized Humanity, and Its Supports*, in his 1984 biography, *Branded Hand: Struggles of an Abolitionist*.

*   *   *   *

Jonathan Walker's record was ultimately unparalleled. He was probably the only American ever whose flesh was marked by a United States marshal on order of a court jury and judge.

Some critics, not without justification, have wondered why a man with so many family responsibilities would virtually desert them for the cause of abolition. Critics also have wondered why he would involve himself in such a dangerous mission as his Pensacola flight. Why would a father with several young children at home risk jailing, even death, in order to help seven slaves – legally "owned" in a slave territory more than a thousand miles from his own home?

It is never easy for the many of us who are pragmatists to understand the few of us who follow their visions.

Jonathan Walker The Man with the Branded Hand

During the early years of the American experiment in a democratic government, a visitor from Scotland predicted the future for these people in revolution. Alexander Fraser Tyler, a professor of economics at Edinburgh University, wrote:

> A democracy cannot exist as a permanent form of government. It can only exist until the voters discover that they can vote themselves largesse from the public treasury. From that moment on... a democracy always collapses over loose fiscal policy, always followed by a dictatorship. The average age of the world's great civilizations has been 200 years. These nations have progressed through this sequence:
>
> From bondage to spiritual faith; from liberty to abundance; from abundance to selfishness; from selfishness to complacency; from complacency to apathy; from apathy to dependence; from dependence back to bondage.

A simpler, and more hopeful, outlook comes from Nate Shaw, the son of two former slaves. Born in Alabama in 1885, he died there on November 5, 1973. He told oral historian Theodore Rosengarten:

> I've noticed many things through the past history of my life – uneducated man that I am – that point to a plan. Time passes and the generations die. But the condition of the people that's livin today ain't like it was for the people that's gone. And it ain't now like it's goin to be for the people that comes after us. I can't say exactly what the future way of life will be, but I has a idea. My color, the colored race of people on earth, goin to shed theirselves of these slavery ways. But it takes many a trip to the river to get clean... I'd like to live; and... I'd love to know that the black race had fully shed the veil from their eyes and the shackles from their feet.

Jonathan Walker did more than dream of an America practicing equality; he dedicated most of his life to helping his country uphold this daring vision. He can be credited with helping to achieve some of the progress towards equality, generation to generation, that Nate Shaw cited. That there has been no collapse, as Tyler predicted, can be attributed to the spirit of independence and compassion that Walker left as his legacy for all Americans.

Henry David Thoreau, writing about Cape Cod, said: "A man may stand and put all America behind him." Jonathan Walker saw his stance the other way around. Coming out of Cape Cod and into the heart of the anti-slavery battle, he chose to put all America before him.

BIBLIOGRAPHY

This is a listing of some of the books I have read or consulted during the many years I have been researching this subject. I apologize to those who may wonder why I have not listed volumes they consider necessary for a well-rounded knowledge of the broad subject of slavery and in particular the abolitionist movement. My research was not conducted in the form of a scientifically-designed raking of all available material. I therefore list below some of the books I found helpful for my purposes and that I can confidentally recommend to others.

Abbott, Richard H. - *Cotton and Capital, Boston Businessmen and Antislavery Re form, 1854-1868*, 1992, University of Massachusetts Press, Amherst, MA

Atwood, W.F. - *The Pilgrim Story*, 1940, The Memorial Press, Plymouth, MA

Bennett, E.D. - *American Journeys*, 1975, TravelVision, Convent Station, NJ

Berger, Josef (Jeremiah Diggs) - *Cape Cod Pilot*, 1985, Northeastern University Press, Boston

Berman, Eleanor - *Cape Cod and the Islands*, 1985, Chartwell Books, Inc., Secaucus, NJ

Blockson, Charles L. - *Escape from Slavery*, July 1984 *National Geographic*

Bibliography

Boswell, Thomas D. - Bahama Islands entry in *Global Encyclopedia*, 1986, Global Industries, Inc., Arlington, VA

Bradford, William - *History of Plimouth Plantation*

Brandon, William - *The American Heritage Book of Indians*, 1988, Bonanza Books, New York

Breyfogle, William, *Make Free, the Story of the Underground Railroad*, 1958, J.B. Lippincott Co., New York

Brown, Sterling A. - "A Century of Negro Portraiture in American Literature," *Black Voices*, reprinted from *The Massachusetts Review*, Winter, 1966

Buchen, Gustave W. - *Historic Sheboygan County*, 1976 (2nd edition)

Burke, William Jeremiah, *Cape Cod Bibliography*, unpublished work, Nickerson Collection, Cape Cod Community College, West Barnstable, MA

Burner, David; Eugene D. Genovese, Forrest McDonald, Pete Seeger, and Tom West - *An American Portrait*, 1982, Perspectives and Revisionary Press, Winter Park, FL

Cain, Alfred E. (editor-in-chief) - *The Negro Road to Freedom*, 1965, Negro Heritage Library, Stratford Press, New York.

Carter, Clayborne - "Blacks in North America" entry in *Funk & Wagnalls New Encyclopedia*, 1992, Columbus, OH

Cash, Wilbur J. - *The Mind of the South*, 1941, Alfred A. Knopf, Inc., New York

Chapman, Abraham (editor) - *Black Voices*, 1968, New American Library, New York

Clark, Admont G. - "Lighthouse history" entry in *Three Centuries of Cape Cod County*, 1985, County of Barnstable, MA

Cogswell, John B. D. - "Historical Sketch of Barnstable County, Massachusetts," in *Atlas of Barnstable County, Massachusetts*, 1880, George H. Walker Co., Boston

Collier, John - *Indians of the Americas*, 1948, The New American Library of World Literature, New York

Corbett, Scott - *Cape Cod's Way: An Informal History*, 1955, Thomas Y. Crowell Company, New York

Crosby, Katharine - *Blue-Water Men and Other Cape Codders*, 1946, The MacMillan Company, New York

Dangerfield, George - "Mr. Madison's War," in *The American Story*, 1956, Kingsport Press, Inc., Kingsport, TN

Der, Mark - *Some Kind of Paradise, A Chronicle of Man and the Land in Florida*, 1989, William Morrow and Company, Inc., New York

de Tocqueville, Alexis - *Democracy in America*, Volume II, 1840; translation by Henry Reeve 1863; abridgement and editing by Andrew Hacker, 1964; Washington Square Press, New York

Deyo, Simeon L. (editor) - *History of Barnstable County, Massachusetts*, 1890, H.W. Blake & Company, New York

Dollard, John - *Caste and Class in a Southern Town*, 1957, Doubleday &

Bibliography

Company, Garden City, NY

Douglas, Marjory Stoneman - *Florida: The Long Frontier*, 1967, Harper & Row, Boston

Douglass, Frederick - *The Life and Times of Frederick Douglass*, adapted from the second edition, 1892, by Barbara Ritchie, 1966, Thomas Y. Crowell Co., New York

-------- *My Bondage and My Freedom*, 1855, Miller, Orton, and Mulligan, New York

-------- *Narrative of the Life of Frederick Douglass, An American Slave, Written by Himself*; in Black Voices

Dow, George Francis – "Everyday Life in Massachusetts Bay Colony," as quoted in *New England Discovery*; reprinted by permission of the Society for the Preservation of New England Antiquities

Drewry, Henry - "Black Americans" entry in *Global Encyclopedia*, 1986, Global Industries, Inc., Arlington, VA

Edwards, Agnes - *Cape Cod – Old and New*, 1925, Houghton Mifflin, Boston

Ellis, Richard - *Men and Whales*, 1991, Alfred A. Knopf, New York

Feagin, Joe R. - Black Nationalism entry in *Global Encyclopedia*, 1986, Global Industries, Inc., Arlington, VA

Fernald, Edward - Florida entry in *Global Encyclopedia*, 1986, Global Industries, Inc., Arlington, VA

Finger, Ben, Jr. - *Concise World History*, 1960, Philosophical Library, Inc., New York

Freeman, Frederick - *The History of Cape Cod*, 1862

Frost, J. William - George Fox biography in *Global Encyclopedia*, 1986, Global Industries, Inc., Arlington, VA

Furnas, J.C. - *Goodbye to Uncle Tom*, 1956, William Sloane Associates, New York

Gagnon, Paul - "Why Study History?", November 1988, *The Atlantic* magazine.

Gerlach, Larry R. - Boston Massacre entry in *Global Encyclopedia*, 1986, Global Industries, Inc., Arlington, VA

Gilchrist, David T. (editor) - *The Growth of the Seaport Cities, 1790-1825*, 1967, The University Press of Virginia, Richmond, VA

Greene, Lorenzo Johnston - *The Negro in Colonial New England*, 1969, Athaeneum, New York

Hale, Judson D., Sr. (editor) - The 1992 edition of *The Old Farmer's Almanac*, 1991, Yankee Publishing Inc., Dublin, NH

Hale, Nancy (editor) - *New England Discovery*, 1963, Coward-McCann, Inc., New York

Hale, William Harlan - "General Eaton and His Improbable Legion," in *American Heritage*, February 1960

Haley, Alex - *A Different Kind of Christmas*, 1988, Doubleday, New York

Harris, Sheldon H. - *Paul Cuffe, Black America, and the African Return*, 1972, Simon and Schuster, New York

Bibliography

Hart, Albert Bushnell (editor) - *Commonwealth History of Massachusetts*, 1930, States History Co., New York

Harwich Historical Commission - *Indian History of Harwich, Massachusetts*, 1972, published by Harwich Historical Society

Hayden, Robert C. - *The African Meeting House in Boston*, 1987, The Museum of Afro American History, Boston

Herrick, James W. - The Five Civilized Tribes entry in *Global Encyclopedia*, 1986, Global Industries, Inc., Arlington, VA

Hodges, Margaret, *Hopkins of the Mayflower, Portrait of a Dissenter*, 1972, Farrar Strauss Giroux, New York

Hotten, John Camden (editor) - *Original Lists of Persons of Quality 1600-1700*, 1976, Genealogical Publishing Company, Inc., Baltimore

Isaac - *Memoirs of a Monticello Slave: As Dictated to Charles Campbell in the 1840s by Isaac, one of Thomas Jefferson's Slaves*; 1951, University of Virginia

Ivanoff, Josephine Buck - *Pieces of Old Cape Cod*, 1985, printed by Jack and Claire Viall, West Harwich, MA

Jordan, Winthrop D. - *Tumult and Silence at Second Creek*, 1993, Louisiana State University Press

Josephy, Alvin M., Jr. - *Now That the Buffalo's Gone*, 1982, Alfred A. Knopf, New York

Keene, Annie C. - *Early Days of Manomet*, date unknown, Wareham Courier Press, Wareham, MA

Kellogg, Louise Phelps - *The French Regime in Wisconsin and the Northwest*, 1968, Cooper Square Publishers, Inc., New York

Kennedy, John F. - *Profiles in Courage*, 1956, Harper & Brothers, New York

Kittredge, Henry C. - *Cape Cod: Its People and Their History*, 2nd edition, 1968, Houghton Mifflin Company, Boston

-------- *Sailmasters of Cape Cod*, 1935, Houghton Mifflin Company, Boston

Knight, Franklin W. - Blacks in the Americas, in *Funk & Wagnalls New Encyclopedia*, 1992, Columbus, OH

Koppelmann, Elmer - *Branded Hand: The Struggles of an Abolitionist*, 1984, BH Press, Sheboygan Falls, WI

Langer, William L. (editor) - *An Encyclopedia of World History*, 1948, Houghton Mifflin, Boston

Lester, Julius - *To Be a Slave*, 1974, Dell Publishing Co., Inc., New York

Little, Shelby - *George Washington*, 1962, Capricorn Books, New York

Locke, Mary Stoughton - *Anti-Slavery in America*, 1901, Ginn & Company, Boston

Lowell, D.O.S. - *A Munsey-Hopkins Genealogy*, 1920, privately printed, Boston

Mather, Cotton - The Big Snow of 1717, a letter to Mr. Woodward, quoted in *New England Discovery* by permission of the Massachusetts Historical Society.

Maxwell, James A. (editor) - *America's Fascinating Indian Heritage*, 1984,

Bibliography

Readers Digest Association, Pleasantville, NY

McFeely, William S. - *Frederick Douglass*, 1991, W. W. Norton & Company, Inc., New York

McKee, Russell - *Great Lakes Country*, 1966, Thomas Y. Crowell Company, New York

Miers, Earl Schenck (editor) - *The American Story*, 1956, Channel Press, Great Neck, NY

Miller, Douglas T. - Fugitive Slave Laws entry in *Global Encyclopedia*, 1986, Global Industries, Inc., Arlington, VA

Mitchell, J. H., and Whit Griswold - *Hiking Cape Cod*, 1978, East Woods Press Books, Charlotte, NC

Moore, George H. - *Notes on the History of Slavery in Massachusetts*, 1866, D. Appleton & Company, New York

Myrdal, Gunnar - *An American Dilemma*, 1964, McGraw-Hill, New York

Nichols, Roy F. - *The Stakes of Power*, 1961, Hill and Wang, New York

Nickerson, Joshua Atkins, II - *Days to Remember*, 1988, Chatham Historical Society, Chatham, MA

Nickerson, Sean - *Land Ho!*, 1620

Oates, Stephen B. - *To Purge This Land with Blood*; 1970, Harper & Row, New York

Paine, Josiah - *The History of Harwich*, 1971, Parnassus Imprints, Yarmouthport, MA

Pettengill, Samuel B. - *Yankee Pioneers — A Saga of Courage*, 1971, Charles E. Tuttle Co., Inc., Rutland, VT

Richardson, Joe M. - (See Walker, Jonathan)

Riznik, Barnes - *Medicine in New England 1790-1840*, 1969, Meriden, CT

Roe, Merwin (editor) - *Speeches and Letters of Abraham Lincoln*, 1832-1865, 1912, E.P.Dutton & Co., New York

Rosengarten, Theodore, *All God's Dangers (The Life of Nate Shaw)*, 1974, Alfred A. Knopf, New York

Ruchames, Louis (editor) - *John Brown – The Making of a Revolutionary*, 1969, Gosset & Dunlap, New York

Ryder, Marion Crowell - *Cape Cod Remembrances*, 1972, William S. Sullwood Publishing, Taunton, MA

Sable, Joel - "Spanish Trail Half Among Rarest Commemoratives," October 27, 1991, Boston Globe, Boston, MA

Salvador, George Arnold - *Paul Cuffe, The Black Yankee*, 1962, Reynolds-DeWalt Printing, Inc., New Bedford, MA

Sandburg, Carl - *Remembrance Rock*, 1948, Harcourt, Brace and Company, Inc., New York

Schlesinger, Arthur M., Jr., *The Disuniting of America, Reflections of a Multicultural Society*, 1992, Norton, New York.

Sellers, Charles, *James K. Polk, Jacksonian*, 1968 (third printing), Princeton University Press, Princeton, NJ

Bibliography

Shay, Edith, and Shay, Frank - *Sand in Their Shoes*, 1951, Houghton Mifflin Company, New York

Small, Isaac M. - *Shipwrecks on Cape Cod*, 1928, reprinted 1967, Chatham Press, Chatham, MA

Smith, William C. - *History of Chatham, Massachusetts*, 1971 edition, Chatham Historical Society, Inc., Chatham, MA

Snow, Edward Rowe - *A Pilgrim Returns to Cape Cod*, 1946, Yankee Publishing Co., Boston

-------- *Legends, Maps, and Stories of Boston and New England*, 1965, George W. Prescott Publishing Company, Quincy, MA

Sprague, S.W. – "Barnstable Sea Captains," *in Cape Cod Library of History and Genealogy*, C. W. Swift, Yarmouthport, MA

Stackpole, Edouard - *Life Saving -- Nantucket*, 1972, Stern-Majestic Press, Inc.

Stampp, Kenneth M. - *The Peculiar Institution*, 1963, Alfred A. Knopf, New York

Sterling, Dorothy - *Ahead of Her Time*, 1991, W. W. Norton & Co., Inc., New York

Stern, Philip VanDoren (editor) - *Prologue to Sumter*, 1961, Fawcett Publications, Inc., Greenwich, CT

Stowe, Harriet Beecher - *Uncle Tom's Cabin*, 1966, sixth edition, The New American Library, New York

Sumner, William Graham - *Folkways*, 1940, Ginn and Company, Boston

Tarbell, Arthur Wilson - *Cape Cod Ahoy!*, 1932, A.T. Ramsay & Company, Boston

Thoreau, Henry David - *Cape Cod*, 1865; 1961 edition arranged with notes by Dudley C. Lunt; W.W. Norton & Company, Inc., New York

-------- "Slavery in Massachusetts," in *A Yankee in Canada*, with Anti-Slavery and Reform Papers, 1969; 12th edition, Haskell House Publishers Ltd., New York

Trefousse, Hans L. - "Admiral Farragut" entry in *Funk & Wagnalls New Encyclopedia*, 1992, Columbus, OH

Vuilleumier, Marion - *Churches on Cape Cod*, 1974, Wm. S. Sullwold Publishing, Taunton, MA

Walker, J.B.R. - *Memorial of the Walkers of Old Plymouth County*, 1861, Metcalf & Company, Northampton, MA

Walker, Jonathan - *Trial and Imprisonment of Jonathan Walker at Pensacola, Florida, for Aiding Slaves to Escape from Bondage*, 1974, with introduction and index by Joe M. Richardson; facsimile reproduction by the University Press of Florida of 1845 edition published by the Anti-Slavery Office, Boston

-------- *A Brief View of American Chattelized Humanity and Its Supports*, 1847, Dow & Jackson, Boston.

Walsh, Catherine - "The Columbus Quicentennial: A Moment of New Discovery," October 1991, *St. Anthony Messenger*, Cincinnati

Bibliography

Warden, G.B. - *Boston 1689-1776*, 1970, Little, Brown, & Company, Boston

Warren, Robert Penn - *Band of Angels*, 1955, Random House, Inc., New York

Weber, Dianne - "Wisconsin Wish," September 10, 1991, The Mass Media, University of Massachusetts/Boston student newspaper.

Weekes, Mabel - *The Man with the Branded Hand*, 1902, Harwich High School, Harwich, MA ("Printed, Not Published")

Weymouth, Charles. H., Jr. (chairman, history committee) - *History: First Congregational Church*, Harwich, Massachusetts, 1972, printed by Jack Viall, West Harwich, MA

Whitney, Ralph - "The Unlucky Collins Line," *American Heritage*, February 1957

Whittier, John Greenleaf, *The Complete Poetical Works of John Greenleaf Whittier*, 1894, Houghton, Mifflin & Company, Boston

Wilson, George F. - "The Fertile Germ of Democracy," in *The American Story*, 1956, Kingsport Press, Inc., Kingsport, TN

Wilson, Woodrow - *A History of the American People*, 1918 edition, Harper & Brothers, New York

Wood, Donald - *Cape Cod – A Guide*, 1973, Little, Brown & Company, Boston

Zesmer, David M. - John Bunyan biography in *Global Encyclopedia*, 1986, Global Industries, Inc., Arlington, VA

Zobel, Hiller B. - *The Boston Massacre*, 1970, W. W. Norton & Company, Inc., New York

OTHER SOURCES

275th Anniversary, Anniversary Committee, 1969, Jack Viall, printer, West Harwich, MA

American Heritage Book of the Presidents and Famous Americans, 1967, Dell Publishing Co., Inc., New York

American Heritage New Illustrated History of the United States, Dell Publishing Co., Inc., New York

Boston *Globe*, Boston, MA

Cape Cod *Times*, Hyannis, MA

Civil War Times Illustrated, Volume XXXII, Number 2, May/June 1993
  - Patterson, Gerard, "The Beast of New Orleans"
  - Zebrowski, Carl, "Jeff Davis' Living Tomb"

Compex Directory, Chicago, 1984, "Postal History of Sheboygan County, Wisconsin," by Ray Van Handel, Jr.

Correspondence Concerning Moore's Notes on the History of Slavery in Massachusetts, 1866, New York; see George T. Davis letter to George H. Moore.

Harwich *Independent*, Harwich, MA

Historical Journal of Western Massachusetts, Vol. III, No. 2, Fall 1974:
  - Boilard, David, and Carvalho, Joseph III, "Private John E. Bisbee, The 52nd Mass. Volunteers, and the Banks Expedition"

Bibliography

- Doyle, John E., "The Epidemic Cholera in Springfield, 1832 and 1849"
- Morin, Edward M., "Springfield During the Civil War Years"

Inaugural Addresses of the Presidents of the United States, 1961, U.S. Government Printing Office, Washington, DC

The Journal of American History, Vol. 72, No. 2, September 1985, "Nantucket Whalemen in the Deep-Sea Fishery: The Changing Anatomy of an Early American Labor Force," by Daniel Vickers

Mangelinkx, Paul M. - *Keeping It Before the People: The Emergence of the Yarmouth Register, 1836-1850*, master's degree thesis at UMass/ Boston, Department of American Civilization, 1988.

Massachusetts Soldiers and Sailors of the Revolutionary War, 1891, Massachusetts Secretary of the Commonwealth

Monomoy Wilderness, 1972, prepared and published by the Massachusetts Audubon Society, South Wellfleet, MA

The National Cyclopedia of American Biography, Volume I, 1892, James T. White & Co., New York

Negroes in Michigan During the Civil War, 1965, Michigan Civil War Centennial Observance Commission

The New American Desk Encyclopedia, 1989, Concord Reference Books, Inc., New York

New Bedford *Republican Standard*

The Oxford Dictionary of English Etymology

Pensacola Historical Society Quarterly, Pensacola, FL (Vol. 3, No. 1, January 1967) "Blacks and Slaves in Pensacola 1780-1880," by Leora M. Sutton, 1980

Vital Records of Chatham, Massachusetts, 1696-1850

Vital Records of Harwich, Massachusetts, 1692-1800

World's Popular Encyclopedia, 1937, World Syndicate Publishing Co., Cleveland

Index

Index

Index

Index

Index

Index

Index

Index

Y

Z

ORDER FORM

Jonathan Walker **The Man with the Branded Hand**
Want another copy, or more? Check your local bookstore, or order directly from:

Lorelli Slater Publisher
Post Office Box 69
Everett, MA 02149-0001

Discount prices are available for purchase of five or more copies shipped to a single address. For more information, contact the publisher at the numbers at the bottom of this form.

Please send _____ (number of copies) at $12.00 each plus shipping/handling to:

Name_____

Street or P.O. _____

City, State, Zip _____

Payment enclosed:
_____ copies x $12.00 each $_____
Mass. residents add Sales Tax 5%:
_____ copies x $.60 each $_____
Shipping and Handling ($3.00 for one) $ 3.00_____
____additional copies x $1.50 each $_____

                                  Total $ _____

Payment via Money Order/personal check must be enclosed, made out to Lorelli Slater Publisher. For more information, contact:

Lorelli Slater Publisher
Telephone (617) 389-2532   FAX (617) 389-1697
P.O. Box 69, Everett, MA 02149   E-mail: LSPub@juno.com